Qur'an 30 for 30

Thematic *Tafsir*

Dr. Omar Suleiman
Sh. Ismail Kamdar

Qur'an 30 for 30: Thematic *Tafsir*

First published in England by
Kube Publishing Ltd
Markfield Conference Centre
Ratby Lane, Markfield
Leicestershire, LE67 9SY
United Kingdom

Tel: +44 (0) 1530 249230
Website: www.kubepublishing.com
Email: info@kubepublishing.com

In Associassion with
Yaqeen Institute for Islamic Research
7750 N. MacArthur Blvd Suite 120237
Irving, TX 75063, USA
E-mail: info@yaqeeninstitute.org
Website: www.yaqeeninstitute.org

ISBN 978-1-84774-253-7 Paperback
eISBN 978-1-84774-254-4 Ebook

Written by Dr. Omar Suleiman and Sheikh Ismail Kamdar
Layout and typesetting by Jannah Haque

 Cataloguing-in-Publication Data is available from the British Library.

Contents

Introduction

In the Name of Allah, Most Gracious, Most Merciful.

All praise is for Allah, the Absolute, the Perfect. Peace be upon His final messenger Muhammad, and all those who follow the path of guidance until the end of time. Alhamdulillah, the Qur'an 30 for 30 series has become an annual tradition, reaching and benefiting hundreds of thousands of people, in both video and written formats.

The purpose of the series is to help connect Muslims with the Qur'an and understand its message on a deeper level. Alhamdulillah, our fifth season of Qur'an 30 for 30 will air this Ramadan, and to supplement it, we have combined the notes from all previous seasons into one book.

We have divided this book into thirty chapters, each focusing on one *juz* (one of the thirty equal conventional divisions) of the Qur'an. Each chapter is divided into four sections representing the past four seasons of Qur'an 30 for 30. Season 1 focused on a **thematic overview** of the Qur'an, Season 2 on **Seerah-related passages** and *surahs* (chapters), Season 3 on **Judgement Day**, and Season 4 on the **Qur'anic worldview**. In this book, you will find each *juz* discussed from all four angles.

The rest of the introduction focuses on key terminology for understanding this book and maximising benefits from its content. This includes definitions of the terms *tafsir*, Seerah, *asbab al-nuzul* and thematic *tafsir*, which are explained below.

Tafsir and its types

Tafsir refers to the science of interpreting the Qur'an and extracting its deeper meanings. Over the centuries, many experts have researched and deeply reflected on the Qur'an, coming up with thousands of pages of in-depth interpretations of it. The field of *tafsir* seems to have no end, with new methods and books being produced every year for over fourteen centuries. This depth is part of the miraculous nature of the Qur'an and a reflection of the infinite nature of Allah's speech.

Asbab al-nuzul (Reasons for revelation)

The term *Asbab al-nuzul* refers to narrations about why and when specific verses of the Qur'an were revealed. The Qur'an was revealed in pieces over a period of twenty-three years. During this period, many *surahs* and verses were revealed in relation to specific events in the life of the Prophet ﷺ. These events were narrated by his companions and form a core part of narrated *tafsir*. Such narrations help us understand the Qur'an better by providing us with important context and background.

These narrations are crucial for understanding the Qur'an properly. We hope the few examples provided throughout this book help revive the study of this field in our time. When the reason for revelation of a verse or *surah* is known, the depth and beauty of the Qur'an is appreciated so much more.

The concept of Seerah

The Seerah, in this context, refers to the life of the Prophet ﷺ from which we draw our inspiration. It is the story of the greatest human to ever walk the face of this earth. The Seerah and the Qur'an are directly intertwined.

At each phase across twenty-three years of preaching Islam, the Prophet ﷺ faced particular challenges that led to immediate revelation of verses and *surahs*. This is why many of the narrations on *asbab al-nuzul* can be found in books of Seerah as well.

By focusing on the Seerah in this book, we hope to give the reader an appreciation for both the message (the Qur'an) and the Messenger ﷺ, allowing the reader to understand the fundamental role that the prophetic model plays in the field of *tafsir*.

A note on translations

Most of the translations of Qur'anic verses in this book are taken from *Quran in English* by Talal Itani with slight modifications. The translations of hadiths from major hadith collections are mostly taken from the Darus Salam translations with slight modifications. Some hadiths are translated directly by the authors, when no previously available translation could be sourced.

Most quotations from early *tafsir* works have been translated directly by the authors.

How to use this book

This book can benefit the reader in many ways. You can read it as a companion piece to our daily YouTube videos, or on its own as a companion to your daily Qur'an recitation during Ramadan. You could use it to review the core meanings of the Qur'an or to teach your kids the meanings of the Qur'an.

We tried to write this in a way that makes it an easy read, while providing a deeper understanding of the Qur'an. We hope that our readers all find it beneficial and will continue to benefit from it for years to come.

We ask Allah to accept this small effort to promote and explain His words. We ask Allah to forgive our mistakes and overlook our faults, and to bless this effort and all those involved in making it a reality.

We ask Allah to accept this endeavour and to make it a means of guidance for all. We ask Allah to add this to our scale of good deeds on the Last Day and make it a means of forgiveness of our sins. *Ameen.*

Omar Suleiman & Ismail Kamdar
Yaqeen Institute for Islamic Research
Ramadan 1445

The Qur'an itself is guidance for those who are conscious of Allah and our guidance lies entirely in understanding, reflecting on and living by its essential, divine teachings.

Juz one

Juz one
Thematic overview

1 Qur'an 1:5.

2 Qur'an 1:6–7.

3 Qur'an 2:2.

The Qur'an begins with a supplication (*dua*) for guidance, and an answer to that *dua*. Guidance is the main theme that flows throughout the first *juz* of the Qur'an. The opening chapter of the Qur'an, Surah al-Fatiha (the Opening), is a beautifully structured *dua* for guidance. It begins with praising Allah by His beautiful names and attributes, then reminds us to worship Allah alone. This verse establishes our relationship with Allah as a relationship of worship. Allah is our Lord whom alone we worship and seek help from.[1]

This is followed by the core of the *dua* in which we are shown the path of those whom Allah has favoured. We are also shown the two paths that lead away from Allah; misguidance by blindly following wrong beliefs and arrogantly rejecting the truth when it is clear, thereby earning the anger of Allah.[2]

Surah al-Fatiha is immediately followed by a declaration that the Qur'an consists of guidance for those who are conscious of Allah.[3] The opening verses of Surah al-Baqarah (the Cow) clarify that the Qur'an is here to guide us, but we can only access that guidance if we have sincerity and strive for righteousness. The rest of the *surah* builds on this theme by discussing various topics related to the theme of guidance.

The opening passages of Surah al-Baqarah describe the three ways in which people react to the guidance of the Qur'an. The righteous believe in it, embrace it, and strive to follow it. The disbelievers reject it and turn away from it. The third group, the hypocrites, get the most attention as this is a subtle dangerous path that people rarely realise they are upon. The hypocrites outwardly embrace the guidance of the Qur'an, yet internally reject it. They are Muslim on a surface level, yet their attitude towards the revelation is closer to that of the disbelievers. This passage calls on us to introspect and ensure we do not have any of the traits of the hypocrites.[4]

4 Qur'an 2:3–20.

The opening verses of Surah al-Baqarah clarify for us that the Qur'an is here to guide us, but we can only access that guidance if we have sincerity and strive for righteousness.

Whether we embrace the guidance of the Qur'an or not depends on our attitude and intention towards it. People who approach the Qur'an with an antagonistic mindset are more likely to reject it. Those who sincerely seek the truth are more likely to follow it, this is why it is "Guidance for the God-conscious."

The various stories in Surah al-Baqarah show us the different reactions to Allah's guidance. Humans by our nature will slip up but how we react to our own mistakes indicates our overall attitude towards Allah. The story of Adam ﵇ in Surah al-Baqarah is a reminder that the best of people also make mistakes, but in their humility, they acknowledge their mistakes and repent. This is the path of guidance.[5]

Contrast this with the stories of Satan (Shaytaan or Iblis) and Pharaoh. Both of them actively rejected the truth, even though they recognised it, because of their arrogance. Their arrogance blocked them from the path of guidance and led them towards Hellfire. This is a strong warning against the evil trait of arrogance and its effects on the heart.

Another story mentioned in Surah al-Baqarah is the story of Solomon (Arb., Sulayman) ﵇. In this *surah,* Allah declares that Sulayman ﵇ did not disbelieve, rather it was the devils who disbelieved.[6] Sulayman ﵇ was blessed with every worldly privilege, but he did not allow any of these blessings to distract him from the purpose of life. Sulayman ﵇ is proof that worldly success can come with spiritual success, as he achieved both.

The final story in this *juz* is about Prophet Ibrahim ﵇. Ibrahim ﵇ was guided and wanted guidance for his descendants. Allah praises his beautiful character in this *surah* with a special emphasis on the *dua* he made for his descendants.

5 Qur'an 2:30–39.
6 Qur'an 2:102.

Ibrahim ﷺ wished for people from his descendants who would continue the work of calling towards Allah's guidance. Allah answered his *dua* through his descendants and their descendants.[7]

7 Qur'an 2:124–36.

The story of Adam ﷺ in Surah al-Baqarah is a reminder that the best of people also make mistakes, but in their humility, they then acknowledge their mistakes and repent.

The *juz* ends with a reminder that we profess our belief in all these prophets and confirm everything that was revealed to each of them. Our *ummah* is called the balanced nation that will bear witness for every other nation, while our Prophet is a witness over us. The next *juz* begins with the changing of the *qiblah* (direction of prayer), signifying the transition of revelation from the Jewish descendants of Ibrahim ﷺ to his Arab descendants.

As Surah al-Baqarah is the longest *surah* in the Qur'an, its main theme continues into the second and third *juz* in which we will explore other lessons related to guidance and misguidance.

Juz one
The Seerah

Surah al-Baqarah was revealed gradually throughout the Medinan era. The various verses and themes found in this, the longest *surah* in the Qur'an, reflect the questions and situations of early Medinan society. Many of these verses have clear reasons for revelation that have been passed down through narrations.

In Medina, the Prophet ﷺ dealt directly with various Jewish tribes whose leaders recognised that he was the foretold prophet, but most rejected him because he was not from their tribe.

The early years in Medina were a period of settling down, establishing a city-state, and building the foundations of the Islamic community. The various laws of the Shariah related to acts of worship like prayer, fasting, and charity were elaborated during this period, as were the early community laws related to marriage, divorce, war, business, and inheritance. This is why this *surah* contains so many verses related to the laws of Islam; most of them are found in the second *juz* of the Qur'an.

The first *juz* focuses more on the spiritual states of people. The descriptions of believers and disbelievers are briefly listed at the start of the *surah*. These two categories had already been elaborated on in various Meccan *surahs*. This is followed by two entire pages focused on describing a new group of people that the Muslims had to deal with in Medina: the hypocrites. Hypocrites did not exist in Mecca, making this a new challenge. This is why the Qur'an opens with a detailed description of this category of people, those who pretend to be Muslim for worldly reasons. Right at the start, the Qur'an begins with a warning that belief should be sincere.

Among the people are those who say, "We believe in Allah and in the Last Day," but they are not believers. They seek to deceive Allah and those who believe, but they deceive none but themselves, though they are not aware.

In their hearts is sickness, and Allah has increased their sickness. They will have a painful punishment because of their denial. And when it is said to them, "Do not make trouble on earth," they say, "We are only reformers." In fact, they are the troublemakers, but they are not aware.

And when it is said to them, "Believe as the people have believed," they say, "Shall we believe as the fools have believed?" In fact, it is they who are the fools, but they do not know.

And when they come across those who believe, they say, "We believe"; but when they are alone with their devils, they say, "We are with you; we were only ridiculing." It is Allah who ridicules them and leaves them bewildered in their transgression.[8]

The bulk of the first *juz* focuses on stories of the past prophets, specifically on the story of the Prophet Moses and his trials with the Israelites. In Medina, the Prophet ﷺ dealt directly with various Jewish tribes. The leaders of these tribes recognised that he was the foretold prophet, but most rejected him because he was not from their tribe.

These stories were reminders to the People of the Book (Jews and Christians) of their covenant to obey the messengers. They also served as a reminder to the Muslims to be true in their belief and their obedience to the Prophet ﷺ.

And when a scripture came to them from Allah, confirming what they have—although previously they were seeking victory against those who disbelieved—but when there came to them what they recognised, they disbelieved in it. Allah's curse is upon the disbelievers.[9]

8 Qur'an 2:8–15.
9 Qur'an 2:89.

Juz one

Judgement Day

The afterlife is a core theme of the Qur'an. A primary goal of the Qur'anic message is to prepare our hearts for the Last Day. This preparation begins with building a core foundation of faith in our hearts, cementing that faith with good deeds, and living our lives with the afterlife as our priority.

In Surah al-Baqarah, those who believe are described as having conviction (yaqeen) in the afterlife. Those who disbelieve are given a strong warning regarding the consequences of rejecting the truth.

Surah al-Fatiha serves as a fundamental reminder of these realities. It is a prayer for guidance that will benefit us in both worlds, and especially on the Last Day. This *surah* reminds us of three core attributes of Allah related to the Last Day. He is the *Rabb* (Lord) of all the worlds, those that we see and those that we cannot see. He is Most Merciful, with special mercy reserved for His worshippers on the Last Day. And He is the Master/King of the Day of Judgment, a day on which all of humanity will be held to account for their beliefs and deeds.[10]

10 Qur'an 1:1–3.

11 Qur'an 2:4.

Reciting Surah al-Fatiha in every unit of every daily prayer serves as a constant reminder that we all will stand before the King of the Last Dsay and be held to account for how we spent our lives.

This focus on the fundamentals of faith flows into Surah al-Baqarah. It begins with a description of the three reactions humans have to the truth: belief, disbelief, or hypocrisy. Those who believe are described as having conviction (*yaqeen*) in the afterlife.[11] Those who disbelieve are given a strong warning about the consequences of rejecting the truth. The hypocrites are given the longest description in this passage. Hypocrisy is associated with the worst outcome on the day of Judgment.

Strong faith leads to certainty and preparation, which will benefit us on Judgment Day. Hypocrisy and disbelief both lead to negligence which will be regretted that day.

Hypocrites claim to believe in Islam, yet their hearts are empty of any real faith. They are described as people who sell the afterlife for this world. Hypocrites tend to be obsessed with worldly success and will compromise the fundamentals of faith to achieve it.

To the hypocrite, religion is just another tool for attaining worldly goals. Allah gives a very stern warning to these people in this passage:

They are those who have traded misguidance for guidance; but their trade does not profit them, and they are not guided. Their likeness is that of a person who kindled a fire; when it illuminated all around, Allah took away their light, and left them in darkness, unable to see. Deaf, dumb, blind. They will not return.[12]

This message and warning are repeated later in the same *surah*.

They are those who bought the present life for the hereafter, so the punishment will not be lightened for them, nor will they be helped.[13]

Our attitude towards the Day of Judgment begins with our faith. Strong faith leads to certainty and preparation, which will benefit us on that day. Hypocrisy and disbelief both lead to negligence which will be regretted that day. It all begins with one simple choice: to believe with conviction and to commit to living by our beliefs.

12 Qur'an 2:16–18.

13 Qur'an 2:86.

Juz one

Qur'anic worldview

14 Qur'an 2:3–4.

Surah al-Baqarah is one of the first *surahs* revealed in Medina; as such it played a crucial role in shaping the worldview of the first generation. The Islamic worldview is rooted in developing a conviction in specific beliefs. True believers are described as "Those who believe in the unseen, and perform the prayers, and give from what We have provided for them. And those who believe in what was revealed to you, and in what was revealed before you, and are certain of the Hereafter."[14]

Two opposing worldviews are detailed. The disbelievers are described as those who were blinded from the truth by their preoccupation with worldly affairs. Worse than them are the hypocrites who pretend to have faith, while holding worse spiritual diseases in their hearts than the disbelievers. The Muslim worldview begins with having the correct faith and conviction in it.

From this perspective, we understand that we are a creation of Allah, created for a specific purpose. We are aware that other creations exist, including unseen beings like the jinn and angels. This humbles us and prevents us from seeing ourselves as the most important beings in existence. The Muslim worldview is also built around the concept of the afterlife as we see this life as a journey in which we prepare for the afterlife.

The origin story of humanity in this *juz* gives us an idea of our role and purpose on earth. Allah said to the angels, "I am creating a representative (caliph) on the earth."[15] One of the interpretations of caliph here is a representative of Allah's Will. This means that we were created to ensure Allah's laws are upheld. This includes caring for His Creation, upholding justice, establishing morality, and calling people to live a life that is pleasing to Him. In the Muslim worldview, life is purposeful, God-centric, and a powerful responsibility.

15 Qur'an 2:30.

We were created to ensure Allah's laws are upheld. This includes caring for His Creation, upholding justice, establishing morality, and calling people to live a life that is pleasing to Him.

The story of Moses (Arb., Musa) ﷺ again gives us these three types of approaches. Pharaoh rejected the message, some of the Tribes or the Children of Israel (Banu Israel) embraced it, and some of Banu Israel were hypocrites who embraced the message outwardly while harbouring spiritual diseases internally. The emphasis is once again on the importance of pure faith in a pure heart, which is the foundation of the Islamic worldview.

The story of Banu Israel showcases the dangers of treating one's religion as an identity. Some of them thought that all that mattered was that they identified as believers and that would be enough to earn Paradise. Because of this, they were rebellious and caused a lot of problems for Prophet Musa ﵇. Islam is not an identity; it is a way of life. A Muslim must submit to Allah and follow His laws to earn His pleasure. Our success lies in living an Islamic lifestyle with true faith, not in simply calling ourselves Muslims.

The story of Banu Israel showcases the dangers of treating one's religion as an identity. Islam is not an identity; it is a way of life.

Juz two

Juz two

Thematic overview

16 Qur'an 2:185.

The theme of guidance continues to run throughout the second *juz* of the Qur'an. The focus moves towards the laws Allah has revealed. In this *juz,* Allah explains to us various laws of Islam related to every area of life. The laws of fasting in Ramadan, Hajj, marriage, divorce, warfare, and criminal law are all detailed in this *juz*. The believer will strive to obey these laws as they constitute guidance from our Creator.

The theme of guidance appears in the verses on Ramadan, in which Allah reminds us that He revealed the Qur'an in Ramadan as guidance for mankind.[16] Notice that Allah referred to the Qur'an as guidance for the God-conscious at the beginning of the *surah*. In the middle, He refers to it as guidance for mankind.

This is because the message is meant for all of humanity and is accessible to anyone, but only the God-conscious will pay heed and follow it.

Allah revealed the book of guidance during the month of guidance and calls on us to thank Him for that guidance. This is followed by a verse reminding us about the importance of *dua*. *Dua* is another important theme that flows throughout the first three *juz* of the Qur'an.

In this *juz,* Allah reminds us, "Whenever my servant asks of Me, tell him I am near."[17] This is a beautiful reminder to draw near to Allah through *dua*. He also reminds us to "enter into submission completely, and do not follow the footsteps of Shaytaan."[18] Guidance cannot transform us if we pick and choose what we want to follow. We must submit completely to experience the benefits of Allah's guidance.

17 Qur'an 2:186.

18 Qur'an 2:208.

19 Qur'an 2:249.

Guidance cannot transform us if we pick and choose what we want to follow. We must submit completely to experience the benefits of Allah's guidance.

The *juz* ends with the story of the Children of Israel when they asked for a king but then refused to follow him. The few who followed him were successful, despite being outnumbered. This is a reminder that success lies in following the guidance of Allah, even if only a minority of people follow it. The truth will prevail: "How often has a small group defeated a larger group with Allah's permission? Indeed, Allah is with the patient."[19]

20 Qur'an 2:255.

21 Qur'an 2:285–86.

Towards the end of Surah al-Baqarah (the Cow), you will find the greatest verse in the Qur'an known as Ayat al-Kursi (lit. Verse of the Throne).[20] Ayat al-Kursi is both a *dua* for protection and a reminder that Allah is the greatest and we are constantly in need of Him.

Surah al-Baqarah contains the greatest verse in the Qur'an known as Ayat al-Kursi, which is both a dua for protection and a reminder that Allah is the greatest and we are constantly in need of Him.

The *surah* then ends with another *dua*. The closing verses are a confirmation that we believe in the guidance that Allah has revealed to His prophets, followed by a *dua* in which we admit that we are weak and often slip up. We ask Allah to keep us firm upon guidance and to overlook our mistakes and sins.[21]

Juz two

The Seerah

There is a shift in the core content of the *surah* at this point. The earlier verses in the first *juz* focused more on the stories of past prophets, while the second *juz* includes a heavy emphasis on laws.

This *juz* may be the most law-focused *juz* in the entire Qur'an, as it includes verses related to prayer, charity, fasting, war, marriage, divorce, and many more topics.

In the early years of Islam, Jerusalem was the qiblah to distinguish the believers of Mecca from the pagans who worshipped the idols that surrounded the Kabah.

The bulk of this *juz* was revealed during the second year after Hijrah. It was a time in which the companions had many questions, and the laws of Islam were starting to take shape. Many of these passages begin with "They ask you about," showing how keen the companions were to learn more about their religion.

The laws revealed in this *juz* became the foundations of the faith, as the various pillars of Islam like the pilgrimage and fasting were crystallised.

The *juz* begins with the changing of the qiblah from Jerusalem to Mecca. In the early years of Islam, Jerusalem was the qiblah to distinguish the believers of Mecca from the pagans who worshipped the idols that surrounded the Ka'bah.

In Mecca, Muslims were able to stand on one side of the Ka'bah so that they would be facing both the Ka'bah and Jerusalem at the same time. In Medina, the Ka'bah and Jerusalem were on opposite sides, so facing both was impossible.

The Prophet ﷺ and his companions continued facing Jerusalem until the verses were revealed, making the Ka'bah the permanent qiblah until the end of time.

We have seen your face turned towards the heaven. So, We will turn you towards a direction that will satisfy you. So, turn your face towards the Sacred Mosque. And wherever you may be, turn your faces towards it. Those who were given the Book know that it is the Truth from their Lord; and Allah is not unaware of what they do.[22]

22 Qur'an 2:144.

The passage that follows includes a strong reminder that life is a test, and the believer should be prepared for various trials and difficulties in this world. These verses put the migration into context, while preparing the companions for the trials yet to come, including the battles against the Quraysh.

23 Qur'an 2:155–57.

The Battle of Badr took place during the first Ramadan in which fasting was obligated.

We will certainly test you with some fear and hunger, and some loss of possessions and lives and crops. But give good news to the steadfast. Those who, when a calamity afflicts them, say, "To Allah we belong, and to Him we will return." Upon these are blessings and mercy from their Lord. These are the guided ones.[23]

These verses prepared the companions for the Battle of Badr (2 AH/ 624 CE) that occurred that same year. It was the year in which the verses of fasting were revealed. We often overlook this point that the Battle of Badr took place during the first Ramadan in which fasting was obligated. The blessings of Ramadan included the first major victory of Islam, as the Muslims finally turned the tide against their oppressors at Badr.

Juz two

Judgement Day

24 Qur'an 2:200–202.

Preparing for the afterlife does not mean ignoring this world. Balance lies in prioritising the afterlife without neglecting our worldly responsibilities and goals. This concept is highlighted in a comprehensive supplication mentioned in this *surah*:

Among the people is he who says, "Our Lord, give us in this world," yet he has no share in the Hereafter. And among them is he who says, "Our Lord, give us goodness in this world, and goodness in the Hereafter, and protect us from the torment of the Fire." These will have a share of what they have earned. Allah is swift in reckoning.[24]

The supplication mentioned in this passage is one of the most popular and important prayers in the Qur'an. It is a reminder to prioritise the afterlife without neglecting this world. The hypocrite is obsessed with this world and has no goals related to the afterlife. The believer finds balance in prioritising the afterlife without neglecting this world.

The supplication is made up of three parts. The first is for goodness in this world, which does not necessarily mean wealth or fame. Worldly success in Islam refers to a good life that is pleasing to Allah. It could be a simple life or a life full of luxury; either way, it is only good if it is pleasing to Allah. Goodness in this supplication includes contentment, piety, inner peace, and happiness.

The second part of the supplication is a prayer for goodness in the afterlife, which refers to Paradise. This is the greatest reward and the end goal of every believer. A Muslim must strive for Paradise and prioritise this over everything else. We must be willing to sacrifice the goodness of this world for Paradise if needed. Every one of us is tested with situations in which we must choose between the two. When tested with such choices, the goodness of the afterlife is the obvious choice.

The third part of the supplication is a prayer for protection from the Hellfire. This makes two-thirds of the supplication focused on the afterlife, showing what our priority should be. Entering Paradise does not necessarily mean protection from the Hellfire, as some people will initially enter Hellfire before going to Paradise. To make this prayer comprehensive and inclusive of all goodness, it concludes with asking for protection from the Hellfire.

Allah knows what is best for us in both worlds. A Muslim must have firm faith in this. Even when we do not understand the wisdom behind an Islamic ruling, we must trust Allah's perfect wisdom and submit to it.

Juz two

Qur'anic worldview

In the second *juz,* the story of Prophet Abraham (Ibrahim) ﵇ showcases the perfect example of a true believer. Prophet Ibrahim ﵇ submits wholeheartedly to Allah, obeys without question, even when commanded to leave his family in the desert, and stands firm on his beliefs even when facing great trials for the sake of Allah.

Compare this with the story of Banu Israel in the first *juz*. They asked too many questions, questioning both the laws and the wisdom of Allah. They rebelled often and submitted reluctantly. They looked for loopholes to avoid the law or bypass it. And they antagonised their prophet often.

Prophet Ibrahim ﵇ on the other hand looked for ways to increase his faith and gain deeper conviction. He remained firm upon the truth even when his life was at risk and he was the only one believing in it. And he bravely debated a tyrannical king in his own court. These two stories showcase the differences between the true believer and the hypocrite.

Islam means to submit to Allah and that is the essence of our worldview. We trust Allah and obey Him even when we do not understand the laws or the wisdom behind these laws. This lesson is repeated later in this *juz* in a verse about military duty.

Fighting is ordained for you, even though you dislike it. But it may be that you dislike something while it is good for you, and it may be that you like something while it is bad for you. Allah knows, and you do not know.[25]

25 Qur'an 2:216.

There is wisdom in every law of Islam even when the rational mind cannot understand it. We must submit to it with full trust in the Perfect Wisdom of Allah.

This verse teaches us one of the most important maxims in our relationship with Allah: we must trust Allah's Wisdom. Allah's Knowledge and Wisdom are infinite, and His Law is based on this infinite Wisdom. So, there is wisdom in every law of Islam even when the rational mind cannot understand it. When you are unable to understand the wisdom behind a particular law, submit to it with full trust in Allah's Perfect Wisdom. It may be that later in life you will understand the wisdom and be grateful that you had chosen to submit. And even if you never fully understand it, you will be rewarded for your trust and submission.

Juz three

Juz three

Thematic overview

Surah Ali 'Imran (the Family of Joachim) begins in the third *juz* of the Qur'an and continues into the fourth *juz*. Hence, it will be the focus of the next two chapters of this book. A large portion of Surah Ali 'Imran was revealed in 3 AH and reflects the political climate of that year. During the third year after Hijrah, Muslims encountered Christian delegations who wanted to learn about Islam and its teachings about Jesus and Mary.

In Surah Ali 'Imran, we are reminded that the Gospel and Torah were revealed as guidance from Allah for those who came before us.

They also had interactions with the Jews of Medina, and most importantly, engaged in the Battle of Uhud (3 AH/ 625 CE). This *surah* therefore gives us some insights into the challenges and events of that year.[26] This *surah* addresses the People of the Book more than any other *surah* in the Qur'an due to the many interactions that the Prophet ﷺ had with both Jews and Christians during that year.

26 Ismail Kamdar, Themes of the Quran (Durban: Islamic Self Help, 2016), 18; Muhammad al-Ghazali, A Thematic Commentary on the Quran (London: IIIT, 2000), 30.

27 Qur'an 3:3–4.

A beautiful link between Surah al-Baqarah (the Cow) and Surah Ali 'Imran is the topic of piety. Surah al-Baqarah focuses on guidance towards piety, while Surah Ali 'Imran gives us multiple examples of piety in the families of Joachim (Imran) and Zechariah (Zakariyya). Multiple stories are narrated throughout this *surah* giving us many examples of the piety, miracles, prayers, and attitudes of these righteous people.

We learn that Allah provides for whomever He wills without any limits. He provided Mary with fruits that were out of season, and with a miracle child.

The *surah* itself begins with a reminder about the core beliefs of Islam. We are reminded that the Gospel and Torah were revealed as guidance from Allah for those before us. This is followed by stories of those who followed this guidance. Allah begins this *surah* with this reminder, "He sent down to you the Book with the Truth, confirming what came before it; and He sent down the Torah and the Gospel. Aforetime, as guidance for mankind; and He sent down the Criterion. Those who have rejected Allah's signs will have a severe punishment. Allah is Mighty, Able to take revenge."[27]

This is followed by the verse describing the unclear verses of the Qur'an and people's attitudes towards these verses. The previous *surah* began with a description of believers, disbelievers, and hypocrites. We see all three attitudes shown in those who believe in the unclear verses, those who reject them and those who seek to reinterpret them due to a "sickness in the heart"; i.e., hypocrisy.

Allah says, "It is He who revealed to you the Book. Some of its verses are definitive; they are the foundation of the Book, and others are unspecific. As for those whose hearts have deviation, they follow the unspecific part, seeking dissent, and seeking to derive an interpretation. But none knows its interpretation except Allah, and those firmly rooted in knowledge say, "We believe in it; all is from our Lord." But none recollects except those with understanding."[28]

This is immediately followed by a beautiful *dua* for guidance, continuing the theme of *dua*s for guidance in Surah al-Fatiha and the closing verses of Surah al-Baqarah. "Our Lord, do not cause our hearts to swerve after You have guided us, and bestow on us mercy from Your presence; You are the Giver."[29]

28 Qur'an 3:7.

29 Qur'an 3:8.

30 Qur'an 3:67.

31 Qur'an 3:27, 37.

32 Qur'an 3:35–50.

Through the stories of this *surah*, we are taught the beautiful manners, beliefs, and practices of Islam. We learn that Ibrahim ﷷ was a Muslim and preached Islam.[30] We learn that Allah provides for whomever He wills without any limits.[31] He provided Mary with fruits that were out of season, and with a miracle child. He provided Zakariyya with a miracle child when he asked Allah for an heir. He can provide for us too in such miraculous ways if we ask with conviction.[32]

The stories of Mary and those around her form the central narrative of this *juz*. It is worth taking the time to read these stories and reflect on them as they are full of powerful lessons about what piety and guidance look like in practice.

Through the amazing stories of Mary and Zakariyya, we are taught that Allah can provide for us in miraculous ways if we ask from Allah with conviction.

Juz three

The Seerah

Surah Ali 'Imran was mostly revealed in the third year after Hijrah. The various themes discussed in this *surah* reflect the core events in Medina during that year.

The themes of the Battle of Uhud, correct beliefs regarding Jesus ﷺ, and discussions about hypocrisy and relationships with the People of the Book all reflect the primary political events of 3 AH. During that year, the Prophet ﷺ dealt with all these issues.

The Battle of Uhud occurred a year after the Battle of Badr. The Muslims faced setbacks both before and during the battle which lead to the only military defeat they suffered during the Medinan phase.

The story of Jesus is narrated in more detail here than in Surah Maryam. Surah Maryam was revealed in Mecca, where Christianity did not really have a presence. This *surah* served more as a theological foundation for the Muslims of Mecca, while also serving as *da'wah* to the leaders of Abyssinia.

In Medina, particularly in 3 AH, the Prophet ﷺ began receiving delegations from Christian lands. To answer the questions of these delegations, Surah Ali 'Imran was revealed with a detailed account of the life of Jesus ﷺ and a firm reminder regarding the correct beliefs about Jesus and His Creator.

Allah revealed that the battles were tests for the believers, and that those who ran away after the Meccans surrounded them were forgiven by His mercy.

Another key event discussed in this *surah* is the Battle of Uhud. The Battle of Uhud occurred a year after the Battle of Badr and was not as successful. The Muslims faced setbacks both before and during the battle. Before the battle, three hundred hypocrites abandoned the ranks of the believers and returned to Medina, leaving the army perplexed, unprepared, and morally deflated.

During the battle, a group of archers abandoned their posts to pursue some loot, leaving the rear of the army exposed to a counterattack. The Meccans took advantage of this and surrounded the Muslims, leading to the only military defeat during the Medinan phase.

Many verses in this *surah* reflect on this Battle and the lessons related to it.

Remember when you left your home in the morning, to assign battle-positions for the believers. Allah is All-Hearing and All-Knowing. When two groups among you almost faltered, but Allah was their Protector. So, in Allah let the believers put their trust.[33]

In this *surah*, Allah revealed that the battles were tests for the believers, and that those who ran away after the Meccans surrounded them were forgiven. He also revealed that obedience to Allah and His Messenger is necessary for success in this world too. Finally, it is revealed that these events also served to expose the hypocrites so that the believers would not be fooled by their schemes.

And that He may know the hypocrites. And it was said to them, "Come, fight in the cause of Allah, or contribute." They said, "If we knew how to fight, we would have followed you." On that day they were closer to infidelity than they were to faith. They say with their mouths what is not in their hearts; but Allah knows what they hide.[34]

In the long run, the events of 3 AH benefited the Muslim community greatly. The discussions with the delegation of Christians clarified the beliefs that Islam and Christianity agreed upon and those they disagreed upon. This made it clear that the fundamental differences between Islam and Christianity regarded the nature of Allah and the humanity of Jesus.

33 Qur'an 3:121–22.

34 Qur'an 3:167.

The events at Uhud served as a powerful lesson for the Muslims which they wholeheartedly embraced. The mistakes made there were not repeated during the Prophet's ﷺ lifetime by those who had witnessed Uhud. The machinations of the hypocrites were exposed, and the believers were able to fend off many of their future schemes.

Surah Ali 'Imran provides a great framework for studying the events of the year 3 AH/624 AD and teaches us fundamental lessons, such as the importance of pure monotheism, sincerity of intention, unity of the believers, and preparing for the unexpected. These are all enduring lessons that continue to have relevance for us.

The events at Uhud served as a powerful lesson for the Muslims and those who witnessed the battle did not repeat those mistakes during the Prophet's ﷺ lifetime.

Juz three

Judgement Day

One of the major sins that leads to a lot of turmoil on the Last Day is consuming *riba* (usury). The modern banking system has normalised *riba* and made it part and parcel of the global economy. Many of us have become so desensitised to *riba* that we sometimes forget that it is a major sin to consume it.

Muslims should never lose sight of the fact that *riba* is a major sin and something of major consequence in both worlds. The warning in this *juz* about *riba* and its results on the Last Day are clear.

Taking advantage of the poor to increase one's own wealth is despicable and immoral, and one of the primary reasons why riba is a major sin in Islam.

Those who swallow usury will not rise [on the Last Day], except as someone driven mad by Satan's touch. That is because they say, "Trade is like usury." But Allah has permitted trade and has forbidden usury. Whoever, on receiving advice from his Lord, refrains, may keep his past earnings, and his case rests with Allah. But whoever resumes, these are the dwellers of the Fire, wherein they will abide forever. Allah condemns usury, and He blesses charity. Allah does not love any sinful ingrate.[35]

35 Qur'an 2:275–76.

36 Qur'an 3:30.

Usury has destroyed the lives of millions as well as entire economies. It nourishes a corrupt system, designed to make the wealthy wealthier at the expense of the poor and desperate. Taking advantage of the poor to increase one's own wealth is despicable and immoral, and one of the primary reasons why *riba* is a major sin in Islam. Believers must try their best to abstain from *riba* and work to transform the system so that it is fairer to the poor. We cannot be mere spectators or, even worse, participants in a system that destroys the lives of so many people.

Surah Ali 'Imran begins with very important reminders about the Last Day, such as the following:

On the Day when every soul finds all the good it has done presented. And as for the evil it has done, it will wish there were a great distance between them. Allah cautions you of Himself. Allah is Kind towards [His] servants.[36]

The above verse is a reminder that every good deed and every sin will be presented to the Creator on the Last Day. This should make us cautious about our lifestyles and actions, as every little good deed could play a role in tipping the scale in our favour on that day.

Juz three

Qur'anic worldview

The early verses of Surah Ali 'Imran highlight some of the most important beliefs and actions that will benefit us on the Last Day. We must submit to Allah completely, accept Islam as the only true path of salvation, follow the Messenger, and live a life of righteousness.

The true religion with Allah is Islam. Those to whom the Scripture was given differed only after knowledge came to them, out of envy among themselves. Whoever rejects the signs of Allah, Allah is quick to take account.[37]

37 Qur'an 3:19.

The good things of this world are a test, and the desire for them should not lead Muslims to the disobedience of Allah. The obedience of Allah and the desire for Paradise should be prioritised over worldly desires.

The Islamic worldview is built on belief in resurrection. Muslims must live their lives as preparation for that day. This inspires us to live a life that is purposeful and righteous. Knowing that we will be answerable on the Last Day for

38 Qur'an 3:25.
39 Qur'an 3:30.
40 Qur'an 3:14.

everything we do shapes our choices and actions.

How about when We gather them for a Day in which there is no doubt, and each soul will be paid in full for what it has earned, and they will not be wronged?[38]

Our belief in the Judgment on the Last Day also shapes how we perceive worldly calamities and injustices. There are many injustices in this world that will never be resolved in this life. Knowing that a day will come which the oppressors cannot escape gives us hope and optimism even during our toughest trials.

On the Day when every soul finds all the good it has done presented. And as for the evil it has done, it will wish there were a great distance between them. Allah cautions you of Himself. Allah is Kind towards [His] servants.[39]

The good things of this world are a test, and our desire for them should not lead to the disobedience of Allah. We must strive to keep things in perspective and prioritise the obedience of Allah and desire for Paradise over all worldly desires, even if these desires are halal.

Adorned for the people is the love of desires, such as women, and children, and piles upon piles of gold and silver, and branded horses, and livestock, and fields. These are the conveniences of worldly life, but with Allah lies the finest resort.[40]

Juz four

Juz four

Thematic overview

A central theme that flows throughout the fourth *juz* of the Qur'an is unity. These verses were revealed shortly after the Battle of Uhud (3 AH/ 625 CE), during which the Muslims encountered their first military defeat due to a moment of disunity. Many of these verses address the aftermath of that battle, reminding the believers that victory is from Allah, and that disunity gets in the way of Divine Assistance.

Internal problems continue to plague us even today, and our external enemies simply take advantage of this issue and utilise it to harm our ummah.

Disunity is written in the destiny of this great *ummah*. The Prophet ﷺ said, "I asked my Lord three things, and He granted me two but withheld one. I begged my Lord that my *ummah* should not be destroyed because of famine and He granted me this. And I begged my Lord that my *ummah* should not be destroyed by drowning [by deluge] and He granted me this. And I begged my Lord that there should be no bloodshed among the people of my *ummah*, but He did not grant it."[41]

41 Sahih Muslim, no. 2890.

It is interesting to note that the previous three verses focused on the mistakes of the past nations in the form of the rebelliousness of the professed followers of Moses and the misguided theology of those who claimed to follow Jesus. Yet this *juz* focuses primarily on the mistakes of the Muslims, our biggest weakness: our disunity. Disunity has always been a problem for the Muslim world. Internal problems continue to plague us even today, and our external enemies simply take advantage of this and utilise it to harm the *ummah*. The following verses in this *surah* all address different aspects of unity.

O you who believe! Revere Allah with due reverence, and do not die except as Muslims. And hold fast to the rope of Allah, all together, and do not become divided. And remember Allah's blessings upon you; how you were enemies, and He reconciled your hearts, and by His grace you became brethren. And you were on the brink of a pit of fire, and He saved you from it. Allah thus clarifies His revelations for you, so that you may be guided.

And let there be among you a community calling to virtue, and advocating righteousness, and deterring from evil. These are the successful. And do not be like those who separated and disputed after the clear proofs came to them; for them is a great punishment."[42]

42 Qur'an 3:102–5.

43 Qur'an 3:110.

44 Qur'an 3:121–29.

These verses implore us to unite and work together, to call towards good and deter evil. This is emphasised further in the following verse in which Allah describes the best of this nation. "You are the best community that ever emerged for humanity: you advocate what is moral, and forbid what is immoral, and believe in Allah. Had the People of the Scripture believed, it would have been better for them. Among them are the believers, but most of them are sinners."[43]

In this verse, we are informed that we are indeed the best of nations if we fulfil the obligations Allah has put upon us. Fulfilling these obligations requires unity and sincerity. The verses of unity are followed by a series of verses describing the Battle of Uhud and what went wrong at this battle.[44] The primary focus is on the lessons from this battle.

We are informed that we are indeed the best of nations if we fulfil the obligations Allah has put upon us. However, fulfilling these obligations requires unity and sincerity.

These lessons include the following:

- Any victory of Muslims is not because of numbers, it is dependent on the assistance of Allah. We should never rely on numbers alone in battle.
- Allah grants us victory when we are united.
- Allah's mercy descends when we are united.
- When we are disunited, we are our own worst enemies.
- We are commanded to strive for Allah, even though the Prophet passed away, the struggle for Islam continues.[45]

The *juz* ends with a reminder that those who made mistakes at Uhud were already forgiven by Allah. Allah did not reveal these verses to humiliate them. He revealed these verses so that we can reflect on these events and derive lessons from them. "Those of you who turned back on the day when the two armies clashed, it was Satan who caused them to backslide, on account of some of what they have earned. But Allah has forgiven them. Allah is Forgiving and Prudent."[46]

45 Qur'an 3:144.

46 Qur'an 3:155.

Juz four

The Seerah

Surah al-Nisa was revealed soon after Surah Ali 'Imran, with some of its verses revealed in late 3 AH/625 CE, while the rest were revealed in early 4/625. This *surah* also deals primarily with the aftermath of Uhud.

The Battle of Uhud had shaken the Muslim community and with this defeat came the loss of many great heroes of Islam like Mus'ab ibn 'Umayr رضي الله عنه and Hamza ibn 'Abd al-Muttallib رضي الله عنه. This tragedy brought new problems to the young community and Surah al-Nisa (The Women) was revealed to address many of these problems.

Surah Ali 'Imran focuses more on the spiritual and theological lessons of Uhud. Surah al-Nisa is more focused on resolving the family and community issues that arose in the wake of this tragedy. With the martyrdom of seventy great men came new problems: problems related to orphans, widows, inheritance, and the stability of society.

The beginning sections of this *surah* address the family issues. Polygamy, which was unrestricted before Islam, was restricted to a maximum of four wives, and proposed as a solution to the problem of war widows and orphans, with a strong reminder that treating wives justly was necessary. Inheritance laws were clarified and discussed in detail. The verses of inheritance are among the most detailed laws in the Qur'an. These verses gave women the right to inheritance over a thousand years before modern society did the same. This was shocking and alien to Arab culture at the time.

The wealth of orphans is also discussed in detail in this *surah*. This included the need for a guardian to take care of their wealth until they reach an age of financial responsibility. Along with this, several verses were revealed warning against usurping the wealth of orphans. The rights and responsibilities of husbands and wives were also clarified in these passages to ensure social cohesion on the most fundamental level.

With the martyrdom of seventy great men in Uhud came new problems in Medina related to orphans, widows, inheritance, and also the stability of society.

Society, however, is not made up only of families. For a society to thrive and not face such a loss again, they had to deal with internal and external threats as well. This is why there are several passages in this *surah* about military laws, the dangers of hypocrisy, and the relationship between Muslims and other groups. All of these were necessary to protect the young city-state from future tragedies.

There are also many verses in this *surah* stressing the importance of obeying the Messenger ﷺ. In the aftermath of Uhud, the reason for these verses was clear.

The archers who disobeyed the Prophet ﷺ caused the defeat of the Muslim army and the martyrdom of many of their friends. Obedience to the Prophet ﷺ was necessary for success then and remains necessary for our success today. The warnings about this in Surah al-Nisa are very strongly worded.

We did not send any messenger except to be obeyed by Allah's permission. Had they, when they wronged themselves, come to you, and prayed for Allah's forgiveness, and the Messenger had prayed for their forgiveness, they would have found Allah Forgiving and Merciful. But no, by your Lord, they will not believe until they call you to arbitrate in their disputes, and then find within themselves no resentment regarding your decisions and submit themselves completely.[47]

Obedience to the Prophet ﷺ was necessary for success then and remains necessary for our success even today.

Whoever obeys Allah and the Messenger, these are with those whom Allah has blessed, among the prophets, and the sincere, and the martyrs, and the upright. Excellent are those as companions.[48]

Whoever obeys the Messenger obeys Allah. And whoever turns away—We did not send you as a watcher over them.[49]

47 Qur'an 4:64–65.

48 Qur'an 4:69.

49 Qur'an 4:80.

Juz four

Judgement Day

Surah Ali 'Imran includes many important reminders about the Last Day and how to prepare for it. The various treasures of this world are described as beautiful and tempting. They are juxtaposed with Paradise and revealed to be nothing in comparison. The message is clear: prioritise the afterlife and do not allow temptation to sway you from this.

The treasures of this world are described as beautiful and tempting but when juxtaposed with Paradise, they are actually worth nothing in comparison.

Beautified for people is the love of desires, such as women, and children, and piles upon piles of gold and silver, and branded horses, and livestock, and fields. These are the joys of this worldly life, but with Allah lies the finest resort.

Say, "Shall I inform you of something better than that? For those who are righteous, with their Lord are Gardens beneath which rivers flow, where they will remain forever, and purified spouses, and acceptance from Allah." Allah is [always] observing [His] servants.

50 Qur'an 3:14–17.

Those who say, "Our Lord, we have believed, so forgive us our sins, and save us from the suffering of the Fire." The patient, and the truthful, and the pious, and the generous, and the seekers of forgiveness at dawn.[50]

Five key qualities of the people of Paradise are listed above: patience in adversity, truthfulness and honesty in every situation, piety as a lifestyle, generosity in dealings with others, and seeking Allah's forgiveness in the early morning.

A similar message is repeated at the end of the *surah* in one of the most powerful passages of the Qur'an. This passage highlights the mindset of the righteous, their attitude towards the afterlife, and the focus on their prayers.

In the creation of the heavens and the earth, and in the alternation of night and day, are signs for people of understanding. Those who remember Allah while standing, and sitting, and on their sides; and they reflect upon the creation of the heavens and the earth: "Our Lord, You did not create this in vain, glory to You, so protect us from the punishment of the Fire.

"Our Lord, whomever You commit to the Fire, You have disgraced. The wrongdoers will have no helpers.

"Our Lord, we have heard a caller calling to the faith: 'Believe in your Lord,' and we have believed. Our Lord! Forgive us our sins, and remit our misdeeds, and make us die in the company of the virtuous.

"Our Lord, give us what You have promised us through Your messengers, and do not disgrace us on the Day of Resurrection. Surely, You never break a promise."

And so, their Lord answered them: "I will not waste the work of any worker among you, whether male or female. You are of one another. For those who emigrated, and were expelled from their homes, and were persecuted because of Me, and fought and were killed, I will remit for them their sins and will admit them into gardens beneath which rivers flow" A reward from Allah. With Allah is the ultimate reward.[51]

This amazing passage was often recited by the Prophet ﷺ late at night before the night vigil prayer,[52] and he once said about it, "A verse has been revealed to me tonight and woe to one who reads it without reflecting upon it,"[53] meaning that if someone never reflects on this verse, it will be a great loss to them. Take some time to reflect on this passage and how it prepares us for the Last Day.

Allah says in the Qur'an that in the creation of the heavens and the earth, and in the alternation of night and day, there are signs for people of understanding.

51 Qur'an 3:190–95.

52 Sahih al-Bukhari, no. 4294.

53 Sahih ibn Hibban, no. 620.

Qur'anic worldview

54 Qur'an 3:103–5.

Ummatic unity is central to the Muslim worldview. When we are united, we will accomplish more and overcome our trials together. When divided, we become our own worst enemies. Muslims must strive to revive ummatic unity by overcoming barriers like sectarianism, nationalism, tribalism, and racism. A united Muslim community is a powerful force that can achieve remarkable results.

We must assess our hearts to ensure that we don't allow evil to consume them and divide us from other Muslims.

And hold fast to the rope of Allah, together, and do not become divided. And remember Allah's blessings upon you; how you were enemies, and He reconciled your hearts, and by His grace you became brethren. And you were on the brink of a pit of fire, and He saved you from it. Allah thus clarifies His revelations for you, so that you may be guided.

And let there be among you a community calling to virtue, and advocating righteousness, and deterring from evil. These are the successful.

And do not be like those who separated and disputed after the clear proofs came to them; for them is a great punishment.[54]

A sign of true unity is desiring good for each other. Likewise, desiring harm for each other is a sign of hypocrisy and diseases in the heart. We must assess our hearts to ensure that we don't allow evil to consume them and divide us from other Muslims.

If something good happens to you, it upsets them; but if something bad befalls you, they rejoice at it. But if you persevere and maintain righteousness, their schemes will not harm you at all. Allah comprehends what they do.[55]

55 Qur'an 3:120.

These passages were revealed after the Battle of Uhud. The lessons from that battle were that disunity and desiring worldly results led to defeat. Another factor that contributed to the defeat was that the hypocrites abandoned the army in large numbers, leaving it weakened and vulnerable. The Battle of Uhud is a great showcase of the importance of unity, true faith, and prioritising the afterlife over this world.

Worldly victories and losses are less important than success on the Last Day. In this world, sometimes we win and sometimes we lose. During times of loss, it is important to focus on learning from our mistakes, trying harder, and striving for future victories. This is a crucial lesson from the Battle of Uhud.

Juz five

Juz five

Thematic overview

Surah al-Nisa was revealed shortly after Surah Ali ‘Imran and continues its theme of addressing the aftermath of Uhud. While Surah Ali ‘Imran focused primarily on the political and theological lessons, Surah al-Nisa primarily focuses on social and legal matters that arose in the aftermath of Uhud. Although the *surah* is named “The Women” due to the high number of gender-related rules that appear in it, the core theme concerns the laws of Islam related to various aspects of society.

We are reminded that although men and women are equal in terms of spirituality and potential for salvation, Allah created them to play different roles in society.

Due to the high number of men who were martyred at Uhud, a variety of issues arose related to widows, orphans, and inheritance. All these issues are addressed in this *surah*. The *surah* begins with a reminder that humanity originated from a single couple, and so due to our common ancestry we must maintain the ties of kinship.[56] This spirit of brotherhood and community runs throughout the *surah*. This verse is also a reminder that although men and women are equal in terms of spirituality and potential for salvation, Allah created them to play different roles in society.

56 Qur’an 4:1.

57 Qur'an 4:4.

58 Qur'an 4:41.

This is another theme that runs throughout the *surah*, the dual roles of men and women, which are meant to complement each other so that society functions smoothly.

The *surah* then reminds us of the permission for and restrictions on polygamy.[57] This verse was revealed during the aftermath of Uhud, giving comfort to the widows and orphans of Uhud that they would be taken care of and not forgotten. Although the permission for restricted polygamy is general, its roots have always been in societal and communal good, with a strong focus on the rights of the women and children involved in such a family structure.

The importance of obeying the Messenger ﷺ is repeated throughout Surah Ali 'Imran and also in Surah al-Nisa.

Surah al-Nisa also continues the theme of defining this *ummah*. The previous two *juz* referred to this *ummah* as a balanced *ummah* and the best of *ummah*s, but in this *juz*, we are told that our *ummah* is a witness over every other *ummah*, and the Prophet ﷺ is a witness over us.[58]

Another beautiful theme that flows through this *surah* is the theme of ease. This *surah* is heavy on legal matters, and this may feel overwhelming to many readers. In between all these laws, Allah assures us that He revealed these laws to make life easier for us and understands that humans are weak.

Allah intends to make things clear to you, and to guide you in the ways of those before you, and to redeem you. Allah is Most Knowing, Most Wise. Allah intends to redeem you, but those who follow their desires want you to turn away utterly. Allah intends to lighten your burden, for the human being was created weak.[59]

Another important lesson that is emphasised in this *surah* is the importance of obeying the Messenger ﷺ. This is a continuation of the lessons from the Battle of Uhud (3 AH/625 CE). The defeat at Uhud was primarily due to the archers disobeying the command of the Prophet ﷺ.

Because of this, the importance of obeying the Messenger is repeated throughout Surah Ali ‘Imran and Surah al-Nisa which includes the powerful command, “But no, by your Lord, they will not believe until they call you to arbitrate in their disputes, and then find within themselves no resentment regarding your decisions and submit themselves completely.”[60]

Surah al-Nisa is the second longest *surah* in the Qur’an and flows through the fourth, fifth, and sixth *juz* of the Qur’an. The themes of law, society, the rights of the weak, and importance of obeying the law all flow throughout this powerful chapter of the Qur’an, giving us a lot to reflect on and more to practice.

59 Qur’an 4:26–28.

60 Qur’an 4:65.

Juz five

The Seerah

The fifth *juz* contains many verses that were revealed in response to specific incidents. These verses were revealed during the early-to-middle years of the Medinan phase in response to various incidents. One of these incidents was related to the loss of Aisha's ﵂ necklace and led to the revelation of the verse of *tayammum* in this *surah*.

'Aisha ﵂ said, "We set out with Allah's Messenger ﷺ on one of his journeys till we reached Al- Bayda' or Dhat al-Jaysh, where a necklace of mine was broken [and lost]. Allah's Messenger ﷺ stayed there to search for it, and so did the people along with him.

There was no water at that place, so the people went to Abu Bakr As-Siddiq and said, "Do you not see what Aisha has done? She has made Allah's Apostle ﷺ and the people stay where there is no water, and they have no water with them.'

Abu Bakr ﵁ came while Allah's Messenger ﷺ was sleeping with his head on my thigh. He said to me, 'You have detained Allah's Messenger ﷺ and the people where there is no water, and they have no water with them.' So, he admonished me and said what Allah wished him to say. Nothing prevented me from moving but the position of Allah's Messenger ﷺ on my thigh.

Allah's Messenger ﷺ got up when dawn broke and there was no water. So, Allah revealed the Divine Verses of dry ritual purification (tayammum).

So, they all performed tayammum. Usaid bin Hudair ؓ said, 'O family of Abu Bakr! This is not the first blessing of yours.' Then the camel on which I was riding was caused to move from its place and the necklace was found beneath it."[61]

61 Sahih al-Bukhari, no. 334.

Even if we cannot understand the wisdom behind a law or a test, trusting Allah and remaining firm in obeying Him in every condition is the path to success.

This story gives us a glimpse of the various challenges the Muslims faced in Medina. A common theme that runs through this *surah* is the importance of trusting Allah and obeying His Messenger ﷺ. Sometimes we cannot understand the wisdom behind a law or a test.

Even in such situations, trusting Allah and remaining firm in obeying Him is the path to success. Very often trials we do not understand today end up becoming the most important moments of our life in the long run.

Juz five

Judgement Day

62 Qur'an 4:42.

63 Qur'an 4:64–65.

Surah al-Nisa focuses on family and societal issues in the aftermath of Uhud. Woven into this discussion are many verses about the Last Day, often focused on the importance of justice and obeying the Messenger ﷺ. These are necessary principles for establishing Islamic families and societies. The theme of obeying the Messenger is repeated multiple times throughout this *surah*.

The authentic hadith narrations teach us the detailed laws of Islam and they are as crucial for formulating Islamic law as the Qur'an is in the life of a Muslim.

On that Day, those who disbelieved and disobeyed the Messenger will wish that the earth was levelled over them. They will conceal nothing from Allah.[62]

We did not send any messenger except to be obeyed by Allah's leave. Had they, when they wronged themselves, come to you, and prayed for Allah's forgiveness, and the Messenger had prayed for their forgiveness, they would have found Allah Relenting and Merciful.

But no, by your Lord, they will not believe until they call you to arbitrate in their disputes, and then find within themselves no resentment regarding your decisions and submit themselves completely.[63]

Obedience to those to whom Allah has given authority is a crucial part of submitting to Allah. The laws of Islam are not suggestions or recommendations; they are necessary for establishing the goals of the Shariah and living a life that is pleasing to Allah. Therefore, all success lies in obeying the Messenger ﷺ.

O you who believe! Obey Allah and obey the Messenger and those in authority among you. And if you dispute over anything, refer it to Allah and the Messenger, if you believe in Allah and the Last Day. That is best, and a most excellent determination.[64]

Obeying the Messenger ﷺ means to follow his way which has been passed down in the hadith narrations. The authentic hadith narrations teach us the detailed laws of Islam and they are as crucial for formulating Islamic law as the Qur'an is. Islamic orthodoxy is not based on the Qur'an alone. It is also based on the collective efforts of righteous scholars in analysing the Qur'an and Sunnah and deducing the laws of Islam from these primary resources. The call to obey the Messenger ﷺ and those in authority is a call to Islamic orthodoxy.

The other core theme in this *surah* related to the Day of Judgment is a reminder about Allah's justice. This *surah* contains many verses about laws intended to promote justice. Inheritance, marriage, caring for orphans and polygamy laws are all explained in this *surah* with an emphasis on justice.

64 Qur'an 4:59.

65 Qur'an 4:40.

Allah then reminds us that He is the Most Just, so He expects us to be just too. It is from His Kindness that He increases the reward for good deeds and multiplies them so that the scale tilts in our favour.

Allah does not commit an atom's weight of injustice; and if there is a good deed, He doubles it, and gives from His Presence a sublime compensation.[65]

It is from His Kindness that He increases the reward for good deeds and multiplies them so that the scale tilts in our favour.

The two main messages to take from this *surah* are the importance of following Islamic orthodoxy and committing to justice. These two concepts will weigh heavily on the Last Day and our success in both worlds depends on how well we commit to both concepts.

Juz five

Qur'anic worldview

The theme of unity remains central in the fifth *juz* which deals with the social fallout from the Battle of Uhud. Various social issues that may cause disunity are addressed specifically in Surah al-Nisa. This *surah* reminds us about the dangers of hypocrisy and disobeying the Prophet.

The various social issues in this *surah* show us the importance of justice as a central tenet of unity. Without justice, it is difficult to maintain peace and unity in a community. The importance of justice is emphasised multiple times in this *surah*, as Muslims are reminded to be just to their spouses, orphans, family, and community. Polygamy is also mentioned in this *surah* with the condition of justice attached.

Surah al-Nisa makes it clear that men and women play different social roles in the Islamic family structure and should not seek what Allah has given the other.

A small yet crucial portion of this *surah* focuses on inheritance law and the crucial need to obey the law in this matter. Injustice in the distribution of inheritance is a primary cause of disunity and dissent among Muslim families. To counter this, inheritance law is explained in a lot of detail in this *surah*. This is exceptional as the Qur'an usually

66 Qur'an 4:32.

67 Qur'an 4:135.

mentions a law briefly and leaves the details to hadith, but on this issue, the details are clearly laid out in the Qur'an to ensure justice.

Regarding gender roles, Surah al-Nisa makes it clear that men and women play different social roles in the Islamic family structure and should not seek what Allah has given the other. Justice here lies in fulfilling the role that Allah has assigned one, as seeking to compete with the opposite gender leads to misuse of Allah's gifts and violating His laws.

Do not covet what Allah has given to some of you in preference to others. For men is a share of what they have earned, and for women is a share of what they have earned. And ask Allah of His bounty. Allah has knowledge of everything.[66]

The *juz* ends with a powerful reminder of the central importance of justice in the Qur'anic worldview as a pillar of unity and peace.

O you who believe! Stand firmly for justice, as witnesses to Allah, even if against yourselves, or your parents, or your relatives. Whether one is rich or poor, Allah takes care of both. So do not follow your desires, lest you swerve. If you deviate or turn away, then Allah is Aware of what you do.[67]

Juz six

Juz six

Thematic overview

68 Qur'an 6:3.

The sixth *juz* of the Qur'an begins at verse 148 of Surah Nisa and ends at verse 41 of Surah Ma'idah. Surah al-Ma'idah was revealed many years after Surah al-Nisa at a very different stage in the Prophet's ﷺ life. Surah al-Ma'idah was one of the last *surahs* to be revealed during the final years of the prophetic era. It was revealed after the conquest of Mecca when Muslims were finally in a position of power. During this phase of power, the Prophet ﷺ began to send letters to the kings of various countries inviting them and their people to Islam. The themes of Surah al-Ma'idah (the Feast) reflect the time in which it was revealed.

The first few *surahs* of the Qur'an give us a glimpse of the Medinan phase of history. Surah al-Baqarah shows us what Islam was like before Badr, while Surah Ali 'Imran and al-Nisa show us glimpses of life after Uhud. Surah al-Ma'idah then shows us the final phase of the *da'wah*, the perfection of the law[68] after the conquest of Mecca. Surah al-Ma'idah essentially revolves around two themes, the final laws of Islam and the principles of *da'wah* to the People of the Book and other nations.

As this was the final lengthy *surah* that was revealed, it contains a lot of details on the various laws of Islam. This includes dietary, marriage, pilgrimage and criminal laws, as well as the foundations and spiritual frameworks of these laws. The *surah* begins with a call to fulfil our covenant with Allah.[69] This is a call for us to take the law seriously and obey it. This includes fulfilling our covenants with people as that is part of obedience to Allah.

Surah al-Ma'idah begins with a call to fulfil our covenant with Allah which is a call for us to take the law seriously and obey it.

This is followed by a series of verses describing the final laws of Islam. In these verses, Allah informs us of the types of food that we are permitted to eat, as well as that which is prohibited. The permission to eat food slaughtered by the People of the Book and marry chaste women of the People of the Book was also revealed in this *surah*.[70] These verses show us how Muslims lived in harmony with the People of the Book in a post-Hudaybiyah society. Hudaybiyah was the site of a peace treaty between the Muslims and the Meccan polytheists which lasted for a few years.

69 Qur'an 6:1.

70 Qur'an 5:3–5.

71 Qur'an 5:7.
72 Qur'an 5:11.

The previous two *surahs* reminded us that victory lies in the obedience of Allah. This *surah*, revealed post-victory, includes a reminder that Allah fulfilled that promise with the conquest of Mecca.

And Remember Allah's blessings upon you, and His covenant which He covenanted with you; when you said, we hear, and we obey. And remain conscious of Allah, for Allah knows what the hearts contain.[71]

O you who believe! Remember Allah's blessings upon you; when certain people intended to extend their hands against you, and He restrained their hands from you. So, revere Allah, and in Allah let the believers put their trust.[72]

In Surah al-Ma'idah, Allah reminds us to remain firm upon justice, and not allow our hatred for anyone to cause us to be unjust.

In between these two verses, Allah reminds us to remain firm upon justice, and not allow our hatred for anyone to cause us to be unjust. It is significant that this verse was revealed after the Muslims were victorious as people often carry out injustices after gaining power. This verse is a powerful reminder to Muslims to remain committed to justice, especially when we have the power to oppress.

O you who believe! Be upright to Allah, witnessing with justice; and let not the hatred of a certain people prevent you from acting justly. Adhere to justice, for that is nearer to piety, and fear Allah. Allah is informed of what you do.[73]

A large portion of this *surah* focuses on the story of Jesus ﷺ, as the Muslims were interacting more with the Christians in this phase; reminders about *tawheed* and how to invite Christians to Islam are frequent throughout this *surah*.

Surah al-Ma'idah also includes the story of Cain and Abel, the two sons of Adam ﷺ and the first murder, once again reminding us that power and greed should not corrupt us and cause us to oppress anyone. This passage includes the famous reminder that killing one innocent person is equivalent in sin to killing all of humanity, and saving a single soul earns one the reward of saving all of humanity.[74]

Surah al-Ma'idah is a reminder of how Muslims should operate when we are in a position of power. Justice, dedication to the law and the fulfilment of covenants all remain priorities for the believer no matter how much worldly power we attain.

73 Qur'an 5:8.

74 Qur'an 5:27–32.

Juz six

The Seerah

This *juz* contains the last long *surah* to be revealed, Surah al-Ma'idah, which was revealed in the 10th year after *Hijrah*. After it, a few small portions of verses and short *surahs* were revealed. This was the final set of laws revealed to the Prophet ﷺ and included the powerful line cementing this Shariah as the perfect law system for humanity.

Today I have perfected your religion for you, and have completed My favour upon you, and have approved Islam as a religion for you.[75]

This verse was so powerful that a rabbi once said to 'Umar ibn al-Khattab ؓ that this was the verse he admired most in the Qur'an.

'Umar ibn al-Khattab ؓ reported: A man from the Jews said, "O leader of the believers, there is a verse you recite in your book and, had it been revealed to us as Jews, we would have taken that day as a celebration."

'Umar ؓ said, "Which verse is it?"

The man recited the verse, "Today I have completed your religion for you, perfected My favour upon you, and have chosen Islam as your religion."[76]

75 Qur'an 5:3.

76 Sahih al-Bukhari, no. 45; Sahih Muslim, no. 3017.

This verse was revealed at Mount 'Arafah during what came to be known as the 'farewell pilgrimage'. Picture the scene. The Prophet ﷺ, after twenty years of struggle, stood humbly on Mount 'Arafah addressing over one hundred thousand Muslims for the last time.

In the 'farewell pilgrimage', the Prophet ﷺ, after twenty years of struggle, stood humbly on Mount 'Arafah addressing over one hundred thousand Muslims in his final year of prophethood.

The Prophet ﷺ worked his way through trial upon trial from a humble beginning of a handful of dedicated followers and was now the most powerful man in Arabia. Soon his followers would continue the growth until within a century, the Muslim world was the dominant civilisation on earth.

At this critical moment, the Prophet ﷺ delivered his final sermon which included the following crucial advice to all his followers until the end of time.

Verily your blood and your property are as sacred and inviolable as the sacredness of this day of yours, in this month of yours, in this town of yours. Behold! Everything pertaining to the Days of Ignorance is completely abolished. Abolished are also the blood feuds of the Days of Ignorance.

Fear Allah concerning women! Verily you have taken them on the security of Allah, and intercourse with them has been made lawful unto you by words of Allah. You too have rights over them, that they should not allow anyone to sit on your bed whom you do not like. But if they do that, you can chastise them but not severely. Their rights upon you are that you should provide them with food and clothing in a fitting manner. I have left among you the Book of Allah, and if you hold fast to it, you will never go astray.

And when you will be asked about me [on the Day of Resurrection], [tell me] what will you say? They [the audience] said: We will bear witness that you have conveyed [the message], discharged [the responsibility of prophethood] and given wise [sincere)] counsel. He [the narrator] said: He [the Holy Prophet] then raised his forefinger towards the sky and, pointing it at the people, [said]: "O Allah, be a witness. O Allah, be a witness," saying it thrice.[77]

77 Sahih Muslim, no. 1218.

It was on this momentous occasion that this beautiful passage was revealed in Surah al-Ma'idah, cementing that the message was complete, and Islam was here to stay.

The Prophet ﷺ delivered his final sermon which included crucial advice for his ummah until the end of time.

The rest of the *surah* contains many other verses related to powerful incidents during that final year of revelation. A common theme in many of these verses is the importance of the Shariah. The entire *surah* focuses on the overall importance of the Shariah, reinforcing that it is the final and perfect system of laws, and the only acceptable path to Allah.

Juz six

Judgement Day

78 Qur'an 5:36.

Surah al-Ma'idah was the last large *surah* to be revealed. Although this *surah* focuses heavily on Islamic law, there are many reminders about the Last Day throughout the *surah*. We are reminded that the things of this world are worthless on the Last Day. Even if someone owned everything in this world, it would count as nothing on that day, and they would not be able to offer it as a ransom to save themselves.

As for those who disbelieve, even if they owned everything on earth, and the like of it with it, and they offered it to ransom themselves from the torment of the Day of Resurrection, it will not be accepted from them. For them is a painful punishment.[78]

Surah al-Ma'idah contains many warnings about trying to tamper with Allah's laws. We are warned that those who were given previous scriptures tried to change the law and will be held accountable for this on the Last Day. Blatant attempts to change Allah's laws are classified as a type of disbelief in this *surah*.

In our time, there is a strong push from a vocal minority to change aspects of Islam to fit with modern ideas. Fundamental aspects of Islamic morality are challenged for not meeting contemporary ideals, and some try to reinterpret the Qur'an and Sunnah to fit these modern ideologies. The following verses serve as severe warnings to those who dare to tamper with Allah's laws.

In Surah al-Ma'idah we are told that the things of this world are worthless on the Last Day. Even if someone owned everything in this world, it would not be enough as ransom to save themselves.

Indeed, We revealed the Torah, containing guidance and light, by which the prophets, who submitted themselves to Allah, made judgments for Jews. So too did the rabbis and scholars judge according to Allah's Book, with which they were entrusted and of which they were made keepers. So do not fear the people; fear Me! Nor trade My revelations for a fleeting gain. And those who do not judge by what Allah has revealed are [truly] disbelievers.[79]

79 Qur'an 5:44.

80 Qur'an 5:47.
81 Qur'an 5:50.

So let the people of the Gospel rule according to what Allah revealed in it. Those who do not rule according to what Allah revealed are sinners.[80]

Is it the laws of the time of ignorance that they desire? Who is better than Allah in judgment for people who are certain?[81]

Severe warnings are given to those who dare to tamper with Allah's laws. The law itself is sacred and will forever stand as the perfect way of life.

The laws of Allah are perfect and the best system of governance for every time and era. Built into this system are methods of flexibility that allow finer details to be adjusted based on necessity, culture, and other considerations. But these adjustments take place within the system using its own principles and do not involve changes to the law itself. The law itself is sacred and will forever stand as the perfect way of life that leads to the best of both worlds.

Juz six

Qur'anic worldview

In the Islamic worldview, this *ummah* is viewed as the best of nations but this is conditional upon sincere belief and active striving to promote good and prevent evil. It is essential to build our faith to a level that it influences every aspect of our lives. This faith though should not be personal or private; it should inspire our public lives as well. This means that Muslims must be forces of good and voices of truth in public, especially in an era in which immorality is so dominant.

You are the best community that ever emerged for humanity: you command goodness, and forbid evil, and believe in Allah.[82]

If someone lacks the authority to change things by their hands, the next step is to be a voice of truth with courage and wisdom to inspire change. The lowest level is to hate evil in one's heart.

82 Qur'an 3:110.

When Muslims live according to the above principles, we become a powerful force capable of global change. True change is inspired by true faith and is built on actively working to build a moral society. The principles of commanding righteousness and forbidding evil (*al-amr bi-l-ma'ruf wa al-nahyy 'an al-munkar*) are essential for developing a truly moral society.

The Messenger of Allah ﷺ said, "Whoever among you sees evil, let him change it with his hand. If he cannot do so, then with his tongue. If he cannot do so, then with his heart, which is the weakest level of faith."[83]

83 Sahih Muslim, no. 49.

There are levels to commanding righteousness and forbidding evil. As per the above hadith, those in authority can change things physically through establishing laws and consequences based on divine morality. If someone lacks the authority to change things by their hands, the next step is to be a voice of truth. This is the level most Muslims are capable of: speaking the truth with courage and wisdom and inspiring change through their words. The lowest level is to hate evil in one's heart, which usually occurs in environments of tyranny. The believer must strive to inspire change through whatever means Allah has blessed them with.

The perfection of the Shariah is central to the Qur'anic worldview. The most famous verse about the perfection of the Shariah has been emphasised in every section of this chapter due to its crucial importance to Muslims. Belief in the perfect Shariah means that we strive to live by Islam's laws and view it as the optimal way for humans to live their lives.

We want people to embrace the optimal way of life and live accordingly. This should inspire us to be actively involved in calling people to the truth.

It also means that we prioritise preaching Islam and spreading the message to others, as we wish goodness for others. We want people to embrace the optimal way of life and live accordingly. This should inspire us to be actively involved in *da'wah* and calling people to the truth.

The Prophet ﷺ said, "By Allah, that Allah guides a man through you is better for you than a herd of expensive red camels."[84]

84 Sahih al-Bukharī, no. 3009; Sahih Muslim, no. 2406.

Juz seven

Juz seven

Thematic overview

The seventh *juz* of the Qur'an begins at verse 83 of Surah al-Ma'idah (the Feast) and ends at verse 110 on Surah al-An'am (the Livestock). The *juz* begins with recognising that many of the People of the Book were righteous and sincere. They recognised the message of Islam as being the same as the previous prophets and accepted it. This was specifically true for many practising Christians.

Satan wants to provoke strife and hatred among us through intoxicants and gambling, and to prevent us from remembering Allah and to abandon prayer.

And you will find that the nearest in affection towards the believers are those who say, "We are Christians." That is because among them are priests and monks, and they are not arrogant. And when they hear what was revealed to the Messenger, you see their eyes overflowing with tears, as they recognise the truth in it. They say, "Our Lord, we have believed, so count us among the witnesses."[85]

One of the greatest examples of this was the Negus King, al-Najashi, the ruler of Abyssinia at that time. He was a just Christian king who sheltered the Muslims.

85 Qur'an 5:82–83.

86 Qur'an 5:90.
87 Qur'an 5:91.

When the verses of Surah Maryam (Mary) were recited in his court, his priests began to weep as described in this verse. Najashi secretly accepted Islam and the Prophet ﷺ performed the funeral prayer (*janazah*) in absence for him when he passed away. He is an exemplary example of a sincere believer.

As the core theme of Surah al-Ma'idah are the laws of Islam, many of these laws are deailed in this *juz*. This includes the prohibition of alcohol and gambling. These two vices were destructive norms in Arab society as they are in many societies today. The laws prohibiting alcohol were revealed slowly over time to allow for gradual change, teaching us the wisest manner of reforming a society.

The final verse prohibiting alcohol completely is this verse in Surah al-Ma'idah: "O you who believe! Intoxicants, gambling, idolatry, and divination are abominations of Satan's doing. Avoid them, so that you may prosper."[86]

The next verse explains the reason for this prohibition, "Satan wants to provoke strife and hatred among you through intoxicants and gambling, and to prevent you from the remembrance of Allah, and from prayer. Will you not desist?"[87]

With so many laws revealed in this *surah*, some believers may have experienced anxiety about their past sins. To comfort them, Allah revealed that He does not hold people accountable for the sins they committed before Islam or before the law was revealed.

Those who believe and do righteous deeds will not be blamed for what they may have eaten, provided they obey, and believe, and do good deeds, then maintain piety and faith, then remain righteous and charitable. Allah loves the charitable.[88]

88 Qur'an 5:93.

The remainder of the *surah* focuses on stories of past nations. There is a parable here between the stories of Moses and Jesus. The followers of Moses asked unnecessary questions out of mockery which led to the religion becoming stricter upon them. The disciples of Jesus, however, asked Allah for a table from Heaven to feast from. They asked this out of sincerity so that they could witness a miracle. Allah answered their prayers, and a beautiful feast was sent down from Heaven for them.

The *surah* ends with a reminder that there is only One Allah, and that Jesus is his messenger. Trinity is an unacceptable belief in Islamic theology, and the sincere followers of Jesus are called once more to abandon the trinity and follow the true message of submission.

The next *surah* in the Qur'an is Surah al-An'am. Here the reader will notice a major shift in both style and content. This is because Surah al-An'am is an early Meccan *surah*, the first after a long series of Medinan *surahs*. While the Medinan *surahs* before it focused on laws and politics, Surah al-An'am focuses purely on the message of *tawhid*. This links up with the ending of Surah al-Ma'idah which called sincere Christians to the doctrine of divine unicity (*tawhid*); the next *surah* is all about the oneness of Allah and His Noble Attributes.

Studying the differences between Surah al-Ma'idah and Surah al-An'am gives us a beautiful example of the differences between Meccan and Medinan revelation. Medinan revelation tends to be more focused on laws, while Meccan revelation focused on beliefs as that is the foundation of the faith. Because of this, the content of Surah al-An'am is very different from the *surahs* before it. It focuses primarily on the oneness of Allah, His Signs, and the story of Abraham (Arb. Ibrahim) confirming the oneness of Allah. It also lists all the major prophets by name, teaching us not only what to believe about Allah, but which prophets we need to believe in as well.

Surah al-An'am focuses primarily on the oneness of Allah, His Signs, and the story of Ibrahim عليه السلام *confirming the oneness of Allah.*

Meccan revelation emphasises the story of Ibrahim as he was an ideal model of Islamic monotheism. Ibrahim submitted to Allah when everyone around him rejected monotheism, and his story became legendary. The Jews, Christians, and even the pagans of Mecca all knew his story well, so it served as a powerful reminder to all of them to return to the way of Ibrahim.

Juz seven

The Seerah

Surah al-An'am marks a break from the themes covered during the first six *juz*s of the Qur'an. While the previous *surahs* were Medinan and closely tied to the events of the Medinan era, Surah al-An'am is a Meccan *surah* focused on theological issues. The themes of prophethood and monotheism flow throughout this *surah* showing us the primary focus of early Meccan revelation.

When we choose to ignore the signs of Allah, we choose to blind ourselves to any proof. Even if a dozen miracles happen before one's eyes, excuses will flow from the mouth when the heart is blind.

Some of the pagans of Mecca refused to believe unless something miraculous happened in front of their eyes. Allah revealed that this was just an excuse and no matter what happened, they would find a way to explain it away and never believe it. Even if a hundred miracles occurred before them, they would reject them by saying each miracle was the result of magic, an illusion, or a hallucination.

89 Qur'an 6:4–5.

90 Qur'an 6:7–10.

This is the reality of many atheists today, too. The Creator has surrounded us with millions of signs of His existence and power. When we choose to ignore these signs, we choose to blind ourselves to any proof. Even if a dozen miracles happen before one's eyes, excuses will flow from the mouth when the heart is blind to the truth. This was the case of Meccans then, and it is the case of many sceptics today.

Not one of their Lord's signs comes to them, but they turn away from it. They denied the truth when it came to them; but soon will reach them the news of what they used to ridicule.[89]

Had We sent down upon you a book on paper, and they had touched it with their hands, those who disbelieve would have said, "This is nothing but plain magic." And they say, "Why was an angel not sent down to him?" Had We sent down an angel, the matter would have been settled, and they would not have been reprieved. Had We made him an angel, We would have made him a man, and confused them when they are already confused. Messengers before you were ridiculed, but those who mocked them became besieged by what they ridiculed.[90]

The revelation of this *surah* was itself a grand event. The revelation was accompanied by so many angels that they filled the horizon. Some narrations stated as much as seventy thousand angels, but as these narrations are weak, we do not list a specific number.

Nonetheless, the fact that the sky was filled with angels shows that this is a powerful and important *surah* with a crucial message.

The leaders of the pagans recognised the Qur'an as a divine revelation. As masters of Arabic poetry, they knew that it was beyond human capacity to produce a book like the Qur'an.

Arrogance and refusal to accept that Allah had chosen Muhammad ﷺ over them as the final messenger caused the Quraysh to reject the truth, even when it was as clear as day.

This was especially the case for al-Waleed ibn Mughirah who eventually wrote it off as magic, despite knowing otherwise. Arrogance and refusal to accept that Allah had chosen Muhammad ﷺ over them as the final messenger caused the Quraysh to reject the truth, even when it was as clear as day. Allah revealed the following verses in response to them.

91 Qur'an 6:20–21.

Those to whom We have given the Book recognise it as they recognise their own children; but those who have lost their souls do not believe. Who does greater wrong than someone who fabricates lies against Allah, or denies His revelations? The wrongdoers will not succeed.[91]

The Meccan revelation focused primarily on the fundamentals of faith. This *surah* gives us a detailed look at the message of Meccan revelation. It is full of strong arguments for the prophethood of Muhammad ﷺ and the oneness of Allah. This *surah* remains a powerful and persuasive message to any sincere seeker of the truth today.

The leaders of the pagans recognised the Qur'an as a divine revelation. As masters of Arabic poetry, they knew that it was beyond human capacity to produce a book like the Qur'an.

Juz seven

Judgement Day

Surah al-Ma'idah ends with a powerful conversation between Allah and the Prophet Jesus ﷺ on the Last Day, narrated in extensive detail. This conversation shows us that the messengers had a task to convey the message to their people and are not responsible for what their people did after their time.

On the Day of Judgment, Allah will say, "This is a Day when the truthful will benefit from their truthfulness." They will be given luxury gardens in which they will remain in enjoyment forever.

And Allah will say, "O Jesus, son of Mary, did you say to the people, 'Take me and my mother as gods, rather than Allah?'" He [Jesus] will say, "Glory be to You! It is not for me to say what I have no right to. Had I said it, You would have known it. You know what is in my soul, and I do not know what is in Yours. You are the Knower of the hidden. I only told them what You commanded me: that you shall worship Allah, my Lord, and your Lord.

"And I was a witness over them while I was among them; but when You took me to Yourself, You became the Watcher over them; You are Witness over everything. If You punish them, they are Your servants; but if You

92 Qur'an 5:116–19.

93 Qur'an 6:63–65.

forgive them, You are the Mighty and Wise." [Allah will say], "This is a Day when the truthful will benefit from their truthfulness." They will have gardens beneath which rivers flow, wherein they will remain forever. Allah is pleased with them, and they are pleased with Him. That is the great attainment.[92]

In this *juz*, the themes shift from Medinan to Meccan with Surah al-An'am. Meccan *surahs* focus a lot more on the afterlife as their primary focus is on building our core theology. This includes our belief in the Day of Judgment and the afterlife.

This *surah* includes a warning to worship Allah in good times, not only during difficult times.

Say, "Who delivers you from the darkness of land and sea?" You call upon Him humbly and inwardly: "If He delivers us from this, We will surely be among the thankful." Say, "It is Allah who delivers you from it, and from every disaster. Yet then you associate others with Him."

Say, "He is able to send upon you an affliction, from above you, or from under your feet. Or He can divide you into factions, and make you taste the violence of one another." Note how We explain the revelations, so that they may understand.[93]

The Prophet ﷺ gave a similar message to 'Abd Allah ibn 'Abbas ؓ in this famous hadith:

Be mindful of Allah, and you will find Him in front of you. Recognise and acknowledge Allah in times of ease and prosperity, and He will remember you in times of adversity. And know that what has passed you by [and you have failed to attain] was not going to befall you, and what has befallen you was not going to pass you by. And know that victory will come with patience, relief will come with affliction, and with hardship will come ease.[94]

Preparation for the Last Day begins with mindfulness of Allah. When we are mindful during good times, we grow stronger in our faith and can engage in more good deeds in preparing for that day.

O assembly of jinn and humans, did there not come to you messengers from among you, relating to you My revelations, and warning you of the meeting of this Day of yours? They will say, "We testify against ourselves." The life of the world seduced them. They will testify against themselves that they were disbelievers. That is because your Lord would not destroy towns for injustice while their inhabitants were unaware.[95]

Be mindful of Allah, and you will find Him in front of you. Recognise and acknowledge Allah in times of ease and prosperity, and He will remember you in times of adversity.

94 Al-'Arba'un al-Nawawiyya, no. 19.

95 Qur'an 6:130–31.

Juz seven

Qur'anic worldview

96 Qur'an 6:12.

Say, "To whom belongs what is in the heavens and the earth?" Say, "To Allah." He has inscribed for Himself mercy. He will gather you on the Day of Resurrection, in which there is no doubt. Those who lost their souls do not believe.[96]

There is no concept more central to the Islamic worldview than monotheism. This refers to belief in One God, who is unique in His Names and Attributes, has power over all things, and is the only one worthy of worship. The concept of monotheism is so central to the Islamic worldview that the only unforgivable sin is to die in a state of polytheism (*shirk*).

The Qur'an reminds us constantly, especially in the seventh juz, of the power and glory of the Creator with an emphasis on the correct understanding of monotheism.

Surah al-An'am focuses primarily on the oneness of Allah and proofs of His existence and power in His Creation. The Creation around us is a miracle, a proof of the existence of the Creator. Spending time in nature and reflecting on the creations around us aid us in increasing and solidifying our faith. There are many verses in this *surah* that remind us to do this.

And they say, "If only a sign could come down to him from his Lord." Say, "Allah is able to send down a sign, but most of them do not know."

There is no animal on land, nor a bird flying with its wings, but are communities like you. We neglected nothing in the Scripture. Then to their Lord they will be gathered.

Those who reject Our revelations are deaf and dumb, in total darkness. Whomever Allah wills, He leaves astray; and whomever He wills, He sets on a straight path.[97]

The Qur'an reminds us constantly, especially in this *juz*, of the power and glory of the Creator. A correct understanding of monotheism is essential for living an Islamic life. Reflecting on this *surah* helps shape our understanding of who our Creator is.

It is He who created the heavens and the earth in truth. On the Day when He says: "Be," it will be. His saying is the truth, and His is the sovereignty on the Day when the trumpet is blown. The Knower of secrets and declarations. He is the Wise, the Expert.[98]

97 Qur'an 6:37–39.

98 Qur'an 6:73.

Juz eight

Juz eight
Thematic overview

The eighth *juz* begins at verse 111 of Surah al-An'am (the Livestock) and ends at verse 87 of Surah al-A'raf (the Heights). Both *surahs* were revealed during the early Meccan era. As a result, they share several themes and flow together as one discussion. The common theme that runs throughout these two *surahs* is Islamic theology (*'aqidah*) and its various

The miracle of the Qur'an and the proofs of prophethood are all clear and evident, yet some still disbelieve in the message, insisting on their disobedience even when they are reminded.

branches. Surah al-An'am focuses more on the concept of monotheism, while Surah al-A'raf continues with further emphasis on the afterlife and the messengers. All the primary beliefs of Islam can be found in this *juz* of the Qur'an, making it a *juz* of *'aqidah*.

The *juz* begins with a firm reminder that those who reject the truth will do so regardless of what evidence is provided to them. Allah says, "Even if We sent down the angels to them, and the dead spoke to them, and We gathered all things before them, they still would not believe, unless Allah wills; but most of them are ignorant."[99]

99 Qur'an 6:111.

100 Qur'an 6:116.

The problem, therefore, is not with the message but with the recipients of the message.

This verse condemns radical scepticism. Scepticism, when taken to its natural conclusion, will cause a person to doubt everything, even when the proof is clear in front of them. It is the same with those who reject the truth. The miracle of the Qur'an and the proofs of prophethood are all clear and evident, yet they still disbelieve. Even if angels descended, they would claim it is a hallucination, bewitchment, or something else. Those who do not want to believe will find every reason to not do so.

We are then reminded that the truth is not always with the majority. Truth has its own criterion and can often be found with minorities.

If you were to obey most of those on earth, they would divert you from Allah's path. They follow nothing but assumptions, and they only conjecture.[100]

The reality is that truth is uncomfortable, and most people do not want to leave their comfort zones. We become complacent with the dominant culture and political correctness. This is easier than seeking the truth and following hard truths that the rest of society may reject.

The parables of truth and falsehood continue throughout the *surah* as Allah compared the guided to the living and the misguided to the dead. "Is he who was dead, then We gave him life, and made for him a light by which he walks among the people, like he who is in total darkness, and cannot get out of it? Thus, the doings of disbelievers are made to appear good to them."[101]

101 Qur'an 6:122.

This verse shows us how Islam brings light to the hearts of people and softens the hearts of even the harshest of critics. 'Umar ibn al-Khattab ﷺ is a good example of this. Initially, he was a dedicated enemy of Islam, but when the light of Islam entered his heart, he became a beacon of light for others whose example continues to light our way today. The parable of guidance and misguidance continues in the next few verses.

Whomever Allah desires to guide, He spreads open his heart to Islam; and whomever He desires to misguide, He makes his heart narrow, constricted, as though he were climbing up the sky. Allah thus lays defilement upon those who do not believe.[102]

102 Qur'an 6:125.

We are in constant need of Allah's sustenance, mercy, and guidance. Guidance can only come from Him and He guides whoever proves worthy of guidance.

103 Qur'an 6:133.
104 Qur'an 6:161–63.

Concluding the section on guidance, Allah reminds us that He does not need anything. We are in constant need of His sustenance, mercy, and guidance. Guidance can only come from Allah and He guides whoever proves worthy of guidance.

Your Lord is the Rich Beyond Need, the Possessor of Mercy. If He wills, He can do away with you, and substitute whomever He wills in your place, just as He produced you from the descendants of another people.[103]

Surah al-An'aam ends with a reminder to submit entirely to Allah. It is not enough to recognise that Allah is the Creator. To fulfil the purpose of life, we must submit entirely to Allah. Our entire lives must be dedicated to the service of Allah. Reminding us about this, the *surah* ends with a powerful set of verses.

Say, "My Lord has guided me to a straight path, an upright religion, the creed of Abraham the monotheist, who was not a polytheist." Say, "My prayer and my worship, and my life and my death, are devoted to Allah, the Lord of the Worlds. No associate has He." Thus, I am commanded, and I am the first of those who submit.[104]

Surah al-A'raf continues this theme of theology and guidance. It begins with the story of Adam and the devil. Allah describes to us how the devil refused to prostrate because he believed that he was better than Adam. Arrogance led him astray. Arrogance remains the primary cause of misguidance. When a person is arrogant, they cling to their opinions and beliefs even when they know that they are wrong. Guidance then lies in purifying our souls from arrogance.

105 Qur'an 7:43.

The devil promises to lead people astray and that many people will be ungrateful. When describing the people of Paradise in this *surah*, Allah shows us that the devil will fail in this mission with the sincere believers. They will be in Paradise, praising Allah, expressing gratitude for all His favours.

Allah describes to us how the devil refused to prostrate because he believed that he was better than Adam. Arrogance led him astray.

We will remove whatever rancour is in their hearts. Rivers will flow beneath them. And they will say, "Praise be to Allah, who has guided us to this. Had Allah not guided us, we would never be guided. The messengers of our Lord did come with the truth." And it will be proclaimed to them, "This is the Garden you are made to inherit, on account of what you used to do."[105]

Juz eight

The Seerah

Surah al-A'raf is the first of many *surahs* in the Qur'an that highlight the stories of perished nations. These stories are narrated and repeated collectively across multiple *surahs*. They include the stories of Prophets Noah (Nuh), Hud (possibly the Biblical Eber), Saleh, Shu'ayb (possibly the Biblical Jethro), Lot (Lut), and Moses (Musa) ﷵ. The collective narration of these six stories is a common feature across Meccan revelation.

The pagans of Mecca were familiar with many of these stories. Some of these nations were Arab nations and the stories of their destruction had been passed down through the generations. What had been lost was the reason for their destruction. These *surahs* were revealed to remind the Meccans about why these past nations were destroyed: for rejecting their messenger and his message.

The story of Noah and the great flood is found across all cultures. It was the first time in human history that a civilisation was wiped out for rejecting the Creator. The stories of how Pharaoh was defeated, and how the people of Lot were destroyed are also very well-known across many cultures and religions.

The other three stories are less known outside of Muslim circles. Hud was sent to the nation of 'Aad who were destroyed for their tyranny and polytheism. Saleh was sent to the nation of Thamud, who were destroyed for similar reasons.

Shu'ayb was sent to the city of Madyan whose inhabitants engaged in unjust business practices.

106 Qur'an 7:4–6.

These three nations, and their stories, were well known to the Meccans. The purpose of these narrations in the Qur'an was to bring the Meccans' attention to the key point of these stories; the importance of believing in and obeying the Messenger of Allah. The Meccans were being warned through these stories that if they rejected the messenger sent to them, a similar fate would await them.

The story of Noah and the great flood is found across all cultures. It was the first time in history that a civilisation was wiped out for rejecting the Almighty Creator.

How many a town have We destroyed? Our might came upon them by night, or while they were napping. When Our might came upon them, their only cry was, "We were indeed wrongdoers." We will question those to whom messengers were sent, and We will question the messengers.[106]

The content of these stories can be rather heavy for some readers. The Qur'an alternates between reminders of Allah's mercy and punishment. This creates a balanced attitude. A believer should not rely on Allah's mercy so much that they stop doing good deeds and live a life of sin,

107 Qur'an 7:56.

expecting full forgiveness. At the same time, they should not despair of Allah's mercy and feel that their sins cannot be redeemed.

Reflecting on and understanding the various stories in the Qur'an helps us achieve this balance. To maintain this balance, it is crucial to reflect on these stories of perished nations, just as much as we reflect on the stories of hope like the stories of Joseph (Yusuf), David (Dawud), and Solomon (Sulayman). Each story plays a role in shaping our faith and our relationship with our Creator.

And do not cause corruption on earth after its reformation. Pray to Him with fear and hope. Allah's mercy is close to the doers of good.[107]

The Qur'an alternates between reminders of Allah's mercy and punishment which creates a balanced attitude to worship.

As an early Meccan *surah*, there is also a strong focus on the afterlife in Surah al-A'raf. The afterlife was a foreign concept to the Quraysh, who did not think there was anything beyond death. As a new concept to them, it needed a lot of elaboration. To achieve this, this *surah* is full of descriptions of the afterlife. Each description creates a detailed picture in the mind and helps increase one's conviction in the reality of the next life.

Juz eight

Judgement Day

Surah al-A'raf is named after a scene on the Last Day that is mentioned in this *juz* only. On the Last Day, a group of believers whose good and bad deeds are equal will have to wait for their fate to be decided. Our goal should be to live a life of righteousness that protects us from ending up in this situation. The scene is described in detail in the following verses.

The people of Hell will call on the people of Paradise to pour some water over them. They will respond that it has been forbidden for the disbelievers.

And between them is a partition, and on the elevations are men who recognise everyone by their features. They will call to the inhabitants of the Garden, "Peace be upon you." They have not entered it, but they are hoping. And when their eyes are directed towards the inmates of the Fire, they will say, "Our Lord, do not place us among the wrongdoing people."

And the dwellers of the elevations will call to men they recognise by their features, saying, "Your hoardings did not avail you, nor did your arrogance." "Are these the ones you swore Allah will not touch with mercy?" "Enter the Garden; you have nothing to fear, and you will not grieve."

108 Qur'an 7:46–50.
109 Qur'an 7:8–9.
110 Qur'an 7:38–39.

The inmates of the Fire will call on the inhabitants of the Garden, "Pour some water over us, or some of what Allah has provided for you." They will say, "Allah has forbidden them for the disbelievers."[108]

This amazing scene is preceded by other verses describing the Last Day in vivid detail. These verses describe the scales, the state of the disbelievers, and the reward for the righteous believers on that day.

The scales on that Day will be just. Those whose scales are heavy; it is they who are successful. But as for those whose scales are light, it is they who have lost their souls because they used to mistreat Our revelations.[109]

He will say, "Join the crowds of jinn and humans who have gone into the Fire before you." Every time a crowd enters, it will curse the other crowd. Until, when they are all in it, the last of them will say to the first of them, "Our Lord, these are the ones who misled us, so inflict on them a double punishment in the Fire." He will say, "Each will have double, but you do not know." The first of them will say to the last of them, "You have no advantage over us, so taste the torment for what you used to earn."[110]

As for those who believe and do righteous work, We never burden any soul beyond its capacity; these are the inhabitants of the Garden, abiding therein eternally. We will remove whatever rancour is in their hearts. Rivers will flow beneath them.

And they will say, "Praise be to Allah, who has guided us to this. Had Allah not guided us, we would never be guided. The messengers of our Lord did come with the truth."

And it will be proclaimed to them, "This is the Garden you are made to inherit on account of what you used to do." And the inhabitants of the Garden will call out to the inmates of the Fire, "We found what our Lord promised us to be true; did you find what your Lord promised you to be true?" They will say, "Yes." Thereupon a caller will announce in their midst, "The curse of Allah is upon the wrongdoers."[111]

111 Qur'an 7:42–44.

Surah al-A'raf is full of incredible descriptions of the Last Day. Every believer should take time to study this *surah* and reflect on its themes.

The people of Paradise will say, "Praise be to Allah who has guided us to this. Had Allah not guided us, we would never be guided..."

Juz eight

Qur'anic worldview

112 Mohammad Elshinawy, The Final Prophet (Leicestershire: Kube Publishing, 2022), 4.

Belief in prophets is central to the Islamic worldview. Surah al-A'raf focuses on the stories of the prophets. There is a beautiful link between Surah al-An'am and Surah al-A'raf, both of which shape our beliefs. In Surah al-An'am, we are given details about the most important tenet of faith, monotheism, then in Surah al-A'raf we are informed about the stories of the prophets. Our faith revolves around these two concepts: testifying to the oneness of Allah, and belief in and obedience to His prophet.

The prophets are links between humans and their Creator. It is through the prophets that revelation is received and guidance is spread. Without their messages and examples, we would be left to figure out too much for ourselves. The prophets, all of them, must be revered and respected. The final prophet must be obeyed and emulated. This is an essential part of Islam.

Shaykh Mohammad El-Shinawy explains the need for prophets as follows:

Another reason why believing in the messengers is inseparable from being a good person is that only the messengers can thoroughly define good, through the inspiration they receive from Allah.[112]

Tawḥīd (pure monotheism), which is to single Allah out in everything unique to Him, is the ultimate supreme good, and this would also be impossible without the messengers. Humanity cannot know Allah, nor know His beauty and grandeur, nor know the path to His pleasure, nor know His promises and threats, nor embody His prescriptive will which He lovingly ordained for the betterment of His creation, without the prophets and messengers.[113]

113 Elshinawy, The Final Prophet, 5.

A key focus of the stories of the prophets in this *juz* is on the consequences for rejecting the messengers. As their guidance is necessary for our salvation, rejecting them leads to destruction in this world and the next. The following passages give us stern reminders about what awaits those who reject the prophets.

It is an essential part of Islam that all the prophets must be revered and respected. The final prophet ﷺ must be obeyed and emulated.

Do the people of the towns feel secure that Our might will not come upon them by night, while they sleep?

Do the people of the towns feel secure that Our might will not come upon them by day, while they play?

114 Qur'an 7:97–101.

Do they feel safe from Allah's plan? None feel safe from Allah's plan except the losing people.

Is it not guidance for those who inherit the land after its inhabitants, that if We willed, We could strike them for their sins? And seal up their hearts, so that they would not hear?

These towns, We narrate to you some of their tales. Their messengers came to them with clear signs, but they would not believe in what they had rejected previously. Thus Allah seals the hearts of the disbelievers.[114]

The guidance of the prophets is necessary for our salvation. Rejecting the prophets leads to our destruction both in this world and in the next.

Juz nine

Juz nine

Thematic overview

The ninth *juz* of the Qur'an begins at verse 88 of Surah al-A'raf (the Heights) and ends at verse 40 of Surah al-Anfal (the Battle Gains). These two *surahs* contain very different themes. Surah al-A'raf is the second of two *surahs* focused on theology. Surah al-Anfal is the first of two consecutive *surahs* focused on the military struggles of the Prophet ﷺ and his companions. Thus, the theme of theology runs through the first half of this *juz*, then there is a shift to military struggles.

Surah al-A'raf discusses the stories of those who obeyed Allah and, as a result, received Allah's blessings both in this world and in the next.

The shift is not disconnected though; the opening verses of Surah al-Anfal ground it in Islamic theology and remind us that victory is from Allah, and to earn a blessed victory we must be true believers. The necessity of a strong theology for a successful military campaign links these two chapters of the Qur'an.

There are many parallels between Surah al-An'am and al-A'raf. Surah al-An'am tells us that Allah sent worldly possessions as a punishment to those who disbelieved before destroying them. Surah al-A'raf mentions how Allah blesses the worldly possessions of those who obey Him. Surah al-An'am discusses the stories of the perished nations who enjoyed the blessings of this world then were punished. Surah al-A'raf discusses the stories of those who obeyed Allah and, as a result, received blessings in this world and the next. The following two verses are a beautiful illustration of this.

When they forgot the reminders, we opened the doors for all that they wanted. Once they were intoxicated, we seized them suddenly and they were left in a state of despair.[115]

If only the people believed and feared Allah, we would have opened for them blessings (sing. barakah), but they denied so we seized them.[116]

The *juz* begins in the middle of the story of Shu'ayb ﵇ which gives us an example of both types of people. Shu'ayb's ﵇ wealth was blessed due to his piety. His people were wealthy traders who earned Allah's anger due to their cheating. In the end, Allah destroyed his people, yet he and the righteous were spared and continued to be blessed. This story teaches us that when Allah's punishment comes, worldly means have no benefit. Earning the blessings of Allah should be the priority of every believer.

The verse quoted above appears immediately after this story as a reflection on it. Had the people of Madyan believed, they would have experienced *barakah* in their wealth as Shu'ayb ﵇ did. They feared that accepting Islam would cause them to lose their wealth. The reality was the opposite of

115 Qur'an 6:46.

116 Qur'an 7:96.

what they feared. This story was very relevant to the people of Mecca as they shared the same fear. The tribe of Quraysh were wealthy traders who feared losing their wealth if they embraced Islam. Instead, Allah put *barakah* in the wealth of Muslims and made Mecca a center of blessed commerce, which it remains today.

Another story in this *juz* is the story of Moses ﷺ and the magicians of Pharaoh. When the magicians witnessed the miracles of Moses, they immediately believed and gave up everything in this world for Allah. They were threatened and killed by Pharaoh but did not waver in their faith. Believers know that the true blessings await them in the afterlife.

The next *surah* is a shift back to Medinan revelation. Surah Al-Anfal was revealed shortly after the Battle of Badr as a reflection on the battle itself. It is the shortest *surah* in the first third of the Qur'an after al-Fatiha (the Opening) and is placed here due to its relation to Surah al-Tawbah (the Repentance) which some companions considered an extension of it.

When the Qur'an was compiled, 'Abd Allah ibn 'Abbas asked 'Uthman [ibn 'Affan] ﷺ, "What is your reasoning about Surah al-Anfal, which has less than a hundred verses, and Surah At-Tawbah, which has more than a hundred verses, yet you put them together without writing in the name of Allah, the Most Gracious, the Most Merciful between them and you placed them with the seven long surahs. Why did you do that?"

Uthman ﷺ responded, "Al-Anfal was among the first to be revealed in Medina and At-Tawbah was among the last of those revealed of the Qur'an and their discussions resemble each other, so we thought that they were part of each other. Then the Messenger of Allah died, and it was not clear to us if they were part of each other. For this reason, we put them together without writing in the name of Allah, the Most Gracious, the Most Merciful and we included them with the seven long surahs."[117]

117 Jami' al-Tirmidhi, no. 3086, grade of authentication: rigorously authentic (sahih).

118 Musnad Ahmad, no. 4247.

Surah Al-Anfal was revealed shortly after the Battle of Badr as a reflection on the battle itself.

Surah al-A'raf ends with the story of Moses and his followers defeating Pharaoh. Surah Al-Anfal was revealed after the Prophet ﷺ and his companions defeated the Quraysh at Badr. There are many parallels between these stories. The followers of Moses had to flee Egypt; the companions had to flee Mecca. Pharaoh was killed in this event; the "pharaoh of this nation," according to a prophetic statement,[118] 'Amr ibn Hisham, a.k.a Abu Jahl (lit. "father of ignorance"), was killed at Badr. These stories give hope to the oppressed that Allah will grant them victory over their oppressors eventually. This is one of the core themes found throughout this *juz* of the Qur'an, the triumph of the oppressed over the oppressors.

Juz nine

The Seerah

Surah al-Anfal begins in the last quarter of the ninth *juz*. This is an early Medinan *surah* revealed immediately after the Battle of Badr (2 AH/624 CE). The Battle of Badr was the first major battle in Muslim history and a significant event that turned the tide in favour of the Muslims.

Until this moment, the Muslims had faced a lot of oppression at the hands of the pagans of Mecca. For thirteen years, the *da'wah* in Mecca faced resistance, tyranny, and violence. The Muslims were forced to flee and had to relocate to Medina. Here they established a base of operations and grew strong enough to face their oppressors. In the second year after the Hijrah, they had an opportunity to do so.

We are reminded that Allah gives victory to whom He wills. The believers attained victory in battle because they obeyed Allah and His Messenger ﷺ.

At the wells of Badr, the Muslims faced their transgressors in battle for the first time. Despite being outnumbered, the Muslims fought valiantly and, with the help of an army of angels, they defeated the Meccans. The defeat was significant as most of the leaders of Mecca died in battle against the Muslims that night.

After this defeat, a new generation of Meccans had to take over the leadership. There was a significant difference between the two generations of leaders, as seen in the fact that most of the next generation eventually accepted Islam and joined the Prophet's side. The likes of Umayyah ibn Khalaf and Abu Jahl were defeated at Badr, and the Prophet ﷺ would not face an enemy as oppressive as them again.

Surah al-Anfal was revealed on this occasion and each of its passages directly relates to the various events surrounding this battle. This was the first time the Muslims had attained a military victory and were unsure regarding the proper method of dividing the war booty. The opening verses of this *surah* addressed this concern immediately.

They ask you about the bounties. Say, "The bounties are for Allah and the Messenger." So be mindful of Allah, and settle your differences, and obey Allah and His Messenger, if you are believers.[119]

This is followed by a reminder that victory is from Allah. He gives victory to whom He wills. The believers attained victory because they obeyed Allah and His Messenger. This is a common theme found throughout the *surahs* that discuss war.

The believers are those whose hearts tremble when Allah is mentioned, and when His revelations are recited to them, they strengthen them in faith, and upon their Lord they rely. Those who perform the prayer; and from Our provisions to them, they spend.

119 Qur'an 8:1.

120 Qur'an 8:2–4.
121 Qur'an 8:9–11.
122 Qur'an 8:17.

These are the true believers. They have high standing with their Lord, and forgiveness, and a generous provision.[120]

The *surah* contains reminders about many of the miracles the Muslims experienced on the battlefield that day, including the assistance of the angels, a gentle rain that benefited them while damaging the opposition's camp, and the moment when the Prophet ﷺ threw a handful of dirt, and it entered the eyes of all his enemies. All these moments are mentioned in this *surah* as reminders of Allah's blessings.

When you appealed to your Lord for help, He answered you, "I am reinforcing you with one thousand angels in succession." Allah only made it a message of hope, and to set your hearts at rest. Victory comes only from Allah. Allah is Mighty and Wise. He made drowsiness overcome you, as a security from Him. And He sent down upon you water from the sky, to cleanse you with it, and to rid you of Satan's pollution, and to fortify your hearts, and to strengthen your foothold.[121]

And it was not you who threw when you threw, but it was Allah who threw. That He may bestow upon the believers an excellent reward. Allah is Hearing and Knowing.[122]

The Battle of Badr is a lesson to the tyrant and oppressor that their tyranny cannot last forever, and a day will soon come when justice will be served.

The Battle of Badr is one of the most significant events in Muslim history. It is a reminder that Allah will assist the righteous, even if they are few. It is a reminder that miracles happen when Allah wills them. It is also a lesson to the tyrant and oppressor that their tyranny cannot last forever, and a day will come when justice will be served. This powerful *surah* covers all these lessons eloquently, leaving the reader with plenty to ponder.

Juz nine

Judgement Day

123 Qur'an 7:188.
124 Qur'an 8:2–4.

Surah al-A'raf ends with a warning that only Allah knows the unseen, which includes when the Last Day will occur. We cannot know or even speculate as to when the world will end, but what we can do is ensure that we prepare for the afterlife adequately.

Say, "I have no control over any benefit or harm to myself, except as Allah wills. Had I known the future, I would have acquired much good, and no harm would have touched me. I am only a warner, and a herald of good news to a people who believe."[123]

Surah al-Anfal begins with five qualities of true believers and the reward for striving to gain these qualities. The qualities of a true believer are fear of Allah, faith increasing when listening to Qur'anic recitation, trust in Allah, firmness in praying five times a day, and generosity.

The believers are those whose hearts tremble when Allah is mentioned, and when His revelations are recited to them, they strengthen them in faith, and upon their Lord they rely. Those who perform the prayer; and who spend from Our provisions to them. These are the true believers. They have high standing with their Lord, and forgiveness, and a generous provision.[124]

Some commentators mention that the opposites of these qualities are the qualities of the hypocrites; that is a lack of fear of Allah, lack of trust in Allah, not being moved by Qur'anic recitation, being negligent of prayers, and miserliness.[125] Every believer must strive to gain the qualities of a true believer, while being mindful to avoid the qualities of a hypocrite.

125 Tafsir ibn Ashur, 9:261.

126 Qur'an 8:7–10.

In Surah al-Anfal, Allah mentions five qualities of true believers and the reward for striving to gain these qualities which believers should always desire to achieve.

Surah al-Anfal is a Medinan *surah* focused on lessons from the Battle of Badr. Many of these lessons were theological as the victory of Badr helped increase the faith of Muslims and served as a proof of the truth of Islam.

Allah has promised you one of the two groups, that it would be yours, but you wanted the unarmed group to be yours. Allah intends to prove the truth with His words, and to uproot the disbelievers to confirm the truth and nullify falsehood, even though the guilty dislike it. When you appealed to your Lord for help, He answered you, "I am reinforcing you with one thousand angels in succession." Allah only made it a message of hope, and to set your hearts at rest. Victory comes only from Allah. Allah is Mighty and Wise.[126]

127 Qur'an 8:24.

This *surah* is a reminder that victory is from Allah. Success is in the hands of Allah, and we are only successful when we live in a way that is pleasing to Him. Islam is referred to in this *surah* as that which revives the hearts of people.

Islam revives the hearts of people. Without Islam, our hearts are dead, and our lives are meaningless.

Without Islam, our hearts are dead, and our lives are meaningless. It is only when we respond to Allah's call to Islam that we will find true success in both worlds. This is a key message of the Battle of Badr.

O you who believe! Respond to Allah and to the Messenger when he calls you to what revives you. And know that Allah stands between a man and his heart, and that to Him you will be gathered.[127]

Juz nine

Qur'anic worldview

Belief in the prophets must lead to obeying the prophetic law. The final Prophet was sent with the perfect way of life, but we can only benefit from that system if we take it seriously and live by it. Both *surahs* in this *juz* emphasise in multiple passages the importance of obeying the messenger.

Say, "O people, I am the Messenger of Allah to you all—He to whom belongs the kingdom of the heavens and the earth. There is no god but He. He gives life and causes death." So believe in Allah and His Messenger, the Unlettered Prophet, who believes in Allah and His words. And follow him, that you may be guided.[128]

The benefits of believing in and obeying the messengers is that we gain the tools required to ultimately pass the test of life.

O you who believe! Obey Allah and His Messenger, and do not turn away from him when you hear.[129]

O you who believe! Do not betray Allah and the Messenger, nor betray your trusts, while you know.[130]

128 Qur'an 7:158.

129 Qur'an 8:20.

130 Qur'an 8:27.

131 Qur'an 7:94–96.

We are reminded in these chapters that life is a test. We must be ready to handle the trials of life with steadfastness, patience, and firm faith in Allah's Perfect Plan. This is not always easy to do, but it is necessary for passing the test of life and achieving eternal bliss.

We did not send any prophet to any town but We afflicted its people with misery and adversity, so that they may humble themselves.

Then We substituted prosperity in place of hardship. Until they increased in number, and said, "Adversity and prosperity has touched our ancestors." Then We seized them suddenly, while they were unaware.

Had the people of the towns believed and become righteous, We would have opened for them the blessings of the heaven and the earth; but they rejected the truth, so We seized them for what they were doing.[131]

The benefits of believing in and obeying the messengers is that we gain the tools required to pass the test of life. The result is that we may experience ease after our hardships, and even if we do not experience it in this world, eternal ease awaits in the next.

Juz ten

Juz ten

Thematic overview

The theme of war and conflict flows throughout the tenth *juz* of the Qur'an. This *juz* begins at verse 41 of Surah al-Anfal (the Battle Gains) and ends at verse 86 of Surah al-Tawbah (the Repentance). These two *surahs* are known as the warfare chapters and are often misquoted by Islamophobes to project a false image of Islam. There are many verses in this *juz* that are quoted out of context to make Islam look violent and intolerant. Yet there are many other verses in this *juz* that put these verses in context and give the full picture.

Surah al-Anfal was revealed after the Battle of Badr (2 AH/624 CE), Surah al-Tawbah was one of the last Medinan *surahs* and was revealed after the expedition to Tabuk (9 AH/630 CE), northwestern of current day Saudi Arabia. Both *surahs* were revealed during military campaigns and their verses reflect these circumstances. To take these verses out of context is dishonest. It also distracts from the many beautiful lessons we can derive from these two *surahs* as many people shy away from discussing them because of their association with the concept of jihad.

In these two *surahs*, we see the beginning and the end of the military campaigns of the Prophet ﷺ against the tribe of Quraysh. Surah al-Anfal reflects on their first victory reminding us that victory is from Allah, and piety is what matters most. Surah al-Tawbah was revealed after the biggest victory of the Muslims, the conquest of

Mecca, showing the Muslims at the height of their power. Between these two *surahs*, we see various reflections on how Muslims should behave during wartime, times of peace, and when in a position of power. In all situations, justice and piety take precedence over all else.

An often-misquoted verse is verse 60 of Surah al-Anfal; "And prepare against them all the power you can muster, and all the cavalry you can mobilise, to terrify thereby Allah's enemies and your enemies, and others besides them whom you do not know, but Allah knows them. Whatever you spend in Allah's way will be repaid to you in full, and you will not be wronged."[132]

Surah al-Anfal reflects on the first victory of the Muslims reminding us that victory is only from Allah, and piety is what matters most.

This verse is often portrayed as promoting terrorism. Yet its context clearly shows otherwise. The verse promotes the importance of the Muslim nation having a strong military presence so that it is not a target of tyrants and enemies. The goal is to avoid war by establishing a position of power. The following verse helps us understand its proper context, "But if they incline towards peace, then incline towards it, and put your trust in Allah. He is the Hearer, the Knower."[133]

132 Qur'an 8:60.

133 Qur'an 8:61.

134 Qur'an 8:70.

135 Musnad Ahmad, no. 948.

Another important verse in this *surah* is verse 70 which was revealed about the Prophet's ﷺ Uncle al-'Abbas; "If Allah finds any good in your hearts, He will give you better than what was taken from you, and He will forgive you. Allah is Forgiving and Merciful."[134]

Al-'Abbas was forced to fight the Muslims at Badr, but he just stood there and allowed himself to be captured. He was captured by Abu Yusuf al-Sulami, a man small in size, who was assisted by an angel. Allah wanted al-'Abbas captured early, so that he would not be killed. It was painful for the Prophet ﷺ and his companions to see their loved ones as captives. The Prophet ﷺ gave concessions to his uncle and out of justice, he gave the same to all the captives. He even started new methods of ransom including allowing prisoners of war to teach people how to read in exchange for freedom. The Prophet ﷺ asked al-'Abbas to ransom himself and he said that he did not have any money. The Prophet ﷺ told him about some money only he and his wife knew about. Al-'Abbas immediately realised that he was a true prophet, and some narrators claim he accepted Islam then and there. This verse was then revealed promising goodness in both worlds to al-'Abbas and those like him. After paying that ransom, al-'Abbas grew wealthier every day and never lost wealth again.[135]

The Prophet ﷺ returned home from Tabuk with a strong psychological victory, but the event had exposed the hypocrites and those inclined to the temptations of this world.

Surah al-Tawbah was revealed around the time of the expedition to Tabuk and reflects the various political events that took place that year. It flows from Surah al-Anfal like one *surah* sharing a theme of military struggle. Tabuk was a long and brutal expedition in which the Prophet ﷺ and thirty thousand companions set out to face the Byzantine army. It was a long march through the desert in the middle of summer. Leaving Medina for this expedition was itself a test from Allah. Eventually, no battle took place as the Byzantine army did not show up. The Prophet ﷺ returned home with a strong psychological victory, but the event had exposed the hypocrites and those inclined to this world.

Juz ten

The Seerah

Surah Tawbah continues the theme of war from Surah al-Anfal. The themes of these two *surahs* are so similar that some early scholars considered them to be one *surah*. The focus on war ethics in this *juz* can be a bit jarring for some first-time readers who are unfamiliar with the background of these *surahs*. Many verses in Surah Tawbah are context-specific and make a lot more sense when the reasons for revelation are clarified.

The opening passages are a declaration that the peace treaty between the Muslims and pagans was over, and that a war was coming. The Meccans and their allies had violated the peace treaty, which led to the revelation of these verses. It is part of Islamic ethics to announce a declaration of war, instead of surprising the enemy. By doing so, the Muslims were being fair and giving their opponents a fighting chance.

Surah Tawbah was revealed in pieces towards the end of the Medinan era. Many of the passages in this *surah* revolve around the events of Tabuk (9 AH/630 CE) and Hunayn (8 AH/ 630 CE), two of the final skirmishes in the Prophet's ﷺ lifetime. Tabuk marked the first expedition of the Prophet's ﷺ army against the Byzantines, while Hunayn was their final major battle against an Arab tribe.

These two events marked a turning of the tide in Arabia. The Muslims were now the dominant power of Arabia, and the Byzantines saw this as a threat to their power in the region. This led to the great battles between the two nations during the Rashidite era in which many Byzantine lands like Damascus, Jerusalem, and Egypt became Muslim lands.

In the Battle of Hunayn, the Muslims felt confident that they would be victorious and let their guard down. As a result, the Muslim army was taken by surprise and ambushed.

Hunayn was an interesting event. The Muslims were a large army for the first time, and for many, their numbers deceived them. They felt confident that they would be victorious and let their guard down. As a result, the Muslim army was taken by surprise and ambushed. Many ran away, but the Prophet ﷺ and his staunchest supporters remained firm against the onslaught. Seeing the courage of the Prophet ﷺ, the Muslims eventually returned to their positions and were victorious.

136 Qur'an 9:25–26.

Allah mentions this battle and some lessons from it in Surah Tawbah.

Allah has given you victory in numerous regions; but on the day of Hunayn, your great number impressed you, but it availed you nothing; and the land, as spacious as it was, narrowed for you; and you turned your backs in retreat. Then Allah sent down His serenity upon His Messenger, and upon the believers; and He sent down troops you did not see; and He punished those who disbelieved. Such is the recompense of the disbelievers.[136]

Hunayn was the final major battle in Arabia. After this, the Arab tribes throughout the region converted to Islam, one by one. The Byzantines saw this as the rising of a new threat against them and formulated an army to fight the Muslims. In response, the Prophet ﷺ gathered a large army and marched to Tabuk to face the Romans. The Roman army did not show up, and the Muslims returned home victorious and triumphant without any fighting.

The test of Tabuk, however, was in preparing for it. Hypocrites were exposed when they refused to join the army based on the flimsiest of excuses. Others were exposed when they tried to demoralise the army along the way by insulting them. There are many passages in this *surah* about the hypocrites, exposing them one last time.

Those who stayed behind rejoiced at their staying behind the Messenger of Allah. And they hated to strive with their wealth and their lives in Allah's way. And they said, "Do not venture out in the heat." Say, "The Fire of Hell is much hotter, if they only understood."

Let them laugh a little, and weep much; in recompense for what they used to earn. If Allah brings you back to a party of them, and they ask your permission to go out, say, "You will not go out with me, ever, nor will you ever fight an enemy with me. You were content to sit back the first time, so sit back with those who stay behind."[137]

137 Qur'an 9:81–83.

The Prophet ﷺ marched to Tabuk with his army to face the Romans. The Roman army did not show up, so the Muslims returned victorious and triumphant without fighting.

Tabuk was a lesson in sincerity and courage. The believers had to leave their homes, wealth, and families and march in the summer heat across the desert to face an army sent by the superpower of the time. Marching out to face the unknown, the believers showed their sincerity, firm commitment, conviction, and courage. These foundations would serve the first generation of Islam very well in the coming years.

Juz ten

Judgement Day

138 Qur'an 9:9.

139 Qur'an 9:11.

Surah Tawbah focuses on the aftermath of the expedition to Tabuk, with a core focus on warnings to the hypocrites. The events surrounding Tabuk exposed the hypocrites within the ranks of the believers. The expedition was a test for the believers as they had to march in the heat of summer deep into the desert for a potential battle against the Romans.

The anxiety and fear of what could happen laid bare the hypocrites who made every excuse not to fight and not to march. The Romans did not show up and no battle took place, but the march itself was enough to expose the hypocrites and various passages were revealed in this *surah* describing them.

They traded away Allah's revelations for a cheap price, so they barred others from His path. How evil is what they did.[138]

Despite this severe warning, the door of repentance is left open for the hypocrites. Every human can repent and turn their life around before they die.

But if they repent, and perform the prayers, and give the obligatory charity, then they are your brethren in faith. We detail the revelations for a people who know.[139]

Some people may be deluded by the worldly success of some hypocrites and disbelievers. The prosperity doctrine, which is a false belief, leads some people to assume that Allah loves those He blesses with wealth. Allah makes it clear in this *surah* that the wealth of hypocrites is a trial for them, not a blessing.

Let neither their possessions nor their children impress you. Allah intends to torment them by way of them in this worldly life, and that their souls depart while they are disbelievers.[140]

140 Qur'an 9:55.

The prosperity doctrine is a false belief leading some to assume that Allah loves those He blesses with wealth. Allah makes it clear that the wealth of hypocrites is a trial for them, not a blessing.

He criticises the hypocrites for their miserliness. Before Tabuk, some made the excuse that they did not have the wealth needed to participate. Allah exposes this as an excuse and warns that hypocrites remain miserly even when blessed with wealth, as has been proven many times throughout history.

141 Qur'an 9:75–76.
142 Qur'an 9:81.

Among them are those who promised Allah: "If He gives us of His bounty, we will donate and be among the upright." But when He gave them of His bounty, they became stingy with it, and turned away in aversion.[141]

The hypocrites are also criticised for taking joy in staying behind and avoiding the expedition. Their excuses are noted as just that: excuses. The truth is that they simply lacked the faith to go.

Allah criticises the hypocrites for their miserliness. Before Tabuk, some made the excuse that they did not have the wealth needed to participate. Allah exposes this as a false excuse.

Those who stayed behind rejoiced at their staying behind the Messenger of Allah. And they hated to strive with their wealth and their lives in Allah's way. And they said, "Do not venture out in the heat." Say, "The Fire of Hell is much hotter, if they only understood."[142]

The attitude of the hypocrites is contrasted with that of a true believer, in the example of Abu Bakr and his firm faith during the migration.

If you do not help him, Allah has already helped him, when those who disbelieved expelled him, and he was the second of two in the cave. He said to his friend [Abu Bakr], "Do not worry, Allah is with us." And Allah made His tranquility descend upon him, and supported him with forces you did not see, and made the word of those who disbelieved the lowest, while the Word of Allah is the Highest. Allah is Mighty and Wise.[143]

Faith is the primary thing that will benefit us on the Last Day. Hypocrisy on that day will lead a person into deep peril. Every believer must strive to maintain sincerity and avoid the qualities of hypocrisy.

143 Qur'an 9:40.

Juz ten

Qur'anic worldview

144 Qur'an 9:6.

Surah al-Tawbah contains many verses revealed during wartime. These verses are important for understanding how comprehensive the Islamic worldview is, as it even covers the ethics of war, which include the following.

And if anyone of the polytheists asks you for protection, give him protection so that he may hear the Word of Allah; then escort him to his place of safety. That is because they are a people who do not know.[144]

The rules and regulations revealed in the two surahs in juz ten provide a framework of ethical warfare that Muslims take very seriously.

The early Muslims are praised for sacrificing everything to establish Islam. They sacrificed their homes when they had to emigrate for the sake of Allah. Then they had to take a stand and fight for Islam as the Meccans continued to assault them after the migration. Allah promised these great warriors eternal ease in return for their sacrifice.

Those who believe, and emigrate, and strive in Allah's path with their possessions and their persons, are of a higher rank with Allah. These are the winners.

Their Lord announces to them good news of mercy from Him, and acceptance, and gardens wherein they will have lasting bliss.

Abiding therein forever. With Allah is a great reward.[145]

145 Qur'an 9:20–22.

A comprehensive worldview should govern every aspect of life, this includes military ethics and warfare. The two *surahs* in this *juz* focus primarily on war, as they were revealed during times of military struggle. The rules and regulations revealed during these periods provide a framework of ethical warfare that Muslims take very seriously. As a worldview that would govern multiple empires, it was crucial that Islam clarified its stance on war and the rules of engagement early on.

The result is a comprehensive set of rules that minimises casualties, honours peace treaties, and gives preference to peaceful resolutions. Abiding by these ethics, the battles fought between the Muslims of Medina against the pagans of Mecca led to few casualties on either side.

146 Ibn Kathir, al-Bidayah wa al-nihayah (Cairo: Dar ibn Rajab, 2005), 3:226–27.

The ethics were enshrined in the advice of Abu Bakr ﷺ, the First Rightly Guided Caliph, to the first army he sent out after the death of the Prophet, led by Usama ibn Zayd:

Oh people, stop [before me]. For I wish to communicate to you ten rules, so ensure that you memorise them from me. Do not be treacherous or stray from the right path. Do not engage in treachery or mutilate the bodies of the dead. Do not kill a young child, man of old age, or a woman. Do not bring forth any harm to the palm trees whether by cutting them or burning them.

Do not cut any tree that bears fruit. Do not slaughter any sheep, cow, or camel, except that which is for your consumption. You will come across groups of people who have devoted themselves [to worship] in monasteries. Such people should be left uninterrupted and allowed to engage in that to which they have devoted themselves."[146]

Abiding by the revealed ethics of warfare, the battles fought between the Muslims of Medina against the pagans of Mecca led to few casualties on either side.

Juz eleven

Juz eleven

Thematic overview

The eleventh *juz* begins at the 87th verse of Surah Tawbah (the Repentance), the bulk of the *juz* contains Surah Yunus (Jonah), and it ends after the opening five verses of Surah Hud. There is another shift in themes from Surah Tawbah to Surah Yunus. While Surah Tawbah was one of the last *surahs* to be revealed in Medina, Surah Yunus is an early Meccan *surah*, revealed in the second or third year after prophethood. The focus of the next few sections is primarily on Meccan revelation.

The shifts between Meccan and Medinan *surahs* in the Qur'an have a lot of wisdom. One lesson we can take from this is to avoid complacency. Life is a series of ups and downs, times of ease and times of trial. Sometimes we experience difficult situations like the Meccan era, at other times we experience victories like Badr (2 AH/ 624 CE). As life is constantly shifting between these two phases, the order of the Qur'an reflects the ups and downs of life.

Central to this *surah* is the story of Prophet Yunus ﷵ. His story is revealed as a reminder to the Prophet ﷺ not to give up and abandon his people. Prophet Yunus ﷵ left his people, but eventually returned and they embraced Islam. The Prophet ﷺ was forced out by his people many years after this *surah* was revealed but also eventually returned and saw his people embrace Islam.

The next *surah* is named after Prophet Hud ؑ and his story contrasts with that of Prophet Yunus ؑ. While the people of Yunus ؑ eventually embraced Islam, the people of Hud ؑ were stubborn and were eventually destroyed. The enemies of the Prophet ﷺ in Mecca fall into both groups. Some were stubborn and died upon disbelief like Abu Lahab and Abu Jahl, yet others like Suhayl ibn 'Amr and Abu Sufyan eventually softened, repented, and embraced Islam. There are elements of both of these prophets' stories in the life of the final Messenger ﷺ.

> *Life is a series of ups and downs. Sometimes we endure difficult situations like the Meccan era, at other times we experience victories like the Battle of Badr.*

A core theme that flows throughout this *surah* is the reactions of various types of people to the message of the prophets. Some embrace it and some reject it. Those who follow the Messenger will attain eternal bliss, while those who reject his message are responsible for their own choice and final destination. For many, it is their love of this world that holds them back from embracing the truth.

147 Qur'an 10:7–10.

Those who do not hope to meet Us, and are content with the worldly life, and are at ease in it, and those who pay no heed to Our signs. These, their dwelling is the Fire, on account of what they used to do. As for those who believe and do good deeds, their Lord guides them in their faith. Rivers will flow beneath them in the Gardens of Bliss.

Those who entered Jannah. Their call therein is, "Glory be to You, our God." And their greeting therein is "Peace." And the last of their call is, "Praise be to Allah, Lord of the Worlds."[147]

These verses offer us the two paths. Allah is Most Merciful but has the right to punish whomever He wills. To earn eternal Paradise, we must embrace the message of the prophets and submit to our Creator completely. Any other path leads to eternal damnation instead.

Those who chose to follow the Messenger ﷺ will attain eternal bliss, while those who reject his message are responsible for their choice and final destination.

The Seerah

The eleventh *juz* includes the concluding verses of Surah Tawbah, as well as all of Surah Yunus. The *juz* ends at the beginning of Surah Hud. These two *surahs* (Yunus and Hud) were revealed in stages across the Meccan era and reflect the classical Meccan themes of monotheism, prophethood, and preparing for the afterlife.

The Meccans knew that the Prophet ﷺ was the most honest and trustworthy person they had ever met, yet they treated him like he was a stranger whose words they could not trust.

Together they work to balance between hope in Allah's mercy and fear of His punishment. Surah Yunus focuses more on topics of hope and optimism, while Surah Hud has such a strong warning that it even caused some of the Prophet's ﷺ hair to turn grey.

['Abd Allah] ibn 'Abbas ﵄ said, "Abu Bakr ﵁ said: 'O Messenger of Allah! You have become grey.' He said: 'I have gone grey from Surah Hud, al-Waqi'ah (the Inevitable), al-Mursalat (the [Winds] Sent Forth), 'amma yatasa'alun [i.e. Surah al-Naba' (the Announcement)], and idha al-shams kuwwirat [Surah al-Takwir (the Final Enwrapping)].'"[148]

148 Jami' al-Tirmidhi, no. 3297, grade: sahih.

149 Qur'an 10:16.

These two *surahs* reflect the challenges that the Prophet ﷺ faced during the Meccan era. Many of their verses and stories were revealed directly to tackle some of these challenges. The Meccans, for example, knew that the Prophet ﷺ was the most honest and trustworthy person they had ever met, yet they treated him like an unknown stranger whose words they could not trust. In response to this, Allah revealed the following verse.

Say, "Had Allah willed, I would not have recited it to you, and He would not have made it known to you. I have lived among you for a lifetime before it. Do you not understand?"[149]

In this verse, Allah calls on the Meccans to reflect on their lifetime of experience dealing with the Prophet ﷺ. Even in his youth, he was known as the most honest person in the city, so why would he lie about something so great?

The perfect character of the Prophet ﷺ is one of his greatest signs and strongest proofs of prophet-hood. Even in the modern world, it is a key point to discuss when calling people to the truth.

Surah Yunus was revealed during a difficult point in the prophetic mission. The Prophet ﷺ had been preaching in Mecca for years and did not have many followers. Persecution was on the rise, and some of his greatest supporters passed away around this time. The optimism in this *surah* served to inspire him to keep going no matter how dark things seemed to get.

The direct comparison to the story of Yunus ﷺ was very relevant at this point. Prophet Yunus ﷺ gave up on his mission at one point and left his city without Allah's permission. The famous incident of the whale took place, and after he sought Allah's forgiveness and returned to the city, he found that it had become a city of true faith.

The Prophet ﷺ soon after this would also have to leave his city, but this time with Allah's permission. He too would return many years later and Mecca would become a city of true faith until the end of time.

Each of the surahs in juz ten ends with a beautiful description of the Prophet ﷺ and his role as a messenger to this world.

If only there was one town that believed and benefited by its belief. Except for the people of Jonah. When they believed, We removed from them the suffering of disgrace in this worldly life, and We gave them comfort for a while.[150]

150 Qur'an 10:98.

Each of the *surahs* in this *juz* ends with a beautiful description of the Prophet ﷺ and his role as a messenger to this world, with a strong reminder to the Meccans to believe in what had been revealed to them.

151 Qur'an 9:128–29.

152 Qur'an 10:108–9.

There has come to you a messenger from among yourselves, concerned over your suffering, anxious over you. Towards the believers, he is compassionate and merciful. If they turn away, say, "Allah is enough for me; there is no Allah except He; in Him I have put my trust; He is the Lord of the Sublime Throne."[151]

Say, "O people, the truth has come to you from your Lord. Whoever accepts guidance is guided for his own soul; and whoever strays only strays to its detriment. I am not a guardian over you." And follow what is revealed to you, and be patient until Allah issues His judgment, for He is the Best of judges.[152]

The perfect character of the Prophet ﷺ is one of his greatest signs and strongest proofs of prophethood. Even in the modern world, it is a key point to discuss when calling people to the truth.

Juz eleven

Judgement Day

Surah Yunus contains many beautiful reminders about the afterlife and how to prepare for it. The *surah* contains a powerful description of the Qur'an and its role in the life of a believer.

O people! There has come to you advice from your Lord and healing for what is in the hearts and guidance and mercy for the believers. Say, "In Allah's grace and mercy let them rejoice. That is better than what they hoard." [153]

153 Qur'an 10:57–58.

In Surah Yunus, we are reminded of Allah's power, our relationship with Him, and the fact that we will have to return to Him and answer for how we choose to live our lives.

This verse teaches us to seek guidance from the Qur'an which was revealed to heal the spiritual illnesses of our souls. It is a mercy to everyone who lives by it, and we must rejoice in this beautiful gift to mankind.

Earlier in this *surah*, there is a passage that teaches us about the reality of this world. In this passage, we are reminded of the power of Allah, our relationship with Him, and the fact that we will return to Him and answer for how we lived our lives.

154 Qur'an 10:22–24.

It is He who transports you across land and sea. Until, when you are on ships, sailing in a favourable wind, and rejoicing in it, a raging wind arrives. The waves surge over them from every side, and they realise that they are besieged.

Thereupon they pray to Allah, professing sincere devotion to Him: "If You save us from this, we will be among the appreciative." But then when He has saved them, they commit violations on earth, and oppose justice.

O people! Your violations are against your own souls. It is the enjoyment of the present life. Then to Us is your return, and We will inform you of what you used to do.

The likeness of the present life is this: water that We send down from the sky is absorbed by the plants of the earth, from which people and animals eat. Until, when the earth puts on its fine appearance, and is beautified, and its inhabitants think that they have mastered it, Our command descends upon it by night or by day, and We turn it into stubble, as if it had not flourished the day before. We thus clarify the revelations for people who reflect.[154]

The passage above ends with a metaphor comparing this world to water. This metaphor is repeated in Surah al-Kahf (the Cave) and reminds us that this world is temporary, and only beneficial in moderate amounts. Just as not enough water leads to droughts and too much water leads to floods, both ignoring this world and obsessing over it lead to problems. Balance lies in moderation, prioritising the afterlife without neglecting this world.

The metaphor comparing this world to water is repeated in Surah al-Kahf reminding us that this world is temporary, and only beneficial in moderate amounts.

The passage then ends with a reminder to focus on preparing for the afterlife, with Paradise as our goal. Paradise is described as *Dar al-Salam* (The Home of Peace) in this verse, highlighting two of its key features; for the believer it is home and a place of eternal peace.

Allah invites to the Home of Peace, and guides whomever He wills to a straight path.[155]

155 Qur'an 10:25.

Juz eleven

Qur'anic worldview

Muslims must strive to please Allah. This is our primary duty. A part of that duty is to convey the message of Islam and ensure that this message reaches as many people as possible. But our job is simply to convey; the results are in Allah's control. This principle applies to other aspects of our lives too. We work, but our sustenance is in Allah's control, and we plan but the results are in Allah's control. Muslims are required to focus on effort, not on results. We try our best and leave the results to Allah.

The lesson in Surah Yunus is to never give up on our good work, to remain focused on sincere efforts, and to leave the ultimate results with Allah.

The two *surahs* in this *juz* contrast different points in the Prophet's ﷺ life. Surah Tawbah was revealed towards the end of his life, when he had emerged victorious over his enemies after nearly two decades of struggle. Surah Yunus was revealed much earlier, during the Meccan era, in which the results of the *da'wah* had not yet been seen. Yet the message remained consistent across both phases: remain focused on what is in your control and to leave the results to Allah.

There has come to you a messenger from among yourselves, concerned over your suffering, anxious over you. Towards the believers, he is compassionate and merciful.

If they turn away, say, "Allah is enough for me; there is no god except He; in Him I have put my trust; He is the Lord of the Sublime Throne."[156]

Surah Yunus is named after the Prophet Yunus ﷺ known as Jonah in English. His story serves as a reminder to remain focused on the mission regardless of the results. At one point, Yunus became frustrated at his people's lack of response to the message and left town. He did not know that their guidance would come later.

The story that follows is well known. Yunus ﷺ went out to sea, was cast overboard, swallowed by a whale, and repented in the belly of the whale. He then washed ashore and returned to his people to find that they had embraced the message. The lesson is to never give up on our good work, to remain focused on sincere efforts, and to leave the results to Allah.

If only there was one town that believed and benefited by its belief. Except for the people of Jonah. When they believed, We removed from them the suffering of disgrace in the worldly life, and We gave them comfort for a while.[157]

156 Qur'an 9:128–129.

157 Qur'an 10:98.

Juz twelve

Juz twelve

Thematic overview

The twelfth *juz* begins at verse six of Surah Hud and ends at verse fifty-two of Surah Yusuf (Joseph). The core theme of this *juz* is the stories of the prophets. Both *surahs* are focused on stories of the prophets but with very different outcomes.

Surah Hud focuses on the stories of the destroyed nations who refused to listen to the messenger and were punished in this world. Surah Yusuf focuses on the story of Yusuf ﷺ who attained success in both worlds. The first *surah* was sent as a warning to the Quraysh, and the second as glad tidings to the Prophet ﷺ. Together, they achieve the balance between warnings and glad tidings.

The destruction of previous nations was a reminder to the Quraysh and everybody that nobody can escape the divine justice set by Allah.

Surah Hud is an important *surah* that should make us all reflect. It serves as a warning to all, initially Quraysh, the ruling tribe of Mecca and the main enemy of the Muslim community at the time, but to us as well. The stories in this *surah* focus on nations that rebelled against the prophets and were destroyed for their rebellion.

The Muslim nation is not immune to this. We too can be stripped of our blessings and punished in both worlds if we choose to live a life similar to past nations. Although the *ummah* as a whole has been spared from such a fate, it could happen to some countries and empires.

The first story mentioned in this *surah* is the story of Prophet Nuh which runs from verse twenty-five to forty-one. The story of Nuh and the flood is well known to everyone, not only Muslims. It was the first time that Allah destroyed a nation for their sins, and it has been recorded in the histories of every major nation.

This is followed by the stories of Hud, Saleh, Lut, and Shu'ayb and their nations. Each of these stories follows a similar format and they are often repeated together throughout the Qur'an. These nations were not chosen by random, they all existed in or near Arabia and the Arabs were familiar with their histories. The destruction of their nations was a reminder to the Quraysh and everybody else that nobody can escape divine justice. Furthermore, some of these nations had unique sins that they were identified with, like the sodomy of the people of Lot. All these nations arrogantly rejected their prophets and this led to their destruction.

The final story in this *surah* is the story of Musa ﷷ with a strong focus on the downfall of Pharaoh. This ties in per- fectly with the theme of the *surah.* Even the mighty king of Egypt who thought himself a god could not escape Allah's power and justice. As the theme of punishment and destruction runs strongly throughout this *surah,* it is clear to see why it would cause the Prophet ﷺ to worry about his nation.

> *Surah Yusuf is considered by many to be the best of stories. It was revealed at a time when the Prophet ﷺ was in need of comfort and optimism.*

There is another beautiful theme that flows through these three *surahs.* Surah Yunus gives us an example of a prophet who left his people, then returned to them. Surah Hud gives us examples of prophets who stayed with their nations until their nations were destroyed. Surah Yusuf gives us an example of a prophet who was cast out by his people, but they eventually returned to him. These three *surahs,* placed one after the other, show us a variety of reactions to the messages of the prophets.

The rest of this *juz* focuses on Surah Yusuf which is unique in many ways. It is the only story of a prophet told in one flowing manner in just one *surah*. It is considered by many to be the best of stories. It was revealed at a time when the Prophet ﷺ needed comfort and optimism (after his journey to the city of al-Taif ended in a disappointment, a personal attack on him ﷺ, and the 'most difficult' episode of his prophetic mission) and it is one of the most oft-recited and reflected on *surahs* in the Qur'an today.

> *Like Prophet Yusuf ﵇, Prophet Muhammad ﷺ also went through similar phases; favourite, hated, exiled, leader, conqueror.*

A powerful theme that runs throughout this *surah* is that of family. We see the Prophet Yusuf ﵇ facing the rejection of his family, and their eventual reconciliation after he rises to power. This mirrors the story of the Prophet Muhammad ﷺ. Neither Yunus ﵇ or Hud ﵇ had to deal with their families rejecting them. Prophet Muhammad ﷺ at the time of the revelation of Surah Yusuf had just lost the protection of his tribe. His uncle, Abu Talib, had passed away, and Abu Lahab had taken over the tribe. For the first time, the Prophet ﷺ faced persecution without tribal support and this *surah* was sent to give him hope. As Yusuf eventually rose to power in Egypt, Prophet Muhammad ﷺ was destined to rise to power in Medina too.

The theme of jealousy also runs throughout this Surah, and again mirrors the struggles of the Prophet ﷺ. As Yusuf had to deal with the jealousy of his brothers, entire tribes rejected the Prophet ﷺ because he was not from their tribe and they were jealous that the revelation had been sent to an orphan from the tribe of Banu Hashim instead.

The parallels between the two stories continue throughout the *surah*. Yusuf ﷺ went through various stages in his life journey: favourite child, abandoned in a well, slavery, imprisonment, and eventually minister. The Prophet ﷺ went through similar phases; favourite, hated, exiled, leader, conqueror. The story reminds us that not all of Yusuf's ﷺ brothers were evil. Likewise, the family of the Prophet ﷺ included both allies and enemies. Yusuf ﷺ rejected temptation and was ready to face imprison- ment instead. The Prophet ﷺ rejected multiple bribes and offers and accepted exile instead.

The above similarities show us why this *surah* was revealed at that time. It provided the Prophet ﷺ with hope through a story of a great man who went through similar trials. Just as Yusuf ﷺ eventually was successful, it was a sign that the Prophet ﷺ would also one day be successful in his mission.

Juz twelve

The Seerah

The dual themes of hope and fear continue in the twelfth *juz*. Surah Hud focuses on the stories of the perished nations. These were all nations who the Meccans were familiar with. 'Ad, Thamud, Madyan, and the people of Lut were all ancient civilisations that had been destroyed for rejecting Allah's messengers. The message here to the Meccans was clear: they might face the same consequences if they rejected the final messenger.

Surah Yusuf, however, is all about hope and optimism. It was revealed at a time when the Prophet ﷺ needed this the most. Surah Yusuf was revealed during the year of sorrow. The Prophet ﷺ had lost his closest supporter, his beloved wife Khadija ؓ and his external protector, his uncle the tribal chief Abu Talib. Both had passed away in the same year, a few months apart.

Without his uncle's support, the Prophet ﷺ faced renewed persecution in Mecca and sought help elsewhere. He went to Taif seeking their protection. Their response was abusive and traumatising. It was during this difficult year, when things looked bleaker than ever, that Surah Yusuf was revealed. Surah Yusuf tells the entire story of Yusuf in one powerful *surah*.

The story parallels that of the Prophet ﷺ, giving him hope for the future. Just as the Prophet ﷺ faced persecution from his own family (his uncle Abu Lahab), Yusuf too faced persecution from his own brothers.

Just as the Prophet would soon be forced to leave Mecca, move to a new land, and eventually become the leader of that land, Yusuf too was forced to flee to Egypt and eventually became a leader in Egypt.

After the abusive event of Taif, during the difficult year when things looked bleaker than ever, Allah revealed Surah Yusuf.

The message was clear, the Prophet's trials were preparing him for something greater. Just like Yusuf, he would rise above the challenges of life and eventually Islam would dominate the region.

The Prophet ﷺ related to this story so much that the conquest of Mecca mirrored Yusuf's confrontation with his brothers when he was in power. The Prophet ﷺ even told the Meccans the same beautiful words that Yusuf spoke to his brothers; He said, "There is no blame upon you today. Allah will forgive you. He is the Most Merciful of the merciful."[158]

158 Qur'an 12:92.

159 Qur'an 12:111.

The lessons contained in this *surah* are timeless. Every generation finds its message of hope and optimism relevant to their specific circumstances. It remains one of the most beloved and most frequently studied *surahs* in the Qur'an today. The themes of family, hope, true dreams, leadership, redemption, resisting temptation and rising through trials resonate with every believer.

Surah Yusuf remains one of the most beloved and most frequently studied surahs in the Qur'an today.

Surah Yusuf is close to all our hearts. It is the best of stories. In it is a reminder to be optimistic and trust Allah's plan even when life does not seem to go our way. The *surah* ends with a beautiful reminder about the purpose of revelation.

In their stories is a lesson for those who possess intelligence. This is not a fabricated tale, but a confirmation of what came before it, and a detailed explanation of all things, and guidance, and mercy for people who believe.[159]

Juz twelve

Judgement Day

Surah Hud and Surah Yusuf are placed one after the other in the twelfth *juz*. Together they give us a beautiful balance between hope and fear. Surah Hud focuses on warnings of the Day of Judgment, and reminders of the destruction of past nations. Surah Yusuf gives us a story about hope for believers, that Allah is always in control and that whatever happens to believers is best for them.

Only those deeds that are done sincerely for Allah will have value on the Last Day. Anything else will eventually be null and void.

At the beginning of Surah Hud is a stern warning for those who prefer this world over the next. They are reminded that they may get whatever they want in this world, and that too is not guaranteed, but the cost is the afterlife where their deeds will have no value.

Whoever desires the worldly life and its glitter, We will fully recompense them for their deeds therein, and therein they will not be defrauded. These, they will have nothing but the Fire in the Hereafter. Their deeds are in vain therein, and their works are null.[160]

160 Qur'an 11:15–16.

161 Qur'an 11:97–99.

The core message of this verse is to focus on our intentions. It is a reminder to ensure we have *ikhlas* (sincerity) in all our deeds. Only deeds that are done sincerely for Allah have value on the Last Day. Anything else will be null and void.

This *surah* also contains a firm warning that blind following is not an acceptable excuse on the Last Day. On that day, anyone who chose to blindly follow tyrants and false religions will have to answer for their own deeds. This excuse was not accepted from the followers of Pharaoh, despite his tyranny, as we are all responsible for whom we choose to follow.

To Pharaoh and his nobles, but they followed the command of Pharaoh, and the command of Pharaoh was not wise. He will precede his people on the Day of Resurrection and will lead them into the Fire. Miserable is the place he put them in. They were followed by a curse in this, and on the Day of Resurrection. Miserable is the path they followed.[161]

Surah Hud is very firm in its warnings. The focus is on building fear of Allah and the Last Day. The message of this *surah* is balanced by the message of the next *surah* which focuses on hope and optimism in the story of Yusuf.

Juz twelve

Qur'anic worldview

We thus established Yusuf in the land, to teach him the interpretation of events. Allah has full control over His affairs, but most people do not know.[162]

And thus We established Yusuf in the land, to live therein wherever he wished. We touch with Our mercy whomever We will, and We never waste the reward of the righteous.[163]

162 Qur'an 12:21.

163 Qur'an 12:56.

We may not be able to fathom why bad things happen to us, but often it is these same tragic events that help to shape us into the best versions of ourselves.

The story of Prophet Yusuf ﷺ in Surah Yusuf gives us a glimpse at the divine wisdom behind hardship and struggle. There are many tragic things that happen in this world that people cannot understand. These events are guided by the divine will of Allah based on His infinite wisdom. We may not be able to fathom why bad things happen to us, but often it is these same tragic events that shape us into the best versions of ourselves.

164 Qur'an 12:101.

165 Al-'Arba'un al-Nawawiyya, no. 19.

It is during times of trial and tragedy that we discover our true strength and courage. Determination and patience are uncovered in these moments, and they tend to become our defining moments. The story of Yusuf takes us on a journey from one tragedy to another, showing us how these events shaped him into a wise, gentle, and powerful leader. Through these stories, we learn to trust divine wisdom, even when we do not understand it, and this gives us strength during our darkest hours. This wisdom is reflected in the final words of Prophet Yusuf at the end of the *surah*:

My Lord, You have given me authority, and taught me the interpretation of dreams. Creator of the heavens and the earth; You are my Protector in this life and in the Hereafter. Receive my soul in submission and unite me with the righteous.[164]

In life, we will face many tests and deal with great tragedies. Allah is in full control, and He knows what is best for us. We trust this and find peace in trusting divine wisdom.

Take solace in the advice of the Prophet ﷺ when he said, "Be mindful of Allah, and you will find Him in front of you. Recognise and acknowledge Allah in times of ease and prosperity, and He will remember you in times of adversity. And know that what has passed you by [and you have failed to attain] was not going to befall you, and what has befallen you was not going to pass you by. And know that victory comes with patience, relief with affliction, and ease with hardship."[165]

Juz thirteen

Juz thirteen

Thematic overview

The thirteenth *juz* begins at verse fifty-three of Surah Yusuf (Joseph), contains all of Surah al-Ra'd (the Thunder), and ends with Surah Ibrahim (Abraham). A common theme that runs from Surah Yunus (Jonah) to Surah al-Hijr (the Stoneland) is the greatness of the Qur'an itself. In fact, every one of these *surahs* begins with verses describing the greatness of the Qur'an, as a reminder to us, the reader, to take it seriously and reflect upon it.

This *juz* begins around a major turning point in the life of Prophet Yusuf عليه السلام. His story in the previous *juz* focused on his trials. At this point, he begins to work for the king and eventually rises to a position of authority in the kingdom. It is at this stage that we see the amazing character of Prophet Ya'qub (Jacob) and Yusuf. Ya'qub عليه السلام shows us the most beautiful example of optimism and patience, while Yusuf عليه السلام shows us an incredible example of generosity and forgiveness. These are four powerful characteristics that their forefather Ibrahim عليه السلام was known for and we see all these characteristics in this *surah*.

The *surah* ends with the family reunited and all grudges forgiven. Ya'qub عليه السلام is not satisfied to learn that his son Yusuf عليه السلام is still alive, he is only satisfied when he learns that he is still a believer. The true passing of any test in life is to remain firm on the true faith throughout the test. Yusuf عليه السلام himself asks Allah to allow him to die a believer, fulfilling the supplication of his forefathers. In Surah al-Baqarah we learn that Ibrahim and Ya'qub both made *dua* that their progeny would die upon Islam. Yusuf عليه السلام was one of many answers to that *dua*.

The true passing of any test in life is to remain firm on the true faith throughout the test. Yusuf عليه السلام himself asks Allah to allow him to die as a believer, fulfilling the supplication of his forefathers.

A common theme that runs throughout this *juz* is the importance of patience and gratitude. Surah Yusuf gives us the example of beautiful patience in Ya'qub عليه السلام. Surah al-Ra'd reminds us that Paradise is earned through patience. "Peace be upon you because you endured patiently. How excellent is the Final Home?"[166]

166 Qur'an 13:24.

167 Qur'an 13:28.
168 Qur'an 14:7.
169 Qur'an 14:24–26.

Both Surah al-Ra'd and Surah Ibrahim remind us of the crucial importance of gratitude in earning the mercy of Allah.

Those who believe, and whose hearts find comfort in the remembrance of Allah. Surely, it is in the remembrance of Allah that hearts find comfort.[167]

And when your Lord proclaimed: "If you give thanks, I will grant you increase; but if you are ungrateful, My punishment is severe."[168]

Do you not see how Allah presents a parable? A good word is like a good tree—its root is firm, and its branches are in the sky. It yields its fruits every season by the will of its Lord. Allah presents the parables to the people, so that they may reflect. And the parable of a bad word is that of a bad tree—it is uprooted from the ground; it has no stability.[169]

We need to be patient with the trials of life, knowing that victory is from Allah and He does not test us beyond our capabilities. We also need to be grateful for every blessing in our lives.

This is a theme that runs through this *juz*. The two paths to Paradise are patience and gratitude. We need to be patient with the trials of life, knowing that victory is from Allah and He does not test us beyond our capabilities. We also need to be grateful for every blessing in our lives. If we do so Allah will increase our blessings in both worlds. These two qualities can happen at the same time. At almost any time in our lives, there are trials to be patient with and blessings to be grateful for. Victory is achieved by constantly moving between these two states depending on the tests of the day.

Surah al-Ra'd is named after the thunder as this *surah* reminds us that even what we perceive as inanimate are creations of Allah that praise Him in ways that we cannot imagine. "The thunder praises His glory, and so do the angels, in awe of Him. And He sends the thunderbolts, striking with them whomever He wills. Yet they argue about Allah, while He is tremendous in might."[170]

170 Qur'an 13:13.

Juz thirteen

The Seerah

Surah al-Ra'd and Surah Ibrahim were revealed towards the end of the Meccan era, just before the migration of the Prophet ﷺ to Medina. They marked a final reminder to the tribe of Quraysh to follow the Prophet ﷺ or else Allah would give the gift of Islam to another community.

While the majority of Meccans had rejected the message, Islam was spreading quickly through every tribe in Medina. This was primarily due to the *da'wah* efforts of Mus'ab ibn 'Umair ؓ who the Prophet ﷺ had sent to Medina to teach Islam.

This marked a turning of the tide in favour of Islam. In Medina, the Muslims would grow into the majority, establish their new home, and eventually grow into a thriving civilisation that spread across the globe. These *surahs* were revealed when this process was just getting started.

In Medina, the Muslims would grow into the majority, establish their new home, and eventually grow into a thriving civilisation that spread across the globe.

Surah al-Ra'd takes a very stern tone in addressing those who continuously rejected Islam after the truth had been made clear to them. The Meccans had known the Prophet ﷺ his entire life, had attested to his honesty and trustworthiness, and had witnessed many miracles in his presence, especially the miracle of the Qur'an itself.

Despite this, they continued to reject the truth, mock the message, criticise the Prophet, and make ridiculous demands for miracles. Surah al-Ra'd addresses this attitude with some stern warnings.

Those who disbelieve say, "If only a miracle was sent down to him from his Lord." Say, "Allah leaves to stray whomever He wills, and He guides to Himself whoever repents."[171]

Even if there were a Qur'an by which mountains could be set in motion, or by which the earth could be shattered, or by which the dead could be made to speak. In fact, every decision rests with Allah. Did the believers not give up and realise that had Allah willed, He would have guided all humanity? Disasters will continue to strike those who disbelieve, because of their deeds, or they fall near their homes, until Allah's promise comes true. Allah never breaks a promise.

Messengers before you were ridiculed, but I granted the disbelievers respite, and then I seized them. What a punishment it was![172]

171 Qur'an 13:27.

172 Qur'an 13:31–32.

173 Qur'an 13:38.

We sent messengers before you, and We assigned for them wives and offspring. No messenger could bring a sign except with the permission of Allah. For every era is a scripture.[173]

Surah Ibrahim reminded the Quraysh that their city was established by Ibrahim as a seat of monotheism. He had in fact prayed for that city, and so in answer to his prayer it would eventually return to being the center of monotheism. The mention of this *dua* here was in fact a prophecy that Islam would eventually become the religion of Mecca.

The *dua* is narrated at length in this *surah* for the Quraysh to reflect on. There are many lessons we can learn from the wording of this supplication.

Recall that Abraham said, "O my Lord, make this land peaceful, and keep me and my sons from worshipping idols.

My Lord, they have led many people astray. Whoever follows me belongs with me; and whoever disobeys me—You are Forgiving and Merciful.

Our Lord, I have settled some of my offspring in a valley of no vegetation, by Your Sacred House, our Lord, so that they may perform the prayers.

So, make the hearts of some people incline towards them, and provide them with fruits, that they may be thankful.

The mention of Ibrahim's ﷺ dua was a reminder to the Quraysh and a prophecy that Islam would eventually become the religion of the city of Mecca.

Our Lord, You know what we conceal and what we reveal. And nothing is hidden from Allah, on earth or in the heavens."[174]

The *surah* ends with a firm warning that tyrants will not escape Allah's punishment. This was a warning to the Meccans to repent and stop oppressing the Muslims. It remains a warning to every tyrant in the world today.

Do not ever think that Allah is unaware of what the wrongdoers do. He only defers them until a Day when the eyes stare.[175]

174 Qur'an 14:35–38.

175 Qur'an 14:42.

Juz thirteen

Judgement Day

176 Qur'an 12:38–40.

Surah Yusuf is a message of hope for believers. It was revealed during the late Meccan period when the Muslims were facing great trials. The story of Yusuf demonstrates how a believer can go through many trials and end up successful and victorious in the end if Allah wills. It was a message to the believers in Mecca that they would eventually triumph over their oppressors.

At one point in the story of Yusuf, he is in prison unjustly and other prisoners ask him to interpret their dreams. They noticed that he was a righteous person, so they confided their dreams to him. Before interpreting their dreams, Yusuf called them towards the straight path with a focus on monotheism and a reminder that the final judgment will be by Allah on the Last Day.

And I have followed the faith of my forefathers, Ibrahim (Abraham), Ishaaq (Isaac) and Ya'qub (Jacob). It is not for us to associate anything with Allah. This is by virtue of Allah's grace upon us and upon the people, but most people do not give thanks.

O My fellow inmates, are diverse lords better, or Allah, the One, the Supreme? You do not worship, besides Him, except names you have named, you and your ancestors, for which Allah has sent down no authority. Judgment belongs to none but Allah. He has commanded that you worship none but Him. This is the right religion, but most people do not know.[176]

This passage is a reminder to always prioritise Islam and its message, even during difficult times. Later in the story, Yusuf's father Prophet Ya'qub is grieving after being separated from him for many decades. In his grief, he shows us the best Islamic manner of dealing with trauma, which he calls beautiful patience (*sabr jamil*).

Yusuf called his fellow prisoners towards the straight path with a focus on monotheism and a reminder that the final judgment will be by Allah on the Last Day.

Then he turned away from them, and said, "O my sadness for Yusuf." And his eyes turned white from sorrow, and he became depressed. They said, "By Allah, you will not stop remembering Yusuf, until you have ruined your health, or you have passed away." He said, "I only complain of my grief and sorrow to Allah, and I know from Allah what you do not know. O my sons, go and inquire about Yusuf and his brother, and do not despair of Allah's comfort. None despairs of Allah's comfort except the disbelieving people." [177]

177 Qur'an 12:84–87.

Prophet Ya'qub teaches us to complain only to Allah. This does not mean that we do not seek counselling. It means that we must not develop a habit of complaining. Counselling can be very beneficial but complaining to people who cannot help can often lead to more harm than good.

The believer remains optimistic even when life is darkest, and the trials of life are unbearable. We must not lose hope that Allah will reward us for our patience.

Prophet Ya'qub also teaches us in this passage to never lose hope in Allah's mercy. The believer remains optimistic even when life is darkest, and the trials of life are unbearable. We must never lose hope that Allah will reward us for our patience, either with victory in this world or something better in the next.

Surah Yusuf is, for many people, their favourite *surah* in the Qur'an. Its powerful messages of hope, optimism, and victory motivate the believer to keep working towards the pleasure of Allah, no matter how difficult the trials of life get.

Qur'anic worldview

The entire universe is the creation of Allah, and they all bow and submit to Him in their own ways. Humans have been given free will and have a choice to submit or face the consequences of refusing to do so. Without free will, the rest of creation demonstrates for us the beauty of submission and praising Allah. There are many verses in Surah al-Ra'd that showcase this submission for us.

It is He who shows you the lightning, causing fear and hope. And He produces the heavy clouds. The thunder praises His glory, and so do the angels, in awe of Him. And He sends the thunderbolts, striking with them whomever He wills. Yet they argue about Allah, while He is tremendous in might.[178]

To Allah prostrates everything in the heavens and the earth, willingly or unwillingly, as do their shadows, in the morning and in the evening.[179]

He sends down water from the sky, and riverbeds flow according to their capacity. The current carries swelling froth. And from what they heat in fire of ornaments or utensils comes a similar froth. Thus Allah exemplifies truth and falsehood. As for the froth, it is swept away, but what benefits the people remains in the ground. Thus Allah presents analogies.[180]

178 Qur'an 13:12–13.

179 Qur'an 13:15.

180 Qur'an 13:17.

181 Rhamis Kent, "Saving Truth and Beauty: The Destruction of Nature and the Islamic Solution," Yaqeen, August 29, 2022

These verses should give us a deep connection with nature. The natural world is not just the creation of Allah, but our fellow submitters. When we submit to the Creator and worship Him, we are at peace with nature, willingly doing what the rest of creation does too. This connection to nature should make us care more for the environment, take care of the earth, and treat all creatures and plants well.

Rhamis Kent explains well the dangers of not protecting nature in his paper; *Saving Truth and Beauty: The Destruction of Nature and the Islamic Solution.*

If the creation consists of Allah's Signs, and those Signs serve as reminders of the Divine, what happens when those Signs are removed from the Earth or allowed to be continually corrupted, distorted, degraded, or destroyed altogether? If these corrupted Signs become the basis of our reflection and remembrance, how would our perspectives not also grow corrupted, distorted, and degraded? What precarious world do we produce by substituting for those Signs a mirror of humanity's basest desires, whims, and caprices? [181]

Caring for nature has always been a strong part of the Muslim worldview. In a time in which capitalism and greed are destroying the environment, this principle remains even more important for us today.

Juz fourteen

Juz fourteen

Thematic overview

182 Qur'an 15:2–4.

183 Qur'an 15:6–8.

Juz Fourteen contains two *surahs* in their entirety: Surah al-Hijr (the Stoneland) and Surah al-Nahl (the Bees). A common theme that runs through this *juz* is the amazing blessings from Allah, and the importance of showing gratitude for those blessings. Both *surahs* continue the theme from Surah Ibrahim of reminding us of the various reasons why we should be grateful to Allah. The greatest gift that Allah has given us is guidance to the straight path. Surah al-Hijr begins by showing the results of following that guidance as well as neglecting it.

Perhaps those who disbelieve will wish they had been Muslims. Leave them to eat, and enjoy, and be lulled by hope. They will find out. We have never destroyed a town unless it had a set time.[182]

The above verses remind us that those who choose to disbelieve are given ample time to seek the truth and embrace it. Allah does not punish them before giving them enough time to follow the truth, but many people are distracted by the pleasures of this world and never seek out the purpose of life. Allah then addresses the excuses of these people for rejecting the messengers.

And they said, "O you who received the message, you are insane. Why do you not bring us the angels, if you are truthful?" We do not send the angels down except with reason, and they will not be held back.[183]

Just as the previous messengers were accused of insanity, falsehood, and magic, the Prophet ﷺ faced similar accusations. Allah, out of divine wisdom, sent human messengers to human societies and did not unleash His angels upon us. This is followed by a promise to preserve the message of Islam, a promise that Allah has fulfilled.

Surely, we revealed the Message, and We will surely preserve it.[184]

Those who choose to disbelieve are given ample time to seek the truth and embrace it, but many are distracted by the pleasures of this world and never seek out the purpose and meaning of life.

Another interesting theme that runs through the next few *juz* is the story of Adam (AS) which is repeated in multiple *surahs* with different focal points. In this *surah*, the focus is on the Creation of Adam and how Allah blew his soul into him. "When I have formed him, and breathed into him of My spirit, fall down prostrating before him."[185]

Adam (AS) was not praiseworthy because of his physical nature; it was because of his soul which is sacred and pure. This shows the value of the soul over the body. Iblis only looked at the exterior, not the interior, and that caused him to stray. In this

184 Qur'an 15:9.

185 Qur'an 15:29.

186 Qur'an 15:42.
187 Qur'an 15:49–50.
188 Qur'an 15:87.

way, Iblis was the first racist, judging another by his skin and not the purity of his soul. In this *surah*, we see that Allah informed Satan that, "Over My servants, you have no authority, except for the sinners who follow you."[186]

The story of Adam is followed by a reminder that Allah is the Most Merciful, but also has the most severe punishment. This is similar to the previous *surah* in which Allah promised to increase the blessings of those who show gratitude, and to punish the ungrateful. "Inform My servants that I am the Forgiving, the Merciful. And that My punishment is the [most] painful punishment."[187]

The bulk of this *surah* again focuses on the stories of the perished nations. This is a theme that runs through multiple *surahs* of the Qur'an, each time focusing on a different lesson from these stories. Here the focus is on what happens to those who reject the messenger, a timely reminder for the Meccan tribe of Quraysh who denounced the Prophet's message, but also for us.

Towards the end of the *surah*, Allah again reminds us of the greatness of the Qur'an, this time singling out Surah al-Fatiha for its greatness. "We have given you seven oft-repeated verses, and the Grand Qur'an."[188] The seven oft-repeated verses are Surah al-Fatiha (the Opening) that we repeat in every unit of prayer multiple times a day.

The *surah* ends with comfort for the Prophet ﷺ when Allah says, "We are aware that your heart is strained by what they say. So, glorify the praise of your Lord, and be among those who bow down. And worship your Lord in order to attain certainty."[189]

The next *surah* is al-Nahl named after the bee. The bee and the honey that it produces are simply two of many great favours of Allah listed in this *surah*. The message of this *surah* is clear; Allah has blessed us with more than we can ever imagine, and we must be grateful for it. Surah al-Hijr reminds us of what happens to those who are ungrateful, while Surah al-Nahl lists for us dozens of reasons for why we should be grateful to Allah.

Allah reminds us that He has blessed us with more than we can ever imagine, so we must always be grateful to Him.

The *surah* begins with a beautiful list of many blessings from Allah that we take for granted, followed by the powerful reminder, "And if you tried to enumerate the favours of Allah, you would not be able to count them. Allah is Forgiving and Merciful."[190]

This *surah* does not require a lot of explanation. It is sufficient to recite the verses, read their translations, reflect on them and express gratitude.

189 Qur'an 15:96–99.

190 Qur'an 16:18.

Juz fourteen

The Seerah

191 Qur'an 15:10.

192 Qur'an 15:14–15.

Surah Hijr continues the same theme as *Surahs* al-Ra'd and Ibrahim. Revealed in the late Meccan era, it focuses on reminding people to believe in the Prophet ﷺ and obey him. The stories of the perished nations are repeated in this *surah* as a final reminder to the Meccans not to follow in their footsteps.

The following verses show how the Quraysh were adamant in their disbelief, even though the signs of Allah were all around them.

We sent others before you, to the former communities.[191]

Even if We opened for them a gateway into the sky, and they began to ascend through it, they would still say, "Our eyes are hallucinating; in fact, we are people bewitched."[192]

Surah al-Nahl focuses on many of the blessings Allah has given us that we often take for granted. We are reminded that our food, drink, homes and so much more are all gifts from Allah that we should be grateful for.

He created the human being from a drop of fluid, yet he becomes an open adversary. And the livestock—He created them for you. In them are warmth and benefits for you, and of them you eat. And there is beauty in them for you, when you bring them home, and when you drive them to pasture.

And they carry your loads to territory you could not have reached without great hardship. Your Lord is Compassionate and Merciful. And the horses, and the mules, and the donkeys—for you to ride, and for luxury. And He creates what you do not know.[193]

In Surah al-Nahl, we are reminded that our food, drink, homes and so much more are all gifts from Allah that we should be grateful for. We can never count all of the blessings of Allah in our lives.

This *surah* contains the beautiful reminder that we can never count all of the blessings of Allah in our lives. Reflecting on this *surah* should fill our hearts with gratitude and cause us to worship Allah out of gratitude for all His blessings.

And if you tried to enumerate the favours of Allah, you would not be able to count them. Allah is Forgiving and Merciful.[194]

193 Qur'an 16:4–8.

194 Qur'an 16:18.

Juz fourteen

Judgement Day

195 Sahih Muslim, no. 2999.

196 Qur'an 16:30.

Surah al-Nahl is also known as the *surah* of blessings. In this *surah,* Allah lists and explains many of His various favours upon us. The core message of the *surah* is to be grateful to Allah for all His favours, those that we know and those that we do not realise too.

Some parts of life are tough and require patience, while others are easy and require gratitude to remain firm in our worship. When a believer lives a life of patience and gratitude, the result is a constant state of worship that will be of great benefit on the Last Day.

The Messenger of Allah ﷺ said, "Wondrous is the affair of a believer, as there is good for him in every matter; this is not the case for anyone but a believer. If he experiences pleasure, he thanks Allah, and it is good for him. If he experiences harm, he shows patience, and it is good for him."[195]

The greatest favour that Allah has blessed us with is faith itself. Among the various favours mentioned in this *surah,* the most emphasised is the concept of faith and the goodness it brings into our lives.

And it will be said to those who maintained piety, "What has your Lord revealed?" They will say, "Goodness." To those who do good in this world is goodness, and the Home of the Hereafter is even better. How wonderful is the residence of the pious.[196]

Then We inspired you: "Follow the religion of Abraham, the monotheist. He was not an idol-worshipper." Invite to the way of your Lord with wisdom and good advice, and debate with them in the most dignified manner. Your Lord is aware of those who stray from His path, and He is aware of those who are guided.[197]

The greatest favour that Allah has blessed us with is faith itself. The most emphasised favour mentioned in Surah al-Nahl is the concept of faith and the goodness it brings into the lives of all the believers.

A core message of this *surah* is that we will all answer on the Last Day for our choices in life. Every human has blessings from Allah that they will be held accountable for. This *surah* contrasts the response of a disbeliever on the Last Day with that of a righteous believer.

Those wronging their souls while the angels are taking them away will offer [full] submission [and will say]: "We did no wrong." [The angels will say] "Yes, you did. Allah is aware of what you used to do."[198]

To those who are in a wholesome state when the angels take them, [the angels] will say, "Peace be upon you; enter Paradise, for what you used to do."[199]

197 Qur'an 16:123–25.

198 Qur'an 16:28.

199 Qur'an 16:32.

Preparing for the Last Day includes understanding when to be patient and when to be grateful. Gratitude (*shukr*) is a religious obligation. It emanates from within the heart and is expressed practically through acts of worship and obedience to Allah. It also manifests in acts of generosity, kindness, and gratitude to others.

Among the many benefits of *shukr* is that it builds optimism and resilience, motivating believers to work hard, with patience and steadfastness to overcome challenges, to attain balance and a more holistic well-being and to reap the rewards of this world and the Hereafter. When we choose to live a life of gratitude, we benefit in many ways in both worlds.[200]

200 Check out Yaqeen Institute's gratitude journal, The Shukr Lifestyle, to learn more on how to cultivate an attitude of gratitude.

Gratitude (shukr) emanates from within the heart and is expressed practically through all the acts of worship and obedience to Allah. It builds optimism and resilience, motivating believers to work hard.

Juz fourteen

Qur'anic worldview

As indicated above, Surah al-Nahl focuses on the blessings of Allah, and the importance of gratitude to Allah for those blessings. This is a late Meccan *surah* that focuses on this core aspect of Islamic theology. One of the primary goals of Meccan revelation was to teach people correct beliefs, and why they should worship the Creator alone. Gratitude is considered the highest level of worship as it was the reason that the Prophet ﷺ himself excelled at worship.

Allah has blessed some people with more gifts than others which include wealth, power, knowledge, and intelligence. These gifts must be used responsibly to establish justice on earth and to please Allah.

'Aisha ؓ narrates that the Messenger of Allah ﷺ performed the ritual prayer until his feet became swollen, so he was asked, "Must you burden yourself with this, when Allah has already forgiven you your former and your latter sins?" He replied, "Shall I not be a thankful servant?"[201]

201 Sahih Muslim, no. 2819.

202 Qur'an 16:90.

Worshipping the Creator has many levels, the highest of which includes worshipping out of pure gratitude, as was the station of the Prophet ﷺ. By acknowledging the gifts and blessings of Allah, of which many are described in this *surah*, we draw closer to Allah, and our worship is transformed into pure gratitude. This is a level of faith we must all aspire to.

Towards the end of the *surah* is a powerful verse that is often quoted by scholars. It is considered a comprehensive verse that summarises the commands and prohibitions of Islam.

Allah commands justice and righteousness and generosity towards relatives. And He forbids immorality, injustice and oppression. He advises you, so that you may take heed.[202]

Justice and righteousness are central to the Islamic worldview. Allah has blessed some people with more gifts than others. These gifts include wealth, power, knowledge, and intelligence. These gifts must be used responsibly to establish justice on earth. Justice, righteousness, and generosity are all avenues through which we can use our gifts in ways that are pleasing to Allah.

Juz fifteen

Juz fifteen

Thematic overview

The fifteenth *juz* of the Qur'an contains all of Surah al-Isra (the Night Journey), also known as Surah Banu Israel, and the bulk of Surah al-Kahf (the Cave), ending at verse seventy-four of Surah al-Kahf in the middle of the story of Prophet Musa عليه السلام.

Surah al-Isra and Surah al-Kahf complement each other and flow together. Surah al-Isra begins with an invocation of glorification of Allah (*tasbih*), while Surah al-Kahf begins with an invocation of praise to Allah (*tahmid*); these are the two primary forms of *dhikr* (remembrance of Allah). Both are Meccan *surahs* from the late Meccan period focused on miracles, answered *dua*s and Allah's Power and Wisdom. These themes continue in the next *juz* with Surah Maryam (Mary) and Surah Taha as well.

Surah al-Isra is named in reference to the Prophet's ﷺ night journey to Jerusalem in which he led the previous prophets in prayer, and then ascended to visit the world of the unseen. It was a turning point in his life as it established his status as the leader of the prophets. Surah al-Isra is named after the amazing miracle of Prophet Muhammad ﷺ, while the next few *surahs* focus on the miracles of past prophets and righteous people. The theme of miracles runs strong over the next few *surahs*.

A large portion of Surah al-Isra focuses on the early laws of Islam. The bulk of Islamic law was revealed in Medina but in Surah al-Isra we get a glimpse of the laws that were revealed in Mecca. A primary focus of these earlier laws was the importance of respecting one's parents and treating them well. This remains a core component of our religion today.

203 Qur'an 17:23–26.

The Prophet's ﷺ night journey to Jerusalem was a turning point in his life as it established his status as the leader of all the prophets.

Your Lord has commanded that you worship none but Him, and that you be good to your parents. If either of them or both of them reach old age with you, do not say to them a word of disrespect, nor scold them, but say to them kind words. And lower to them the wing of humility, out of mercy, and say, "My Lord, have mercy on them, as they raised me when I was a child." Your Lord knows best what is in your minds. If you are righteous—He is Forgiving to the obedient. And give the relative his rights, and the poor and the wayfarer and do not squander wastefully.[203]

204 Qur’an 17:61.
205 Qur’an 18:50.
206 Qur’an 17:65.
207 Qur’an 17:82.

Notice how the verse flows from the rights of parents to the rights of relatives, the poor, and others. This shows the comprehensive teachings of Islam. We are called upon to treat everyone well, but our parents deserve a special level of kindness, especially when they reach old age. This kindness during their old age is one of the gateways to Paradise.

The story of Adam عليه السلام is mentioned in Surah al-Isra with a focus on the arrogance of Shaytaan. It is repeated in the middle of Surah al-Kahf, focusing on the origins of the devil. Surah al-Isra shows us that the devil looked down upon Adam for being created from mud,[204] while Surah al-Kahf reminds us that the devil was a jinn,[205] which is not automatically better than a human. The devil had no real reason to feel superior; this is the trap of arrogance, it is a false sense of superiority.

The devil is then reminded that he has no authority over the righteous. It is only the rebellious who fall for the devil’s tricks. “As for My devotees, you have no authority over them. Your Lord is an adequate Guardian.”[206]

Towards the end of Surah al-Isra, we are reminded that the Qur’an is a mercy and a healing for us.[207] In Surah al-Hijr, Allah promised to preserve the Qur’an. In this *surah,* He reminds us that the Qur’an was revealed for our benefit. Allah fulfilled His promise, and the Qur’an remains the primary source of spiritual healing and mercy for humanity today.

Surah al-Isra ends with a series of verses about Prophet Musa ﷺ.[208] Prophet Musa ﷺ was the main prophet that Prophet Muhammad ﷺ communicated with during the night journey; he also resembled him the most in story and mission and is a primary focus of the next *surah*. In the story of Musa ﷺ in Surah al-Isra, we see the punishment of Pharaoh and understand why Allah punishes tyrants in this world. In the story of Musa ﷺ in Surah al-Kahf, we see good people facing trials and learn to understand why bad things happen to good people in this world.

208 Qur'an 17:101–2.

209 Qur'an 17:111.

210 Qur'an 18:1.

In Surah al-Hijr, Allah promised to preserve the Qur'an. Allah fulfilled His promise, and the Qur'an remains the primary source of spiritual healing and mercy for humanity today.

Surah al-Isra ends with praising Allah who has no son. Surah al-Kahf begins with similar verses. "Praise be to Allah, who has not begotten a son, nor has He a partner in sovereignty, nor has He an ally out of weakness, and glorify Him constantly."[209] "Praise be to Allah, who revealed the Book to His servant, and allowed in it no distortion."[210]

211 Al-Sunan al-Kubra, no. 5856, grade: sahih.

Surah al-Kahf focuses on four core stories, each dealing with a different test of life. First, the sleepers of the cave were tested for their faith, and Allah rewarded them through a miracle. Second, the owner of the garden was tested with wealth, and it was taken away from him when he failed to show gratitude. Third, the people in the story of Musa and Khidr ﷤ were tested with a variety of trials. Their patience with these trials was the path to passing the test. Finally, Dhu al-Qarnayn was tested with power over others, and he passed this test by ruling with justice.

In Surah al-Kahf, the people in the story of Musa and Khidr ﷤ were tested with a variety of trials. Their patience with these trials was the path to passing the tests in their lives.

The core lesson in this *surah* is that each of us will face similar trials in life. Surah al-Kahf teaches us how to pass each of the tests. In this way, a weekly recitation of Surah al-Kahf on Fridays serves as a reminder and a guiding light for the rest of the week. Abu Sa'id al-Khudri reported that the Prophet ﷺ said, "Whoever recites Surat al-Kahf on Friday will have a light between one Friday and the next."[211]

Juz fifteen

The Seerah

The two *surahs* in this *juz,* Surah al-Isra and Surah al-Kahf, share a reason for the revelation for some of their verses. The Quraysh wanted to prove that the Prophet ﷺ was a false prophet, so they asked the rabbis in Medina for questions to ask him that only a true prophet would know the answers to.

Imam al-Tabari has reported from 'Abd Allah ibn 'Abbas ﷺ that the Quraysh of Mecca (disturbed by the rising influence of the Holy Prophet ﷺ as a prophet) sent two of their men, Nadr ibn al-Harith and 'Uqbah ibn Abi Mu'ayt, to the Jewish scholars of Medina.

Their mission was to find out what they said about him as they were learned in past scriptures of the Torah and the Gospel (Injil). The Jewish scholars told them, "Put three questions before him. If he answers these correctly, you should know that he is a prophet and messenger of Allah, and if he fails to do that, you should know that he is a pretender and not a messenger. Firstly, ask him about the young men who had left their city in the distant past and what had happened to them, for this is a unique event.

Secondly, ask him about the person who had travelled through the East and West of the earth and what had happened to him. Thirdly, ask him about the ruh (soul, spirit) as to what it was?"

The two Quraysh emissaries returned to Mecca, informed their tribesmen that they had come back with a decisive plan of action and told them all about their encounter with the Jewish scholars of Medina. Then, these people took these questions to the Holy Prophet ﷺ. He heard the questions and said that he would answer them tomorrow.

But he forgot to say 'Insha'Allah' at that time. These people went back, and the Prophet ﷺ kept waiting for divine revelation in the hope that he would be told the answers to these questions through wahy (revelation).

But no revelation came the next day. In fact, fifteen days went by, and things stood as they were, with no new revelation. The Quraysh of Mecca started taunting the Prophet ﷺ which caused him significant pain.

After fifteen days, the angel Gabriel (Jibril) came with Surah al-Kahf (in which the pause in revelation was explained as being due to not having said 'Insha'Allah' when promising to do something in the future).

This surah also narrates the event about the young men known as the People of the Cave and the event concerning the travel of Dhu al-Qarnayn from the East to the West.

Also included therein was a brief answer to the question asked about the 'ruh.' This question was addressed separately at the end of Surah Banu Israel (17:85) and this is the reason why Surah al-Kahf was placed after Surah Banu Israel.[212]

212 Al-Tabari; al-Suyuti.

Surah al-Kahf narrates the event about the young men known as the People of the Cave, and the story of Dhu al-Qarnayn's great travel from the East to the West.

The opening verses of Surah al-Isra have a different reason for revelation. These verses were revealed soon after the miraculous night journey of the Prophet ﷺ.

This night journey served as proof of prophethood and a test of the sincerity of the believers. It was at this event that Abu Bakr ؓ gained his title *al-Siddiq* due to his immediate testifying to the truth without any hesitation.

Both *surahs* were revealed in Mecca during the early to mid Meccan era and focus on matters of faith. Surah al-Isra clarifies some of the fundamental moral foundations of Islam, while Surah al-Kahf clarifies the various tests of life that people will face. From these two *surahs*, many fundamental lessons in theology can be derived. Surah al-Kahf also holds a special virtue of serving as a protection against the Antichrist.

Abu al-Darda' reported that the Messenger of Allah ﷺ said, "If anyone learns by heart the first ten verses of the Surah al-Kahf, he will be protected from the Dajjal." [213]

Surah al-Kahf clarifies the various tests of life that people will face and it also holds a special virtue of serving as a protection against the Antichrist.

213 Sahih Muslim, no. 809.

Juz fifteen

Judgement Day

The fifteenth *juz* contains two powerful Meccan *surahs*, al-Isra and al-Kahf. Surah al-Isra begins with a reminder of the beautiful miracle in which the Prophet ﷺ journeyed to the heavens and saw the realities of the afterlife with his own eyes. This is followed by a warning to us all that our book of deeds will be presented to us on that day.

We are reminded that Allah created this earth to test which of us are best in deeds. We are warned about the day when we will all have to stand in front of Allah to answer for how we used our blessings.

For every person We have attached his fate to his neck. And on the Day of Resurrection, We will bring out for him a book which he will find spread open. "Read your book; today there will be none but yourself to call you to account." Whoever is guided is guided for his own good. And whoever goes astray goes astray to his detriment. No burdened soul carries the burdens of another, nor do We ever punish until We have sent a messenger.[214]

214 Qur'an 17:13–15.

215 Qur'an 18:49.
216 Qur'an 18:7–8
217 Qur'an 18:45.

Surah al-Kahf contains four powerful stories, each relating to a different test that we face in life. In between each of these stories are reminders about the Last Day, including a specific reminder that not only will our books be presented to us that day, but they will include every little deed that we did.

And the book will be placed, and you will see the sinners fearful of its contents. And they will say, "Woe to us! What is with this book that leaves out nothing, small or big, but it has enumerated it?" They will find everything they have done present. Your Lord does not wrong anyone.[215]

Surah al-Kahf is full of powerful imagery regarding the tests of life, and the severity of the Last Day. We are reminded that Allah created this earth to test which of us are best in deeds. We are given the parable of this world being like rain, which means it is temporary and beneficial in moderate amounts. And we are warned about the day when we will all stand in front of Allah to answer for how we used our blessings.

We made what is upon the earth an ornament for it, to test them as to which of them is best in conduct. And We will turn what is on it into barren waste.[216]

And cite for them the parable of the present life: it is like water that We send down from the sky; the plants of the earth absorb it; but then it becomes debris, scattered by the wind. Allah has absolute power over everything.[217]

On the Day when We set the mountains in motion; and you see the earth emerging; and We gather them together and leave none of them behind. They will be presented before your Lord in a row. "You have come to Us as We created you the first time. Although you claimed We would not set a meeting for you."[218]

218 Qur'an 18:47–48.

The various stories in this *surah* remind us about the Last Day too. The miracle of the sleepers of the cave being resurrected after 300 years showcases Allah's ability to bring the dead back to life. The story of the two men and the garden is a reminder that those who reject the Last Day out of arrogance may lose everything in this world too. The story of Musa and al-Khidr reminds us that there are many trials and blessings that we will not understand in this world that may only become clear in the afterlife. And the story of Dhu al-Qarnayn is a reminder of the signs of the Last Day which includes the return of Gog and Magog.

In Surah al-Kahf, the miracle of the sleepers of the cave being resurrected after 300 years showcases Allah's ability to bring the dead back to life.

The theme of the Last Day appears throughout Surah al-Kahf, creating powerful imagery that leaves a lasting impression. It is recommended to recite this *surah* every Friday, serving as a weekly reminder of the tests of this world and the reality of the next.

Juz fifteen

Qur'anic worldview

219 Qur'an 18:7–8.

When we think about life being a test, we tend to focus on the negative aspects of life: trials, tragedies, and trauma. Surah al-Kahf draws our attention to the fact that even the good things in life are tests for us. Wealth, children and all things beautiful are a test from Allah. If these things are utilised in a way that is pleasing to Allah, we pass the test. However, if we become arrogant and obsessive, we risk losing it all in both worlds.

We are reminded first that the beautiful things of this world are a fleeting test, and one day they will all cease to be.

We made what is upon the earth beautiful for it, to test them as to which of them is best in conduct. And We will turn what is on it into barren waste.[219]

Then we are reminded through a parable that wealth is a test. In this parable, a man is gifted great wealth in the form of two farms. He boasts about this wealth, becomes arrogant and entitled, and ignores his neighbour's warnings to be grateful to Allah.

And cite for them the parable of two men. To one of them We gave two gardens of vine, and We surrounded them with palm trees, and We placed between them crops.

Both gardens produced their harvest in full and suffered no loss. And We made a river flow through them.

And thus he had abundant fruits. He said to his friend, as he conversed with him, "I am wealthier than you, and greater in manpower."[220]

In the end, he loses it all. A powerful reminder about the fleeting nature of the beauty of this world.

And ruin closed in on his crops, and so he began wringing his hands over what he had invested in it, as it lay fallen upon its trellises. And he said, "I wish I never associated anyone with my Lord."[221]

This parable is followed by a powerful reminder that wealth and family are beautiful blessings, and tests, from Allah. But our priority should always be righteous deeds and the pleasure of Allah.

Wealth and children are the adornments of the present life. But the things that last—virtuous deeds—are better with your Lord for reward, and better for hope.[222]

In life, we are always being tested. Sometimes with hardship and sometimes with blessings. Often with both at the same time. We must remain committed to the obedience of Allah in all situations, and neither let the hardships of life bring us down, nor the pleasures of this world make us heedless.

220 Qur'an 18:32–34.

221 Qur'an 18:42.

222 Qur'an 18:46.

Juz sixteen

Juz sixteen

Thematic overview

The sixteenth *juz* begins at verse 75 of Surah al-Kahf (the Cave) in the middle of the story of Musa and al-Khidr ﵇. The *juz* contains all of Surah Maryam (Mary) and Surah Taha, ending at the conclusion of Surah Taha. The story of Musa ﵇ is a theme that flows throughout this *juz*. It begins in the middle of the story of Musa's adventure with Khidr, the bond between Musa and his brother Aaron (Arb. Harun) ﵇ is mentioned in Surah Maryam, and then Surah Taha focuses entirely on the story of Musa ﵇. Between these three *surahs*, we see three different parts of the journey of Musa ﵇, as a student, a brother, and a messenger.

The theme of miracles is another theme found consistently throughout the *juz*. The *juz* begins with the miracles of Khidr ﵇ and Dhu al-Qarnayn in the second half of Surah al-Kahf. Khidr ﵇ was a prophet who was granted many miracles and a deep understanding of *qadar* (destiny). During Musa's ﵇ journey with him, they encountered many strange things and Musa ﵇ learned the importance of trusting Allah's *qadar*. Dhu al-Qarnayn was a great leader who was given control over a large portion of the earth. As a miracle, Allah allowed him to construct a wall that protected the world from Gog and Magog.[223] Gog and Magog will remain hidden behind this wall until the end-times.

223 Qur'an 18:94–99.

Surah Maryam describes two miraculous births: those of John the Baptist (Yahya) and Jesus ('Isa). Yahya was granted to his parents at an old age after his father made *dua* for an heir. 'Isa is the only human created from a mother without a father.[224] The core lesson in these stories is to never lose hope in Allah's mercy and to ask Allah for whatever we need as He is capable of all things. Some of the miracles of Musa are listed in Surah Taha as well.

Surah Maryam is an early Meccan *surah* that was revealed before the migration to Abyssinia. We know this because Jafar recited this *surah* in the court of the Negus King, al-Najashi. The *surah* has a powerful rhythmic flow that, along with its meaning, really touches the heart. A core concept in this *surah* is the mercy of Allah, which is referred to repeatedly throughout it. The divine name the Merciful (al-Rahman) appears in this *surah* sixteen times.[225]

In the stories of Maryam and al-Khidr, there is an interesting contrast. Khidr took away the child of a couple to protect them from the child growing up to harm them. They viewed losing their child as a tragedy and were unaware that it was to protect them. Maryam was blessed with a child that was initially viewed as a test. She did not realise then that her child would be a great blessing for her. In these two stories, we see how both gaining and losing a child can be perceived differently. Both can be tests from Allah, and whatever Allah wills for us is ultimately what is best for us.

224 Qur'an 19:2–34.

225 Muhammad al-Ghazali, A Thematic Commentary on the Quran, 323.

In the story of Prophet Ibrahim ﷺ, we have an excellent role model of how to call people to Islam. Throughout the story, Ibrahim ﷺ calls on his father with compassion and wisdom, despite his father's rejection and harshness towards him. This passage in Surah Maryam should be recited and reflected on for lessons in *da'wah* methodology.[226] The Prophet ﷺ sees in Ibrahim ﷺ an optimistic message. Ibrahim's father rejected his message, yet others would later embrace it. Likewise, the uncle of the Prophet ﷺ rejected his message, but many were going to embrace it in the future.

226 Qur'an 19:41–50.

Surah Maryam has a powerful rhythmic flow that, along with its meaning, can really touch the heart. The divine name the Merciful (al-Rahman) appears in this surah sixteen times.

A variety of other prophets are mentioned in Surah Maryam. The brotherhood between Moses (Musa) and Aaron (Harun), the steadfastness of Ishmael (Isma'il) ﷺ and the raising up of Idris ﷺ are all listed as examples of Allah's blessings on various prophets. The message is clear: obey Allah and He will take care of you in both worlds.

Surah Taha revolves around the story of Prophet Musa ﷺ with a strong focus on his journey as a messenger. Other repetitions of this story in the Qur'an focus on the reactions of the Pharaoh or his people. Here the focus is on Musa's journey and personal struggles, which parallel those of the Prophet Muhammad ﷺ.

Ibrahim عليه السلام calls on his father with compassion and wisdom, despite his father's rejection and harshness towards him. He is an excellent role model of how to call people to Islam.

Juz sixteen

The Seerah

The two *surahs* introduced in this *juz* are each related to a crucial conversion story in early Islamic history. Both are early Meccan *surahs* that are focused on the stories of the prophets. Their powerful rhythm, beautiful imagery, and heart- softening messages were responsible for two of the most important conversions in early Muslim history.

Surah Maryam teaches us about Allah's mercy through stories about the prophets and their families. At its heart is the story of Mary and the birth of Jesus. Ja'far ibn Abi Talib ﵁ recited a portion of this *surah* in the court of the Abyssinian king al-Najashi. This recitation caused the priests to weep and al-Najashi to embrace Islam. Al-Najashi was the first king to embrace Islam, marking a crucial moment in Muslim history.

Due to persecution at the hands of the Meccans, some of the companions had migrated to Abyssinia seeking asylum from its just Christian ruler al-Najashi. The Meccans sent 'Amr ibn al-'Aas to convince the king to send the Muslims back. The king listened to both sides of the story and eventually sided with the Muslims and secretly converted to Islam.

Two key elements led to his conversion. The first was a speech Ja'far ﷺ gave to him describing Islam, which is translated below. The second was the recitation of portions of Surah Maryam.

Ja'far's lecture is legendary and describes some of the most salient features of Islam. He explained to al-Najashi:

O King! we were plunged in the depths of ignorance and barbarism; we worshipped idols, we were unchaste, we ate carrion, and we spoke vulgarities. We disregarded every feeling of humanity, and the duties of hospitality and neighbourhood were neglected.

We knew no law but that of the strong, when Allah raised among us a man, of whose lineage, truthfulness, honesty, and purity we were aware; and he called to the oneness of Allah and taught us not to associate anything with Him.

Ja'far ibn Abi Talib ﷺ recited a portion of Surah Maryam in the court of the Abyssinian king al-Najashi. The recitation made the priests weep and al-Najashi embraced Islam.

He forbade us from worship of idols; and he enjoined us to speak the truth, to be faithful to our trusts, to be merciful and to regard the rights of the neighbours and kith and kin. He forbade us to speak evil of women, or to eat the provisions of orphans. He ordered us to flee from vices, and to abstain from evil; to offer prayers, to render alms, and to observe fasting.

We have believed in him, we have accepted his teachings and his injunctions to worship Allah, and not to associate anything with Him, and we have allowed what He has allowed, and prohibited what He has prohibited.

For this reason, our people have risen against us, have persecuted us to make us forsake the worship of Allah and return to the worship of idols and other abominations.

They have tortured and injured us until, finding no safety among them, we have come to your country and hope you will protect us from oppression.[227]

Surah Taha is related to the conversion of 'Umar ibn al-Khattab ﷺ. The story of 'Umar's conversion is well known. He was on his way to attack the Prophet ﷺ when he learned that his sister had converted to Islam. He went to her house and demanded an explanation. After calming down, he asked to read what they were reciting. He read the opening verses of Surah Taha and that was enough to convince him to accept Islam.

227 Al-Dhahabi, Siyar a'lam al-nubala (Beirut: Dar al-Risala al-'Alamiyya, 2014), 1:215.

These two stories show us the powerful transformational effect of the Qur'an. When its message reaches a sincere heart, it changes a person forever because a sincere heart cannot ignore the fact that this is revelation from their Lord.

The Qur'an has a powerful transformational effect on a sincere heart. When the message of the Qur'an reaches a sincere heart, it changes a person forever.

Juz sixteen

Judgement Day

Surah Maryam focuses on the mercy of Allah, especially on His prophets. A unique feature of this *surah* is its usage of the name *al-Rahman* over a dozen times to emphasise Allah's mercy. The stories in this *surah* demonstrate the mercy of Allah on various prophets including Zechariah (Zakariyya), John the Baptist (Yahya), Jesus ('Isa), and Abraham (Ibrahim) (peace be on all of them). This is followed by a warning to those who do not follow the way of the prophets, particularly those who abandon prayer and follow their desires.

The five daily prayers are our primary link to Allah and the first thing we will be asked about on the Last Day. Commitment to the prayer should be the priority in the life of every sincere believer.

These are some of the prophets Allah has blessed, from the descendants of Adam, and from those We carried with Nuh, and from the descendants of Ibrahim and Israel, and from those We guided and selected. Whenever the revelations of the Most Gracious are recited to them, they would fall into prostration, weeping.

228 Qur'an 19:58–59.

***But they were succeeded by generations who lost the prayers and followed their desires. They will meet perdition.*[228]**

These verses show us that guidance is not guaranteed and that each individual needs to choose to follow the ways of the prophets. They also highlight two key paths that lead to misguidance: abandoning prayer and following desires.

The five daily prayers are our primary link to Allah and the first thing we will be asked about on the Last Day. Commitment to prayer should be the priority of every believer on our journey of spiritual development. Abandoning the prayer is akin to disbelief in that it opens the doors of doubt, spiritual weakness and temptation. Without prayer, we lack a consistent connection to our Creator, leaving us weak and vulnerable to the plots of the devils.

Following desires is a destructive path that will take people away from Allah. In an age of hedonism, following one's desires has become a lifestyle and even a philosophy of many people. Temptation to live one's life experimenting with every immoral desire is rife, creating many paths to spiritual destruction.

Faith is corrupted by doubts and desires. Holding on to faith therefore means holding firm to the five daily prayers, while purifying our souls from immoral desires. The path of the righteous is not easy, but these two fundamental steps are crucial for attaining piety.

Faith is corrupted by doubts and desires. Holding on to faith means holding firm to the five daily prayers, while purifying our souls from immoral desires.

The *surah* ends with a warning to anyone who associates offspring with Allah. This warning is very severe to indicate that this is considered a grave crime in the sight of Allah.

And they say, "The Most Merciful has begotten a son." You have come up with something monstrous at which the heavens almost rupture, and the earth splits, and the mountains fall and crumble. Because they attribute a son to the Most Merciful. It is not fitting for the Most Merciful to have a son.

There is none in the heavens and the earth but will come to the Most Merciful as a servant. He has enumerated them and counted them one by one. And each one of them will come to Him on the Day of Resurrection alone.[229]

229 Qur'an 19:88–95.

230 Qur'an 20:116–21.

Surah Taha focuses on the story of Prophet Moses (Musa) ﷺ but contains a summary of the story of Adam ﷺ as well. This summary serves as a timely reminder about the path to Paradise and the various temptations that can lead us astray from that path.

And when We said to the angels, "Bow down to Adam," they bowed down, except for Satan; he refused. We said, "O Adam, this is an enemy to you and to your wife. So do not let him make you leave the Garden, for then you will suffer. In it you will never go hungry, nor be naked. Nor will you be thirsty in it, nor will you swelter." But Satan whispered to him. He said, "O Adam, shall I show you the tree of immortality, and a kingdom that never decays?" And so, they ate from it, whereupon their bodies became visible to them, and they started covering themselves with the leaves of the Garden. Thus, Adam disobeyed his Lord, and fell.[230]

Juz sixteen

Qur'anic worldview

Islam places a lot of emphasis on the importance of family. A primary goal of Islamic law is the preservation of the family, which is achieved through a comprehensive system of family laws. The importance of family is central in this *juz* as well. Surah Maryam highlights many stories about various family dynamics.

The story of the Prophet Zakariyya ﷺ teaches us about the blessings of children. Prophet Zakariyya never lost hope in the mercy of Allah and continued praying for a child even in old age.

In the story of Prophet Ibrahim ﷺ we have a great example of how to deal with relatives, especially our elders, who disagree with us.

A mention of the mercy of your Lord towards His servant Zakariyya. When he called on his Lord in private. He said, "My Lord, my bones have become feeble, and my hair is aflame with grey and never, Lord, have I been disappointed in my prayer to you. And I fear for my dependents after me, and my wife is barren. So grant me, from Yourself, an heir. To inherit me, and inherit from the House of Jacob, and make him, my Lord, pleasing."[231]

231 Qur'an 19:2–6.

232 Qur'an 19:42–45.

The story of the prophet Ibrahim ﷺ shows us how to deal with relatives, especially elders, who disagree with us. He remains compassionate and respectful in his approach while conveying the message clearly and standing by what he believes.

And mention in the Scripture Ibrahim. He was a man of truth, a prophet. He said to his father, "O my father, why do you worship what can neither hear, nor see, nor benefit you in any way?

O my father, there has come to me knowledge that never came to you. So follow me, and I will guide you along a straight way.

O my father, do not worship the devil. The devil is disobedient to the Most Gracious. O my father, I fear that a punishment from the Most Gracious will afflict you, and you become an ally of the devil."[232]

Islam places a lot of emphasis on the importance of family. A primary goal of Islamic law is the preservation of the family.

Prophet Musa ﷺ chooses his brother to be his partner in *da'wah*, and Prophet Ismail ﷺ is praised for reminding his family to worship Allah and prioritise Islam over everything else.

And mention in the Scripture Musa. He was dedicated. He was a messenger and a prophet. And We called him from the right side of the Mount and brought him near in communion. And We granted him, out of Our mercy, his brother Aaron, a prophet.

And mention in the Scripture Isma'il. He was true to his promise, and was a messenger, a prophet. And he used to enjoin on his people prayer and charity, and he was pleasing to his Lord.[233]

All these stories remind us of the central importance of family in the Muslim worldview. Muslims must strive to build beautiful families that worship Allah and make this world a better place. When families are strong, society is strong.

233 Qur'an 19:51–55.

Juz seventeen

Juz seventeen

Thematic overview

The seventeenth *juz* of the Qur'an contains two *surahs* in their entirety, Surah al-Anbiya (the Prophets), and Surah al-Hajj (the Pilgrimage). The focus of this *juz* is on the third and fourth pillars of faith: the messengers and their messages. Surah al-Anbiya focuses on the messengers, their stories and struggles. Surah al-Hajj focuses on the message of the prophets, the message of monotheism, worship and righteous conduct. The Hajj is focused on as a symbol of all three; Hajj is the ultimate act of worship based on pure monotheism that builds in us the best of character.

Surah al-Anbiya gives us snapshots of the lives of sixteen prophets and glimpses into how each of their stories ended. Every prophet is briefly mentioned except Ibrahim عليه السلام who is a primary focus of both these *surahs*. The pagans of Mecca considered themselves followers of Prophet Ibrahim عليه السلام so a lot of early Meccan revelation focused on reminding them of the true message of Ibrahim which was the same as the message of Prophet Muhammad ﷺ.

Both *surahs* begin with strong warnings about the end of time. These passages serve as firm reminders to embrace the message quickly before the hour comes. Mankind does not have the luxury of time to wait and make excuses for rejecting the truth.

234 Qur'an 21:1–3.
235 Qur'an 22:1–2.
236 Qur'an 21:8–41.

Mankind's reckoning has drawn near, but they turn away heedlessly. No fresh reminder comes to them from their Lord, but they listen to it playfully. Their hearts distracted, the wrongdoers confer secretly, "Is this anything but a mortal like you? Will you take to sorcery, with open eyes?"[234]

O people be conscious of your Lord. The quaking of the Hour is a tremendous thing. On the Day when you will see it, every nursing mother will discard her infant, and every pregnant woman will abort her load, and you will see the people drunk, even though they are not drunk—but the punishment of Allah is severe.[235]

A core theme of Surah al-Anbiya is that Prophet Muhammad ﷺ was not the first prophet and the claims made against him were not made for the first time. Every excuse made by the Quraysh is tackled and they are reminded that every messenger before him was also a human just like them. It is not the way of Allah to send angels as messengers. Allah reminds them further that the message of Muhammad ﷺ is consistent with those who came before him. The *surah* leaves no excuse for disbelieving in the truth.[236]

The core focus of this *surah* is the prophets of the past and their similarities to Prophet Muhammad ﷺ in message and challenges. We learn about the struggles of Lot (Lut), Noah (Nuh), Moses (Musa), David (Dawud), Job (Ayub), and Jonah (Yunus) ﷺ along with many others. In all these stories, the end is the same: victory was given to the prophet and those who followed him. This *surah* was revealed as both a warning to the Quraysh and a source of hope and optimism for the Prophet ﷺ and his followers.

Towards the beginning of Surah al-Hajj is a beautiful verse that summarises our lives on earth. It is worth taking time to reflect on this verse and its implications for how we live our lives.

O people! If you are in doubt about the resurrection—We created you from dust, then from a small drop, then from a clinging clot, then from a lump of flesh, partly developed and partly undeveloped. To clarify things for you. And We settle in the wombs whatever We will for a designated term, and then We bring you out as infants until you reach your full strength. And some of you will pass away, and some of you will be returned to the vilest age, so that he may not know, after having known. And you see the earth still; but when We send down water on it, it vibrates, swells, and grows all kinds of lovely pairs."[237]

237 Qur'an 22:5.

Surah al-Anbiya focuses on the messengers, their stories and struggles. Surah al-Hajj focuses on the message of the prophets, of monotheism, worship and maintaining righteous conduct.

Surah al-Anbiya reflects on the creation of heaven and earth, while this *surah* calls on us to reflect on our own existence. Between the two, we are given a lot to reflect on, all of which should lead to the same conclusion: we must devote our lives to serving our Creator.

The story of Prophet Abraham (Ibrahim) عليه السلام is once again a central focus of this *surah*. The story of how he built the Ka'bah and called people for Hajj is mentioned as a sign of hope. Prophet Ibrahim did not see multitudes arriving for Hajj during his lifetime. Today, millions of people respond each year to his call. This was a powerful and hopeful reminder to the Prophet ﷺ that he too would one day be successful and return to Mecca.

Allah reminds the Quraysh that the message of Muhammad ﷺ is consistent with those who came before him. Surah al-Anbiya leaves no excuse for disbelieving in the message of truth.

Juz seventeen

The Seerah

The *surahs* in the seventeenth *juz* were revealed around the time of the migration from Mecca to Medina. Some of these *surahs* are Meccan, and some are Medinan, even though they were revealed in the same year. This *juz* shows some of the challenges of the year of migration as the Muslims adapted to a new life in a new land.

238 Qur'an 22:11.

Allah mentions a type of people who worship Allah conditionally. They worship Allah expecting prosperity or to gain something in return which goes against the purpose of life and submission.

In Surah al-Hajj, Allah mentions a type of people who worship Allah conditionally. These are people who worship Allah expecting something in return, and when they do not receive what they asked for, they leave the faith or stop trying. This kind of transactional relationship with the Creator goes against the very purpose of life and the essence of *tawhid*, the doctrine of divine unicity.

And among the people is he who worships Allah on edge. When something good comes his way, he is content with it. But when an ordeal strikes him, he makes a turnaround. He loses this world and the next. That is the obvious loss.[238]

This verse was revealed because in Medina, some people had converted to Islam with wrong intentions. They thought that if the religion was true, it would make life easier for them. They converted to test the religion out. If their families and livestock had children, they would say it was a good religion. If not, they would leave Islam saying it was a bad religion. This mindset and approach to Islam is problematic and has no basis in the revelation.

It is similar to the prosperity doctrine that is preached today. Some preachers teach the idea that if you love Allah and believe in Him, then He will bless you with whatever you want in this world and make life easy for you. This causes people to accept the faith and worship Allah insincerely.

The Qur'an, in many places, provides a different framework. It proposes that the believer should expect tests in life and be ready to make sacrifices for the sake of Allah. Life in this world is not Paradise, and we will not always get what we want in this world. Allah put us on this earth to test us and part of that test means facing the hardships of life and being patient through them.

The Medinan Helpers (*ansar*) understood this well. They understood that by accepting Islam, allowing the Meccan Muslims to migrate to their land, and protecting the Prophet ﷺ, they were opening themselves up to new challenges and tests. The Meccans would not sit quietly while Islam spread in a nearby city. They would retaliate and this would lead to war. The Ansar embraced Islam wholeheartedly despite knowing this, proving their sincerity and commitment to the faith.

The result of their pledge was a war between Mecca and Medina, which started very soon after this. In this same *surah,* Allah gave permission to the believers to fight back against the Meccans for the first time.

Permission (to fight back) is given to those who are fought against, and Allah is Able to give them victory.[239]

239 Qur'an 22:39.

This was the first time revelation had come down allowing war. Conditions would be revealed to minimise casualties and prioritise peace. These verses show how things shifted in the year of migration.

The move to Medina brought a lot of good. The Muslims now had their own land, strong community support and protection from the tyrants of Mecca. But they also faced new challenges including war with the Meccans and the rise of hypocrites from within.

The Qur'an proposes that the believer should expect tests in life and be ready to make sacrifices for the sake of Allah. We will not always get what we want in this world.

Juz seventeen

Judgement Day

240 Qur'an 21:1–3.

Surah al-Anbiya and Surah al-Hajj are both Meccan *surahs* that focus primarily on the Last Day. Surah al-Anbiya begins by directly addressing the doubts some Meccans had about the afterlife. They treated the revelation lightly and mocked the Messenger, unaware that the Day of Judgment keeps on drawing closer with each passing day.

Mankind's reckoning has drawn near, but they turn away heedlessly. No fresh reminder comes to them from their Lord, but they listen to it playfully. Their hearts distracted, the wrongdoers confer secretly, "Is this anything but a mortal like you? Will you take to sorcery, with open eyes?"[240]

Surah al-Hajj similarly begins with addressing doubts about the Last Day. The difference is that it gives a very detailed introduction to the day itself. The horrors of the day are described in detail to emphasise the importance of the day. Then the doubts are addressed head on, followed by a reminder of the cycle of life.

Surah al-Hajj mentions people's doubts about the Last Day and it also presents a very detailed introduction to the day itself to emphasise its significance.

O people, be conscious of your Lord. The quaking of the Hour is a tremendous thing. On the Day when you will see it, every nursing mother will discard her infant, and every pregnant woman will abort her load, and you will see the people drunk, even though they are not drunk, but the punishment of Allah is severe.

Among the people is he who argues about Allah without knowledge and follows every defiant devil. It was decreed for him, that whoever follows him, he will misguide him, and lead him to the torment of the Blaze.

O people! If you are in doubt about the resurrection, We created you from dust, then from a small drop, then from a clinging clot, then from a lump of flesh, partly developed and partly undeveloped in order to clarify things for you. And We settle in the wombs whatever We will for a designated term, and then We bring you out as infants, until you reach your full strength.

And some of you will pass away, and some of you will be returned to the vilest age, so that he may not know, after having known. And you see the earth still; but when We send down water on it, it vibrates, swells, and grows all kinds of lovely pairs.[241]

241 Qur'an 22:1–5.

The above passage describes the life journey of every soul. We begin in the womb, are fashioned into humans in a miraculous way, and slowly grow into adulthood. Some adults pass away young, while others are tested with extreme old age.

242 Qur'an 21:47.

Either way, eventually, every human will pass away and return to Allah to face judgment.

The Day of Judgment will be all about justice. It will be the day of perfect justice when not a single soul will face any oppression. Every worldly transgression will be resolved and every soul will get what it deserves. Surah al-Anbiya clarifies this verse with another powerful verse about the scales.

On that day, the scales of justice will be set up and every soul will see all their deeds weighed. Every little good deed and sin will be weighed on the scale, and even the smallest of deeds could make the biggest difference in tilting the scales in one's favour.

We will set up the scales of justice for the Day of Resurrection, so that no soul will suffer the least injustice. And even if it be the weight of a mustard-seed, We will bring it up. Sufficient are We as Reckoners.[242]

The Day of Judgment will be the day of perfect justice when not a single soul will face any oppression.

Juz seventeen

Qur'anic worldview

Revelation connects us to the Creator and guides us to the best and most natural way to live our lives. The various prophets sent by Allah emphasised the same key points in their message: monotheism and obedience to the prophets. These prophets are listed by name in Surah al-Anbiya, connecting us to a rich tradition of righteous role models for every situation.

An important part of the Islamic worldview is the existence of unseen realms. The realms of the angels and jinn, as well as the afterlife and the realm of the dead are all realities. These are not mythologies or beliefs. They are realities that exist outside what we can perceive. Revelation serves as our primary means of learning about these realms, and these *surahs* give us many details about the angels, the afterlife and realities beyond our sight.

Preparations for the Last Day are an especially important aspect of how we deal with this reality. This day is described in vivid detail at the beginning of both *surahs* in this *juz*. These verses should inspire awe in our hearts, forcing us to prioritise actions that are valuable on that day over other deeds. This mindset is summarised in the famous narration in which the Prophet ﷺ was asked, "When is the Hour?" To which he replied, "What have you prepared for it?"[243]

243 Sahih al-Bukhari, no. 3688.

244 Qur'an 22:77–78.

Belief in the afterlife should lead to a life of striving to please Allah. This striving is a lifelong commitment in preparation for what is to come, the real life after we pass from this world. This mindset is summarised in the closing verses of Surah al-Hajj.

O you who believe! Kneel, and prostrate, and worship your Lord and do good deeds, so that you may succeed. And strive for Allah, with the striving due to Him. He has chosen you and has not burdened you in religion, the faith of your father Abraham. It is he who named you Muslims before, and in this. So that the Messenger may be a witness over you, and you may be witnesses over the people. So pray regularly, and give regular charity, and cling to Allah. He is your Protector. What an excellent Protector, and what an excellent Helper.[244]

Revelation serves as our primary means of learning about unseen realms, and we are given details about the angels, the afterlife and realities beyond our sight.

Juz eighteen

Juz eighteen

Thematic overview

245 Qur'an 22:78.

246 Qur'an 23:1–11.

The eighteenth *juz* of the Qur'an begins with Surah al-Mu'minun (the Believers), containing all of Surah al-Nur (the Light), and ends at verse twenty of Surah al- Furqan (the Differentiator). A primary focus of this *juz* is on the qualities of a true believer. All three *surahs* emphasise the qualities and characteristics that are expected from Muslims. The closing verse of Surah al-Hajj (the Pilgrimage) was the first verse to refer to this nation as Muslims,[245] the next *surah* begins with a description of believers.

Successful are the believers. Those who are humble in their prayers. Those who avoid nonsense. Those who work for charity. Those who safeguard their chastity. Except from their spouses, or their women, for they are free from blame. But whoever seeks anything beyond that—these are the transgressors. Those who are faithful to their trusts and pledges. Those who safeguard their prayers. These are the inheritors, who will inherit Paradise, wherein they will dwell forever.[246]

The qualities of the believer are all interconnected. Someone who concentrates on their prayers will avoid vain talk. Those who avoid vain talk also avoid the paths to fornication. Abstaining from fornication is a way of fulfilling one's covenant with Allah, which leads us to fulfil our contracts with people. All these qualities are connected and flow together to form the personality of the true believer. The *surah* ends with a beautiful *dua*, "And say, My Lord, forgive and have mercy, for You are the Best of the merciful."[247]

247 Qur'an 23:118.

Surah al-Nur takes its name from the verse of light found in this *surah*. This is a deep powerful verse that would require another book to explain. It is a parable of the greatness of Allah and how He guides the hearts of the believers through the message of Islam. As Surah al-Mu'minun describes the primary characteristics of the believer, Surah al-Nur teaches us the practical ways of living by these characteristics and how we are tested in these areas.

The verse of light in Surah al-Nur is a parable of the greatness and perfection of Allah and how He guides the hearts of the believers through the message of Islam.

A primary focus of this *surah* is sexual morality. This *surah* contains the prohibition of fornication and adultery, the obligation of covering the *'awrah* (private area), the prohibition of slander, the command to lower the gaze, the command to seek permission before entering someone's home and the prohibition of listening to gossip and slander. All these rules work towards the same primary purpose: the establishment of a community that is morally pure.

Surah al-Nur was revealed due to the incident of slander against the Prophet's wife and 'Mother of the Believers' 'Aisha. This is a well-known incident in which hypocrites started slander against the prophet's wife 'Aisha, so Allah revealed verses in this *surah* clarifying her innocence, as well as rules to prevent such incidents from becoming common. Some of the people who spread the slander were not evil hypocrites; they were believers who had a bad habit of gossiping. This incident should serve as a firm warning against spreading gossip and unverified information, a habit that has become even more common with social media.

An additional lesson from this story is the importance of maintaining family ties and forgiving our relatives for their slip-ups. One of the primary gossipers who spread the slander was a relative of 'Aisha who her father was financially supporting. When Abu Bakr al-Siddiq, 'Aisha's father, learned about this, he decided to cut off all monetary support to the man who had slandered his daughter. In response, Allah revealed this powerful verse.

Those of you who have affluence and means should not refuse to give to the relatives, and the needy and the emigrants for the sake of Allah. And let them pardon and let them overlook. Do you not love for Allah to pardon you? Allah is All-Forgiving, Most Merciful.[248]

248 Qur'an 24:22.

One of the primary methods of protecting ourselves from spreading slander is to keep our tongues and minds focused on remembering Allah. This message is repeated throughout this *surah*, especially in the following passage.

In houses (homes or masjids) which Allah has permitted to be raised, and His name is celebrated therein. He is glorified therein, morning and evening. By men who neither trading nor commerce distracts them from Allah's remembrance, and from performing the prayers, and from giving alms. [Note: these are the same qualities mentioned in Surah al-Mu'minun.] They fear a Day when hearts and sights are overturned. Allah will reward them according to the best of what they did and He will increase them from His bounty. Allah provides for whomever He wills without reckoning."[249]

249 Qur'an 24:36–38.

The incident of the slander of 'Aisha رضي الله عنها should serve as a firm warning against spreading gossip and unverified information, a habit that has become even more common with social media.

Surah al-Furqan contains another powerful description of the true believers, herein referred to as the true worshippers of the Most Merciful. This description will be discussed in the next chapter.

Juz eighteen

The Seerah

The three *surahs* in this *juz* share a common theme of describing the qualities of a true believer. The opening verses of Surah al-Mu'minun list the most important of these. The Prophet ﷺ said about these verses, "Ten verses have been revealed to me; whoever practises them will enter Paradise."[250]

Surah al-Mu'minun tells us what laws to follow to get to Paradise; Surah al-Nur shows us the consequences of not following these laws. Together these *surahs* give us a comprehensive overview of the core morals and ethics of our religion.

Surah al-Mu'minun calls on us to avoid idle speech and immorality and to fulfil our promises. Surah al-Nur shows the consequences of immorality, slander and broken promises.

The bulk of Surah al-Nur was revealed because of one incident, known as the slander of 'Aisha ؓ. 'Aisha narrates this story in detail in a narration that is too long to replicate here. It is worth taking the time to open the books of hadith and read the full narration in detail there.[251]

The narration refers to a scandal started by the hypocrites in Medina, the group discussed in Surah al-Baqarah (the Cow) who outwardly embrace Islamic guidance but internally reject it.

250 Al-Qurtubi, Tafsir al-Qurtubi (Beirut: Dar al-Kitab al-'Arabi, 2013), 12:95. The authentication grade of the hadith is rigorously authenticated (sahih).

251 Sahih al-Bukhari, no. 4141.

The Prophet ﷺ was returning from a journey when ‘Aisha رضي الله عنها got lost and left behind. She sat and waited for someone to find her. A young companion found her and took her home to the Prophet ﷺ. The hypocrites started a scandalous rumour upon seeing her enter the city with a stranger.

> *Surah al-Mu’minun and Surah al-Nur provide a comprehensive overview of the core morals and ethics of our religion that we must uphold.*

The scandal shook Medina and many people believed it. At first, ‘Aisha was unaware as she was ill and did not leave her home for a month. When she eventually heard of the slander, she was in shock. She went to her parents’ home and stayed there, hoping that Allah would clear her name. The Prophet ﷺ, in the meantime, investigated the matter fairly and thoroughly.

Eventually, a large section of Surah al-Nur was revealed, declaring her innocence, and criticising those who slandered her and those who believed the slander. ‘Aisha رضي الله عنها was honoured with the revelation of these verses in her defence, verses that we continue to recite today.

252 Qur'an 24:11–17.

Those who perpetrated the slander are a band among you. Do not consider it bad for you, but it is good for you. Each person among them bears his share in the sin. As for him who played the major role—for him is a terrible punishment.

Why, when you heard about it, did the believing men and women not think well of one another, and say, "This is an obvious lie"? Why did they not bring four witnesses to testify to it? If they fail to bring witnesses, then in Allah's sight, they are liars.

Was it not for Allah's favour upon you and His mercy, in this world and the Hereafter, you would have suffered a great punishment for what you have ventured into.

When you spread it with your tongues and spoke with your mouths what you had no knowledge of, you considered it trivial; but according to Allah, it is serious.

When you heard it, you should have said, "It is not for us to repeat this. By Your glory, this is a serious slander." Allah cautions you never to return to the like of it if you are believers.[252]

There are many lessons to take from this incident. Too often we are quick to believe slander against innocent Muslims and treat people as if they are guilty until proven innocent. In the age of social media, slander spreads faster than ever and often the damage done can never be undone. Once slander is out there on the internet, it becomes very difficult to delete it entirely.

As believers, we must firmly hold to the principles in this *surah* and treat people fairly. A person is innocent until proven guilty and we should refrain from believing and spreading rumours until the truth is clearly established.

In the age of social media, slander spreads faster than ever and often the damage done can never be undone.

Juz eighteen

Judgement Day

253 Qur'an 23:57–61.
254 Qur'an 24:21.

Surah al-Mu'minun focuses on the qualities of the true believers. These are the qualities we need to succeed in both worlds and that will benefit us the most on the Last Day. The opening verses are often focused on explanations of these *surahs*, but there is another set later in the *surah* that covers more qualities of true believers. In this second set of verses, the focus is on internal qualities like piety, maintaining monotheism and Allah-consciousness.

Those who, from awe of their Lord, are fearful. And those who believe in their Lord's verses. And those who associate no partners with their Lord. And those who give what they give, while their hearts quake, knowing that to their Lord they will return. It is they who race towards goodness. It is they who will reach it first.[253]

The second *surah* in this *juz* is Surah al-Nur. Surah al-Nur focuses on morality and modesty laws. It teaches us to live lives that are modest and pleasing to Allah, and to avoid the paths of immorality.

O you who believe! Do not follow Satan's footsteps. Whoever follows Satan's footsteps, he advocates obscenity and immorality. Were it not for Allah's grace towards you and His mercy, not one of you would have been pure, ever. But Allah purifies whomever He wills. Allah is All-Hearing, All-Knowing.[254]

The *surah* also includes powerful metaphors about belief and disbelief. Belief is described like a light in a niche that illuminates everything around it.

Allah is the Light of the heavens and the earth. The allegory of His light is that of a pillar on which is a lamp. The lamp is within a glass. The glass is like a brilliant planet, fuelled by a blessed tree, an olive tree, neither eastern nor western. Its oil would almost illuminate, even if no fire touched it. Light upon light. Allah guides to His light whomever He wills. Allah thus cites parables for the people. Allah is cognisant of everything.[255]

Disbelief is compared to a mirage in the desert because it leads to efforts that are in vain on the Last Day. It is also compared to the darkness of the ocean due to the darkness of disbelief blinding people from the truth. These metaphors are deep and important to reflect upon.

As for those who disbelieve, their works are like a mirage in a desert. The thirsty assumes it is to be water. Until, when he has reached it, he finds it to be nothing, but there he finds Allah, who settles his account in full. Allah is swift in reckoning. Or like utter darkness in a vast ocean, covered by waves, above which are waves, above which is fog. Darkness upon darkness. If he brings out his hand, he will hardly see it. He to whom Allah has not granted a light, has no light.[256]

255 Qur'an 24:35.
256 Qur'an 24:39–40.

Juz eighteen

Qur'anic worldview

257 Sunan ibn Mājah, no. 4182.

Modesty (*haya*) is a crucial part of the Islamic worldview. The Prophet ﷺ said, "Verily, every religion has a defining characteristic, and the defining characteristic of Islam is modesty."[257] Modesty is emphasised many times in this *juz*, particularly in Surah al-Nur.

Surah al-Nur summarises the core principles of modesty in Islam, which include dressing modestly, lowering one's gaze, avoiding the paths to fornication, avoiding gossip and slander and not entering anyone's home or room without permission. These principles are integral to establishing a modest chaste culture in which families can flourish.

Modesty is a spiritual barrier that protects the honour of people, the stability of families, and the structure of society. When a society loses its sense of modesty, all of the above begin to decline. Over time this leads to civilisational collapse. To truly live Islamic lives, Muslims must internalise the principles of modesty emphasised in Surah al-Nur and live by them.

To further drive home this point, Surah al-Nur links immodesty to following the footsteps of the devil, while linking modesty and righteousness to political power and stability.

O you who believe! Do not follow the devil's footsteps. Whoever follows the devil's footsteps, he advocates obscenity and immorality. Were it not for Allah's grace towards you and His mercy, not one of you would have been pure, ever. But Allah purifies whomever He wills. Allah is All-Hearing, All-Knowing.[258]

Allah has promised those of you who believe and do righteous deeds, that He will make them successors on earth, as He made those before them successors, and He will establish for them their religion, which He has approved for them, and He will substitute security in place of their fear. They worship Me, never associating anything with Me. But whoever disbelieves after that, these are the sinners.[259]

The decline of past and present nations can be easily linked to the spread of immorality in society. A return to true power must then include a return to modesty, chastity and honourable living becoming the norm again.

When a society loses its sense of modesty, we begin to decline in honour, family stability and the structure of society, over time this leads to civilisational collapse.

258 Qur'an 24:21.

259 Qur'an 24:55.

Juz nineteen

Juz nineteen

Thematic overview

The nineteenth *juz* of the Qur'an begins at verse twenty-one of Surah al-Furqan (the Differentiator), contains all of Surah al-Shu'ara (the Poets), and ends at verse fifty-five of Surah al-Naml (the Ants). Surah al-Furqaan completes the theme of qualities of the true believers covered in the previous two *surahs*.

Surah al-Shu'ara and Surah al-Naml contain stories of the prophets, but they focus on different types of stories. Surah al-Shu'ara focuses on the perished nations who disobeyed the messengers, while Surah al-Naml focuses on the success of Prophet Sulayman ﷺ in his mission. In both, we see the two endings of those who follow the messengers and those who reject them.

The opening verse of the *juz* is a reminder of the kind of excuse the disbelievers make for not following the truth. "Those who do not expect to meet Us say, 'If only the angels were sent down to us, or we could see our Lord.' They have grown arrogant within themselves and have become excessively defiant."[260]

This is followed by a series of verses describing the regrets of the disbelievers and the hypocrites, ending with the complaint of the Prophet ﷺ that his people did not take the Qur'an seriously. We ask Allah to make us from those who take the Qur'an seriously.

260 Qur'an 25:21.

261 Qur'an 25:27–30.
262 Qur'an 25:44.
263 Qur'an 25:77.
264 Qur'an 25:63–76.
265 Ismail Kamdar, Themes of the Quran, 59.

On that Day, the wrongdoer will bite his hands, and say, "If only I had followed the way with the Messenger. Oh, woe to me; I wish I never took so-and-so for a friend. He led me away from the message after it had come to me; for Satan has always been a betrayer of man." And the Messenger will say, "My Lord, my people have abandoned this Qur'an."[261]

It may be difficult to comprehend why some people reject the message of truth even when it is clear to them. The Qur'an reminds us here that many of them are like cattle, which means that they simply follow their leaders without critical thinking or self-reflection. "Or do you assume that most of them hear or understand? They are just like cattle, but even more errant in their way."[262]

This ties in with the closing verse of the *surah* reminding us that Allah does not need us, but we need Him, and rejecting the truth only harms us. "Say, what are you to my Lord without your prayers? You have denied the truth, and the inevitable will happen."[263]

The closing passage of this *surah* highlights further qualities of true believers, which we can summarise as humility, avoiding arguments, performing the night prayer, reflecting on the afterlife, generosity, avoiding major sins, repenting for past sins, avoiding wasting time and praying for guidance for oneself and one's family.[264] These qualities complement those mentioned in Surah al-Mu'minun and help one attain a higher level of spirituality.[265]

Surah al-Shu'ara is a beautiful poetic *surah* focused on the stories of perished nations. Each story is told in a powerful rhythmic tone with an emphasis on how the people rejected their messenger and the result of that rejection. This *surah* is a retelling of the stories of Moses (Musa), Abraham (Ibrahim), Noah (Nuh), Hud, Salih, Lot (Lut), and Shu'ayb with a focus on how their people rejected them and the result of rejecting the messengers in general.

The Qur'an mentions that many of those who reject the truth are like cattle. They simply follow their leaders without doing any critical thinking or self-reflection.

Surah al-Shu'ara begins with a reminder to the Prophet ﷺ not to stress too much over those who reject his message as each person is responsible for their own choices. "Perhaps you will destroy yourself with grief because they do not become believers."[266]

A unique feature of this *surah* is the repetition of the following verses after every story. "In that, there is a sign, but most of them are not believers. Surely, your Lord is the Almighty, the Merciful."[267]

266 Qur'an 26:3.

267 Qur'an 26:67–68, 103–4, 121–22, 139–40, 158–59, 174–75, 190–91.

In these verses, both the mercy and power of Allah are emphasised with His names the Almighty (al-'Aziz) and the Merciful (al-Rahim). This is a reminder to us that in each story, we see both Allah's mercy to the prophets and those who believed in them and His wrath against those who disbelieved.

> *Each story in Surah al-Shu'ara, is told in a powerful rhythmic tone with an emphasis on how the people rejected their messenger and the result of that rejection.*

It is easy to look at this *surah* entirely from the perspective of punishment, forgetting that in each story, Allah saved the believers and gave them victory, demonstrating both His power and His mercy.

The *juz* ends in Surah al-Naml which focuses on the story of Prophet Sulayman عليه السلام. This *surah* will be explained in detail in the next chapter.

Juz nineteen

The Seerah

The theme of the qualities of the true believers continues in the nineteenth *juz*. These three *surahs*, al-Furqan, al-Shu'ara, and al-Naml, were all revealed in Mecca and demonstrate some of the core qualities of the true believers.

The Quraysh argued that the Qur'an was just stories of ancient people and that the Prophet ﷺ wasn't a true prophet because he had normal human needs.

The opening verses of Surah al-Furqan were revealed as a response to the Quraysh tribe. The Quraysh people made many arguments against the Qur'an and the Prophet ﷺ. They argued that it was just stories of ancient people, and that the Prophet ﷺ could not have been a prophet since he had normal human needs. The opening passage of this *surah* addressed all their doubts head on.

Blessed is He who sent down the Criterion upon His servant, to be a warning to humanity. He to whom belongs the kingdom of the heavens and the earth, who took to Himself no son, who never had a partner in His kingship, who created everything and determined its measure.

268 Qur'an 25:1–9.

And yet, instead of Him, they produce for themselves gods that create nothing, but are themselves created; that have no power to harm or benefit themselves; and no power over life, death, or resurrection.

Those who disbelieve say, "This is nothing but a lie that he made up, and others have helped him." They have committed an injustice and a perjury.

And they say, "Tales of the ancients; he wrote them down; they are dictated to him morning and evening."

Say, "It was revealed by Him who knows the Secret in the heavens and the earth. He is always Forgiving and Merciful."

And they say, "What sort of messenger is this, who eats food, and walks in the marketplaces? If only an angel was sent down with him, to be alongside him a warner."

Or "If only a treasure was dropped on him." Or "If only he had a garden from which he eats." The evildoers also say, "You are following but a man under spell."

Look how they invent examples for you. They have gone astray, and cannot find a way.[268]

There are many powerful passages in these *surahs* that showcase the Meccan *da'wah*.

Surah al-Shu'ara narrates the stories of the past nations and their prophets in a powerful rhythmic manner, reminding the Meccans that the Qur'an is beyond poetry and is a miracle they cannot ignore.

Surah al-Shu'ara includes the first call to warn the people of Mecca openly about Islam, "And warn your close relatives."[269] Following the revelation of this verse, the Prophet ﷺ started conveying the message of Islam to his close family, some of whom accepted, while others rejected.

This *surah* ends with a reminder that not all poetry is evil. The Quraysh used poetry to ignite people's desire to sin and to make propaganda against Islam. In response, some *sahaba* who were gifted in this field like 'Abd Allah ibn Rawaha and Hassaan ibn Thabit رضي الله عنهما wrote poems in defence of Islam and the Prophet ﷺ.

Surah al-Shu'ara narrates the stories of the past nations and their prophets in a powerful rhythmic manner, reminding the Meccans that the Qur'an is beyond poetry and is a miracle they cannot ignore.

269 Qur'an 26:214.

270 Qur'an 26:224–27.

This tradition remains strong in every Muslim culture today. The closing verses of this *surah* praised such poets while condemning the rest.

And as for the poets, the deviators follow them.
Do you not see how they ramble in every style?
And how they say what they do not do?

Except for those who believe, and do good deeds, and remember Allah frequently, and defend themselves after they are wronged.
As for those who do wrong, they will know by what overturning they will be overturned.[270]

The Quraysh used poetry to ignite people's desire to sin and to make propaganda against Islam. In response, some sahaba wrote poems in defence of Islam and the Prophet ﷺ.

Juz nineteen

Judgement Day

Surah al-Shu'ara contains a beautiful supplication by Prophet Ibrahim ﷺ in which he mentions the Last Day and asks Allah not to disgrace him on that day. In answer to his prayer, he will be the first human to be clothed on the Last Day, a day when all of humanity will be resurrected naked, barefoot, and uncircumcised.

What matters most on the Last Day is a sound heart. This refers to the spiritual heart, the core of one's faith, emotions and piety.

He said, "Have you considered what you worship? You and your ancient ancestors? They are enemies to me, except the Lord of the Worlds.

"He who created me and guides me. He who feeds me and gives me water. And when I get sick, He heals me. He who makes me die, and then revives me. He who, I hope, will forgive my sins on the Day of the Reckoning.

"My Lord! Grant me wisdom and include me with the righteous. And give me a reputation of truth among the others. And make me of the inheritors of the Garden of Bliss. And forgive my father, he was one of the misguided. And do not disgrace me on the Day

they are resurrected. The Day when neither wealth nor children will help. Except for him who comes to Allah with a sound heart."[271]

The prayer of Prophet Ibrahim ﷺ ends with a clear indicator of what matters most on that day: a sound heart. This refers to the spiritual heart, the core of one's faith, emotions and piety. Every human has a spiritual heart that is affected by our deeds. It needs to be constantly purified from sin through righteous actions and repentance.

The Prophet ﷺ said, "Beware! There is a piece of flesh in the body if it becomes good (reformed), the whole body becomes good; but if it gets spoiled, the whole body gets spoiled, and that is the heart."[272]

Purification of the heart is one of the primary sciences of Islam. Along with theology and law, it is essential for every believer to study the science of heart purification. It is equally important to learn it from an orthodox source to avoid innovated methods of purifying the soul. The soul can only be purified by that which Allah has allowed and instructed. Preparing for the Last Day includes learning how to purify the soul and spending the rest of our lives slowly working on this process. The method is laid out in the following Qudsi Hadith (A divine communication with a prophetic wording).

271 Qur'an 26:75–89.

272 Sahih al-Bukhārī, no. 52.

Allah said: Whoever shows hostility to a friend of Mine, I have declared war upon him. My servant does not grow closer to Me with anything more beloved to Me than the duties I have imposed upon him. My servant continues to grow closer to Me with extra good work until I love him.

When I love him, I am his hearing with which he hears, his seeing with which he sees, his hand with which he strikes, and his foot with which he walks. Were he to ask something from Me, I would surely give it to him. Were he to ask Me for refuge, I would surely grant it to him. I do not hesitate to do anything as much as I hesitate to take the soul of the believer, for he hates death and I hate to displease him.[273]

273 Sahih al-Bukhārī, no. 6502.

Once we have mastered the obligations, we can build upon these with optional good deeds like extra prayer, charity and fasting. The more good deeds, the purer our hearts become.

This hadith teaches us that we begin the process of purification by focusing on religious obligations. We must establish these first, especially the five daily prayers. Once we have mastered the obligations, we can build upon these with optional good deeds like extra prayer, charity and fasting.

274 Qur'an 26:89.

The more good deeds we fill our lives with, the purer our hearts become. The result of mastering this is a close friendship with Allah that has miraculous benefits in both worlds.

A day will come when nothing benefits us more than having a pure heart. Preparing for that day includes working on the heart by prioritising the obligatory acts of worship and building upon them with optional acts of worship. The goal is to be from those "who come to Allah with a sound heart."[274]

Purification of the heart is one of the primary sciences of Islam. Along with theology and law, it is essential for every believer to study the science of heart purification.

Juz nineteen

Qur'anic worldview

Surah al-Furqan ends with a powerful set of verses, describing the qualities of the true believers. Surah al-Mu'minun started with a description of these qualities and Surah al-Furqan ends with a deeper description of similar qualities. This passage should be studied and reflected upon so that we can emulate some of these amazing qualities.

The servants of the Merciful are those who walk the earth in humility and when the ignorant address them, they say, "Peace."

And those who pass the night prostrating themselves to their Lord and standing up. And those who say, "Our Lord, avert from us the suffering of Hell, for its suffering is continuous. It is indeed a miserable residence and destination."

And those who, when they spend, are neither wasteful nor stingy, but choose a middle course between that.

And those who do not implore besides Allah anyone else and do not kill the soul which Allah has made sacred—except in the pursuit of justice—and do not commit adultery. Whoever does that will face penalties.

The punishment will be doubled for him on the Day of Resurrection and he will dwell therein in humiliation forever. Except for those who repent, and believe, and do good deeds. These—Allah will replace their bad deeds with good deeds. Allah is ever Forgiving and Merciful.

Whoever repents and acts righteously has inclined towards Allah with repentance. And those who do not bear false witness; and when they come across indecencies, they pass by with dignity.

And those who, when reminded of the revelations of their Lord, do not fall before them deaf and blind. And those who say, "Our Lord, grant us delight in our spouses and our children and make us a good example for the righteous."

Those will be awarded the Chamber for their patience and will be greeted therein with greetings and peace.[275]

275 Qur'an 25:63–75.

These verses summarise the paths to piety, a central component of the Islamic worldview. There are various acts of worship highlighted in these verses that elevate a person to higher levels of piety including the night vigil prayer (*qiyam al-layl*), repentance, supplicating for one's family and reflecting on the afterlife. Striving to attain higher levels of piety is a fundamental part of living an Islamic lifestyle.

Juz twenty

Juz twenty

Thematic overview

The twentieth *juz* begins with verse fifty-six of Surah al-Naml (the Ants) and ends at verse forty-five of Surah al-'Ankabut (the Spider). In between, we have Surah al-Qasas (the Story). The stories of the prophets continue to flow through this *juz* as a core theme but the focus shifts to the tests of life and how to deal with them.

Surah al-Naml focuses on the beautiful story of Prophet Sulayman عليه السلام and his *da'wah* to the people of Sheba. A primary lesson we can extract from this story is the importance of gratitude during times of ease. When Sulayman عليه السلام was granted blessings and victory, he always responded with gratitude.

He smiled and laughed at her words, and said, "My Lord, direct me to be thankful for the blessings you have bestowed upon me and upon my parents and to do good works that please You. And admit me, by Your grace, into the company of Your virtuous servants."[276]

When Sulayman عليه السلام was granted blessings and victory, he always responded with gratitude. From him, we learn the importance of gratitude during times of ease.

276 Qur'an 27:19.

Verses fifty-nine to sixty-six are a beautiful passage about the majesty of Allah. Take some time to recite these verses, read their translations and reflect on their meanings.

277 Qur'an 27:59–66.

Say, "Praise Allah and peace be upon His servants whom He has selected. Is Allah better or what they associate [with Him]?" Or, who created the heavens and the earth, and rains down water from the sky for you? With it We produce gardens full of beauty, whose trees you could not have produced. Is there another god with Allah? But they are a people who equate [others with Him]. Or, who made the earth habitable, and made rivers flow through it and set mountains on it, and placed a partition between the two seas? Is there another god with Allah? But most of them do not know.

Or, who answers the one in need when he prays to Him, and relieves adversity, and makes you successors on earth? Is there another god with Allah? How little you pay attention. Or, who guides you through the darkness of land and sea and who sends the winds as heralds of His mercy? Is there another god with Allah? Most exalted is Allah above what they associate. Or, who originates the creation and then repeats it, and who gives you livelihood from the sky and the earth? Is there another god with Allah? Say, "Produce your evidence, if you are truthful." Say, "No one in the heavens or on earth knows the future except Allah; and they do not perceive when they will be resurrected." In fact, their knowledge of the Hereafter is confused. In fact, they are in doubt about it. In fact, they are blind to it.[277]

278 Qur'an 27:89.
279 Qur'an 28:5.

In verse eighty-nine, Allah says, "Whoever brings a virtue will receive better than it and they will be safe from the horrors of that Day."[278] This verse relates to the story of Prophet Moses (Musa) ﷺ who will be safe from the horrors of the Last Day due to his righteousness. The previous *surahs* began and ended with descriptions of the horrors of the Last Day. This *surah* shows us how to protect ourselves on that day.

Surah al-Qasas focuses on the story of Prophet Musa ﷺ. This story shows us the power and decree of Allah. Musa as a helpless baby in the water is protected by Allah. Pharaoh with all his wealth and power is drowned by water too. This shows us that whoever Allah wishes to protect, nobody can harm, and Allah is in control of everything.

But We desired to favour those who were oppressed in the land, and to make them leaders, and to make them the inheritors.[279]

Surah al-Qasas gave us the example of Pharaoh who had a false sense of security in his own power, Hamaan, a high-ranking official, who had a false sense of security in Pharaoh's power, and Qarun who had a false sense of security in his wealth. All three lost everything overnight. Surah al-'Ankabut at the end of this *juz* gives us the perfect parable of this false sense of security, the spiderweb.

The likeness of those who take to themselves protectors other than Allah is that of the spider. It builds a house. But the most fragile of houses is the spider's house. If they only knew.[280]

280 Qur'an 29:41.

Musa عليه السلام was protected by Allah as a helpless baby in water while the Pharaoh was also drowned by water. Whoever Allah wishes to protect, nobody can harm, and Allah is in control of everything.

Juz twenty

The Seerah

Surah al-Qasas and Surah al-Ankabut are late Meccan *surahs* that addressed some of the primary issues of that time. The core theme of Surah al-Qasas is the story of Musa ﷺ and the importance of family. Yet it also includes a warning that guidance is from Allah and that it is not always possible to guide your family to the truth.

No matter how much we love someone, if they close their hearts to the truth we cannot change their hearts.

These verses were revealed when the Prophet's uncle Abu Talib was passing away. He was one of the Prophet's strongest pillars of support yet remained firm on the religion of his forefathers. As he was passing away, the Prophet pleaded with him to accept Islam, but he refused to do so. Upon his death, this verse was revealed.

You cannot guide whom you love, but Allah guides whom He wills, and He knows best those who are guided.[281]

281 Qur'an 28:56.

The death of Abu Talib, the Prophet's uncle, was a tragic event with a deep lesson for us all; we cannot guide people. Guidance is a gift from Allah to the sincere seeker of the truth. No matter how much we love someone, if they close their hearts to the truth because of arrogance, blind following or worldly desires, there is nothing we can do to change their hearts. All we can do is pray for the guidance of those who are alive and call them to the truth with gentle and wise preaching.

Surah al-'Ankabut begins with a strong warning that the believer will be tested.

Have the people supposed that they will be left alone to say, "We believe," without being put to the test?

We have tested those before them. Allah will surely know the truthful, and He will surely know the liars.[282]

This continues the lesson that life is a test and that accepting Islam does not automatically mean all of your dreams will come true in this world. These verses were revealed in the final years of the Meccan era before the migration. It prepared the believers for what was to come. The migration to Medina represented a new beginning but it was not going to be easy. Old problems would be replaced with new problems. Each new blessing would come with new challenges.

282 Qur'an 29:2–3.

283 Sahih al-Bukhari, no. 3926.

The migration itself and adjusting to a new climate and culture would in themselves be tests. The following story, related by 'Aisha ﵂ demonstrates some of the difficulties of this adjustment period.

When Allah's Messenger ﷺ came to Medina, Abu Bakr and Bilal got a fever, and I went to both and said, "O my father, how do you feel? O Bilal, how do you feel?"

Whenever Abu Bakr's fever got worse, he would say, "Every man will meet his death one day, for death is really nearer to him than his leather shoelaces (to his feet)."

And whenever the fever deserted Bilal, he would say aloud, "Would that I know whether I shall spend a night in the valley (of Mecca) with Idhkhir and Jalil (i.e., kinds of grass) around me, and whether I shall drink one day the water of Mijannah, and whether I shall see once again the hills of Shamah and Tafil?"

Then I went to Allah's Messenger ﷺ and told him of that. He said, "O Allah, make us love Medina as much as or more than we used to love Mecca, O Allah, make it healthy and bless its measures, and take away its fever to al-Juhfa."[283]

Life is a test and the various passages in this *juz* demonstrate this repeatedly. The believer does not expect a life of non-stop ease in this world. That is what we expect in Paradise. This world is a mixture of trials and ease, hardship and relief, good times and bad times.

The migration to Medina was a new beginning but it was not going to be easy. Old problems would be replaced with new problems and challenges.

Juz twenty

Judgement Day

Surah al-Qasas focuses on the story of Prophet Musa عليه السلام. Towards the end of the story is a brief account of Qarun. Qarun was a wealthy man from the Israelites who became arrogant about his wealth and status. People were jealous of his wealth and he flaunted it before them. He and all his treasures were swallowed by the earth as a lesson to all of mankind.

> *If someone is tested with wealth and they remain humble, grateful and committed to Allah, then it becomes a blessing that is used to benefit others around them.*

Wealth itself is not frowned upon in Islam. Some prophets like Dawud and Sulayman عليهما السلام possessed great wealth, as did many of the blessed companions like 'Uthman ibn 'Affan, 'Abdur Rahman ibn 'Awf, and Talha ibn 'Ubayd Allah رضي الله عنهم. Wealth is a test from Allah. If someone is tested with wealth and they remain humble, grateful and committed to Allah, then it becomes a blessing that is used to benefit others.

But, if a person becomes arrogant, miserly or self-obsessed due to wealth, then that wealth is not something that we should be jealous of. It is a trial that will bring that person down and we ask Allah to protect us from all such trials.

The story of Qarun includes advice that the pious gave him. They warned him to focus on the Last Day, be generous and avoid corruption. This is how we pass the test of wealth.

Qarun belonged to the clan of Musa, but he oppressed them. We had given him treasures, the keys of which would weigh down a group of strong men. His people said to him, "Do not exult; Allah does not love the exultant. But seek, with what Allah has given you, the Home of the Hereafter and do not neglect your share of this world. And be charitable, as Allah has been charitable to you. And do not seek corruption in the land. Allah does not like the seekers of corruption."

He said, "I was given all this on account of knowledge I possess." Did he not know that Allah destroyed many generations before him, who were stronger than him, and possessed greater riches? But the guilty will not be asked about their sins. And he went out before his people in his splendour. Those who desired the worldly life said, "If only we possessed the likes of what Qarun was given. He is indeed very fortunate."

But those who were given knowledge said, "Woe to you! The reward of Allah is better for those who believe and do righteous deeds." Yet none attains it except the steadfast. So, We caused the earth to cave in on him and his mansion. He had no company to save him from Allah and he could not defend himself.

Those who had wished they were in his position the day before were saying, "Indeed, it is Allah who spreads bounty to whomever He wills of His servants and restricts it. Had Allah not been gracious to us, He would have caved [the earth] in on us. No wonder the ungrateful never prosper."

That Home of the Hereafter, We assign it for those who seek no superiority on earth, nor corruption. And the [ultimate] outcome is for the righteous.[284]

284 Qur'an 28:76–83.

Qarun was arrogant with his wealth and all his treasures were swallowed by the earth as a lesson to all of mankind.

Juz twenty

Qur'anic worldview

This world is a place of trial and temptation; this is a consistent message throughout the Qur'an. Surah al-Qasas and Surah al-'Ankabut expand on this concept. Surah al-Qasas narrates the story of Prophet Moses and all the trials he faced in life, including his exile and standing up to a tyrant.

The story of Moses is repeated in the Qur'an more often than any other story due to its timeless relevance to the believers. Muslims in every era can find lessons from this powerful story that apply to their own lives. In this *surah*, we see his journey from boy to man, from exile to leader and from a man without a family to the leader of a mighty family. To achieve success in any field, we must push through our trials. In the process, we learn more about ourselves, unlock new skills and grow into better versions of ourselves.

This concept of life being a trial, especially for the believers and the righteous, is summarised beautifully at the beginning of Surah al-'Ankabut.

Have the people supposed that they will be left alone to say, "We believe," without being put to the test? We have tested those before them. Allah will surely know the truthful, and He will surely know the liars.[285]

285 Qur'an 29:2–3.

286 Qur'an 29:10–11.
287 Qur'an 29:6.
288 Qur'an 29:69.

Later in this *surah*, we are reminded that the hypocrites performed poorly when tested with the trials of life. This should strengthen our resolve to handle the trials of life in a way that is pleasing to Allah.

Among the people is he who says, "We have believed in Allah." Yet when he is harmed on Allah's account, he equates the people's persecution with Allah's retribution. And if help comes from your Lord, he says, "We were actually with you." Is not Allah aware of what is inside the hearts of the people? Allah certainly knows those who believe, and He certainly knows the hypocrites.[286]

We are reminded multiple times in this *surah* that success comes with struggle and striving. The word jihad is used in this *surah* to refer to striving in the general sense, even though it is generally used to refer to war in most *surahs* of the Qur'an. Victory and higher levels of piety cannot be achieved without striving for the sake of Allah.

Whoever strives, strives only for himself. Allah is independent of [all] beings.[287]

As for those who strive for Us, We will guide them in Our ways. Allah is with the doers of good.[288]

We cannot expect guidance to the straight path without struggle along the way: the path to paradise is paved with trials.

Juz twenty-one

Juz twenty-one
Thematic overview

The twenty-first *juz* begins at verse forty-six of Surah al-'Ankabut, contains all of Surah al-Rum (the Romans), Surah Luqman and Surah al-Sajdah (the Prostration), and ends at verse thirty of Surah al-Ahzab (the Joint Forces). As we progress into the final third of the Qur'an, the *surahs* get shorter. The bulk of the *surahs* in this *juz* are Meccan *surahs* focused on the test of life, monotheism and Islamic character. Surah al-Ahzab is the only Medinan *surah* in this *juz*.

A theme that runs through Surah al-Rum concerns proofs of the existence of Allah. Allah calls on us throughout this *surah* to reflect on a variety of things we take for granted. These range from the universe to marriage, from human origins to the diversity of languages.[289] In everything around us are signs of the existence of Allah.

Luqman's advice to his son should be studied by every parent as a great example of what we must focus on when teaching our children Islam.

289 Qur'an 30:20–25.

Surah Luqman focuses on the story of Luqman the Wise and his advice to his son. Luqman was a wise man who was known to the Arabs. He was the subject of many of their anecdotes. In this *surah,* Allah reminds the Arabs that Luqman was also a monotheist and his advice to his son was the same as the message of Islam. The passage containing Luqman's advice to his son should be studied by every parent as a great example of what we must focus on when teaching our children Islam. Luqman taught his son monotheism, humility, prayer, patience and moderation.

We endowed Luqman with wisdom: "Give thanks to Allah." Whoever is appreciative is appreciative for the benefit of his own soul. And whoever is unappreciative, Allah is Sufficient and Praiseworthy. When Luqman said to his son, as he advised him, "O my son, do not associate anything with Allah, for idolatry is a terrible wrong."

We have entrusted the human being with the care of his parents. His mother carried him through hardship upon hardship, weaning him in two years. So, give thanks to Me, and your parents. To Me is the destination. But if they strive to have you associate with Me something of which you have no knowledge, do not obey them. But keep them company in this life, in kindness, and follow the path of him who turns to Me. Then to Me is your return, and I will inform you of what you used to do.

290 Qur'an 31:12–19.

"O my son, even if it were the weight of a mustard seed, in a rock, or the heavens, or on earth, Allah will bring it to light. Allah is Kind and Expert. O my son, observe the prayer, advocate righteousness, forbid evil and be patient over what has befallen you. These are the most honourable traits. And do not treat people with arrogance, nor walk proudly on earth. Allah does not love arrogant showoffs. And moderate your stride and lower your voice. The most repulsive of voices is the donkey's voice."[290]

Surah al-Sajdah is another strong reminder about the oneness of Allah and the signs of Allah that exist all around us. Throughout this *surah*, Allah reminds us of all the powerful proofs of His Existence and calls on us to worship Him. The *surah* also includes another reminder that the believers will be tested and that those who reject the truth will cause them a lot of pain. It ends with a reminder that the ultimate victory is on the Last Day and that victory is for the believers.

And they say, "When is this victory if you are truthful?" Say, "On the day of victory, the faith of those who disbelieved will be of no avail to them, and they will not be granted respite." So, turn away from them, and wait. They too are waiting.[291]

291 Qur'an 32:28–30.

At the end of Surah al-Sajdah, we are reminded that the ultimate victory is on the Last Day and that victory is for the believers.

After three short and powerful Meccan *surahs*, the next *surah* is a slightly longer Medinan *surah*. Surah al-Ahzab was revealed after the battle of Ahzab reflecting on lessons from the battle. A primary focus of this *surah* is the importance of obeying the Messenger. There are several passages throughout this *surah* about the high status of the Prophet ﷺ and the importance of obeying him.

Juz twenty-one

The Seerah

292 Qur'an 30:2–6.

The twenty-first *juz* consists of mostly Meccan *surahs* which revolve around the *da'wah* of the Prophet ﷺ to the people of Mecca. Surah Al-Rum focuses on the many proofs of the existence of Allah and the various signs He has created that point to Him. At the same time, the *surah* is itself a proof of prophethood, as it begins with a prophecy that clearly proves it is from Allah, and not from the mind of any human.

Surah Al-Rum was revealed at a time when the Romans were losing a war against the Persians. The pagans of Mecca were excited by this news, as they viewed the Persians as closer to them religiously than the Romans who were Christians.

The tide had turned strongly against the Roman Empire, and it seemed like the end of this mighty empire. Many of its most important lands had fallen to the Persians and all hope seemed lost. It was at this moment that Allah revealed the following prophecy.

The Romans have been defeated. In a nearby territory. But following their defeat, they will be victorious. In a few years. The matter is up to Allah, in the past and in the future. On that day, the believers will rejoice in Allah's support. He supports whomever He wills. He is the Almighty, the Merciful. The promise of Allah. Allah never breaks His promise, but most people do not know.[292]

This prophecy was very clear and multi-layered. Allah had promised that the Romans would be victorious within a few years. The Arabic word used indicated that it would happen within ten years. Allah also promised that the believers will be rejoicing and enjoying Allah's support on that day. It ends by saying that this is Allah's promise and that Allah never breaks His promise.

Allah had promised that the Romans would be victorious within a few years. Allah also promised that the believers will be rejoicing and enjoying Allah's support on that day.

This was a major prophecy for that time. The integrity of the *da'wah* revolved around these events coming to pass within a decade, events in foreign lands that the Muslims had no influence over at all.

In his book, *The History of the Decline and Fall of the Roman Empire*, Edward Gibbon says, "At the time when this prediction is said to have been delivered, no prophecy could be more distant from its accomplishment, since the first twelve years of Heraclius announced the approaching dissolution of the empire."[293]

293 Edward Gibbon, The History of the Decline and Fall of the Roman Empire (London: Electric Book Co., 2001), 8:94.

Yet the prophecy came to pass exactly as predicted. Within a few years, the Romans were able to turn the tables completely and take back all their territories from the Persians. On the same day that the Romans recaptured Jerusalem, the Muslims had also turned the tables against the Meccans by winning the Battle of Badr (2 AH/624 CE). The prophecy was fulfilled exactly as it was revealed, adding another major proof that the Prophet Muhammad ﷺ was indeed a true prophet and the Qur'an was indeed from Allah.

S'ad ibn Abi Waqqas رضي الله عنه refused to abandon Islam but remained a respectful son to his mother. He became a role model for any convert with relatives who are antagonistic towards Islam.

In the middle of Surah Luqman, there is a strong reminder not to obey our parents when they ask us to commit evil, but to remain kind and merciful to them. This reminder was revealed due to an incident that occurred in the early Meccan period. Sa'd ibn Abi Waqqas رضي الله عنه was one of the early converts to Islam. In fact, he may have been the seventh man to accept Islam. His mother vehemently opposed Islam and threatened to go on a hunger strike if S'ad did not revert to paganism. The following verses were revealed to clarify the rights of parents and the rights of Allah.

We have entrusted the human being with the care of his parents. His mother carried him through hardship upon hardship, weaning him in two years. So, give thanks to Me, and to your parents. To Me is the destination.

But if they strive to have you associate with Me something of which you have no knowledge, do not obey them. But keep company with them in this life, in kindness, and follow the path of him who turns to Me. Then to Me is your return; and I will inform you of what you used to do.[294]

The Prophet's Companion S'ad ibn Abi Waqqas lived by these verses. He refused to abandon Islam but remained a respectful son to his mother. He became a role model for any convert in the future who has to deal with parents or relatives who are antagonistic towards Islam. The revelation was clear: treat them well but do not obey them in the disobedience of Allah.

This *juz* also includes a lot of discussion on the importance of prayer, humility, reflection and good character. These early *surahs* played a pivotal role in shaping the theology and the character of the early Meccan converts.

294 Qur'an 31:14–15.

Juz twenty-one

Judgement Day

Surah al-Sajdah (the Prostration) contains many beautiful reminders about the Last Day and how to prepare for it. It is a short powerful chapter focused on this theme and the oneness of Allah. In this *surah*, we are shown the formula for righteousness: late-night prayer (*qiyam*), balancing hope and fear of Allah and generosity.

Their sides shun their beds, as they pray to their Lord, out of fear and hope; and from Our provisions to them, they give.[295]

In Surah al-Sajdah, Paradise is described as something that is beyond human understanding, and beyond every imagination.

The late-night prayer is one of the most important optional acts of worship. It transforms the lives of those who establish it as a habit. At that time of night when the rest of the world sleeps, the righteous soul connects with the Creator without any distractions. Its prayers are answered and its piety increases. To reach higher levels of faith, establishing the *qiyam* is essential.[296]

Surah al-Sajdah gives us one of the most important descriptions of Paradise. It describes Paradise as beyond human understanding, something that no soul has even imagined.

295 Qur'an 32:16.

296 Read the Yaqeen Paper "Tahajjud: Fuel for the Self and Society" to learn more about this important act of worship.

No soul knows what eye's delight awaits them, a reward for what they used to do.[297]

The delights of Paradise are a motivation to live a life of righteousness. These are rewards that Allah has created for His righteous servants and kept hidden, not just from our eyes but even from our imagination. Only Allah knows what amazing delights await the righteous believer who prepares for the Last Day.

This beautiful description of Paradise is followed by an answer to a question raised by the disbelievers, "Why are these rewards only for the righteous?" Allah's response is that this is from His Divine Justice. He cannot treat the sinners and rejecters the same as He treats the righteous. This is unjust to those who sacrificed for the sake of Allah. Paradise is for those who chose obedience and submission and Hellfire is for those who chose to reject the truth and transgressed Allah's boundaries.

Are the faithful equal to the sinners? They are not equal. As for those who believe and do righteous deeds, for them are the Gardens of Shelter, a reward for what they used to do.

But as for those who transgressed, their home is the Fire. Every time they try to get out of it, they will be brought back into it, and it will be said to them, "Taste the suffering of the Fire that you used to deny." We will make them taste the lesser torment, prior to the greater torment, so that they may return.[298]

297 Qur'an 32:17.

298 Qur'an 32:18–21.

The above verses show the balance mentioned in the verse on *qiyam*. The believers pray the night-prayer in fear and hope. The verses of Paradise inspire hope, while the verses about Hellfire should cause us to fear it. In Islamic theology, this balance between hope and fear is considered essential for living a righteous life.

Hope without fear can lead to negligence, while fear without hope can lead to despair. The Qur'an carefully balances the two topics whenever discussing the Last Day, Paradise and Hell.

Believers pray the night-prayer in fear and hope. The verses of Paradise inspire hope, while the verses about Hellfire should cause us to fear it.

Juz twenty-one

Qur'anic worldview

The universe is full of beautiful signs of the existence of Allah. Surah al-Rum draws our attention to these signs in a series of powerful verses that call on us to reflect on both the internal and external signs of Allah. In this *surah,* we are reminded that the universe, its various mechanisms and creatures, are all signs of the existence of the Creator, and even abstract concepts like love point to the existence of Allah.

Every tree, flower, animal and planet is a creation of Allah. The signs of Allah are all around us, we just need to open our eyes.

His is the praise in the heavens and on earth, and in the evening, and when you reach midday. He brings the living out of the dead, and He brings the dead out of the living, and He revives the land after it has died. Likewise you will be resurrected.

And of His signs is that He created you from dust; and behold, you become humans spreading out.

And of His signs is that He created for you mates from among yourselves, so that you may find tranquility in them; and He planted love and compassion between you. In this are signs for people who reflect.

299 Qur'an 30:18–27.

And of His signs is the creation of the heavens and the earth, and the diversity of your languages and colours. In this are signs for those who know.

And of His signs are your sleep by night and day, and your pursuit of His bounty. In this are signs for people who listen.

And of His signs is that He shows you the lightning, causing fear and hope. And He brings down water from the sky, and with it He revives the earth after it was dead. In this are signs for people who understand.

And of His signs is that the heaven and the earth stand at His disposal. And then, when He calls you out of the earth, you will emerge at once.

To Him belongs everyone in the heavens and the earth. All are submissive to Him. It is He who initiates creation and then repeats it, something easy for Him. His is the highest attribute, in the heavens and the earth. He is the Almighty, the Wise.[299]

This powerful passage shapes the way we interact with all of Creation. Every tree, flower, animal and planet is a creation of Allah. All point to the powerful creative capabilities of the One True Allah. The signs of Allah are all around us, we just need to open our eyes.

Juz twenty-two

Juz twenty-two

Thematic overview

300 Qur'an 33:69.

The twenty-second *juz* of the Qur'an begins at verse thirty-one of Surah al-Ahzab (the Joint Forces). It includes all of Surah Saba (Sheba) and Surah Fatir (the Creator) and ends at verse twenty- seven of Surah Ya-sin. Aside from Surah al-Ahzab, the rest of this *juz* are Meccan *surahs* focused on the oneness of Allah and the pillars of faith. The core content that runs throughout all four *surahs* is related to the fundamental pillars of belief, primarily our relationship with Allah and His Messenger.

Surah al-Ahzab focuses heavily on the rights of the Prophet ﷺ and his wives. We are taught that the Prophet ﷺ is the perfect role model, who was sent as a witness and a bringer of glad tidings and warnings. We are commanded to send *salawat* (salutations) upon him and to obey him. We are taught that his wives are our mothers and have special rules they need to follow because of this status. All these verses focus on the rights of the Messenger ﷺ.

At the end of the *surah*, we are reminded that some nations in the past disrespected their messengers and we are commanded not to be like them. "O you who believe! Do not be like those who abused Moses, but Allah cleared him of what they said. He was distinguished with Allah."[300]

The *surah* ends with a deep verse about the responsibility that lies upon mankind. Other types of creation refused to take up this responsibility, but humanity accepted it. We must use our free will to obey Allah and fulfil the trust upon us.

We offered the Trust to the heavens, and the earth, and the mountains, but they refused to bear it and were apprehensive of it, but the human being accepted it. He was unfair and ignorant.[301]

The Prophet ﷺ is the perfect role model, who was sent as a witness and a bringer of glad tidings and warnings.

The next *surah* gives us two examples of how humanity deals with the responsibilities Allah gives them. In the story of prophets David (Dawud) and Solomon (Sulayman) عليهما السلام, we see the correct response. They were given authority over large kingdoms and responded with gratitude and justice. "O House of David, work with appreciation, but a few of My servants are appreciative."[302]

301 Qur'an 33:72.

302 Qur'an 34:13.

The people of Saba were gifted with great wealth, but they abused that wealth and were ungrateful for it, so it was taken away from them. The test of abundance is passed by expressing gratitude. When we are grateful, Allah gives us more. When we are ungrateful, then the blessings are removed. All success then lies in living a life of gratitude.

Surah Fatir is a powerful reminder of the greatness of Allah. It is a short powerful *surah* focused on monotheism. Both Surah Saba and Surah Fatir begin with *alhamdulillah* (all praise is for Allah); they are the final two out of five *surahs* that begin with this important phrase. As both *surahs* focus on gratitude towards Allah, they both begin with a reminder of the most common way of expressing our gratitude, by saying *alhamdulillah*.

The test of abundance is passed by expressing gratitude. When we are grateful to Allah, He gives us more. When we are ungrateful, then the blessings are removed.

The *juz* ends near the beginning of Surah Ya-sin; a *surah* that is close to the heart of every Muslim and is often recited in our homes. It focuses on the three central pillars of faith: belief in Allah, His Messenger and the afterlife. The *surah* begins with a story about a nation that rejected its messengers and the result of their rejection.

This is a firm reminder to us to obey the Messenger. This is followed by beautiful passages about the signs of Allah and ends with a reminder of the Last Day. The primary beliefs of Islam can all be extracted from this *surah*. Its true importance lies in understanding these verses.

The *juz* ends in the middle of the story of the three messengers. The people of the town rejected all three messengers and only one person believed in them. This individual called his people towards the truth and was eventually murdered for it. Even after death and experiencing paradise, he remained concerned about his people and wished they could see his ending so that they would believe. This is the true heart of the believer; it is always concerned with the guidance of others and wants only good for them.

It was said, "Enter Paradise." He said, "If only my people knew. How my Lord has forgiven me and made me one of the honoured." After him, we sent down no hosts from heaven to his people; nor would We ever send any down. It was just one Cry, and they were stilled.[303]

303 Qur'an 36:26–29.

Juz twenty-two

The Seerah

Surah al-Ahzab was revealed around the time of the Battle of the Trench in 5 AH. Due to the many events occurring in that battle, there are many passages in this *surah* that have clear reasons for revelation. The remaining *surahs* in this *juz* are early Meccan *surahs* focused on monotheism. This chapter, however, will focus on some of the reasons for the revelation of Surah al-Ahzab.

The *surah* gets its name from the confederation (*ahzab*) of tribes that had united against the Muslims that year. Wanting to wipe Islam out once and for all, the Quraysh allied with many other tribes and marched upon Medina in Shawwal 5 AH. The Muslims were heavily outnumbered.

The Prophet ﷺ gathered his companions together to discuss potential strategies and solutions. One companion, Salman the Persian, suggested that they build a ditch around the vulnerable and open sides of Medina like the Persians used to do. The Prophet ﷺ agreed and a ditch was built.

The *ahzab* were unable to cross the ditch in large numbers. As a result, the battle became a siege with multiple skirmishes. Both sides waited it out, but soon began to run out of food supplies. A powerful wind blew through the tents of the aggressors, destroying their supplies and forcing them to retreat. The Muslims had won with the help of Allah. This victory is mentioned in detail in this *surah*.

O you who believe! Remember Allah's blessings upon you, when forces came against you, and We sent against them a wind, and forces you did not see. Allah is Observant of what you do.

When they came upon you, from above you, and from beneath you; and the eyes became dazed, and the hearts reached the throats, and you harboured doubts about Allah. There and then the believers were tested and were shaken most severely.[304]

Salman the Persian, suggested that they build a ditch around the vulnerable and open sides of Medina like the Persians used to do. The Prophet ﷺ agreed and a ditch was built by the Muslims.

There are many passages in this *surah* related to other important events that occurred that year. The concept of adopting a child as one's own (*tabanni*) was abrogated in this *surah*.

Allah did not place two hearts inside any man's body. Nor did He make your wives whom you equate with your mothers, your actual mothers. Nor did He make your adopted sons, your actual sons. These are your words coming out of your mouths. Allah speaks the truth and guides to the path.

304 Qur'an 33:9–11.

305 Qur'an 33:4–5.
306 Qur'an 33:35.

Name them after their fathers; that is more equitable with Allah. But if you do not know their fathers, then your brethren in faith and your friends. There is no blame on you if you err therein, barring what your hearts premeditates. Allah is Forgiving and Merciful.[305]

When these verses were revealed, all such relations were changed to reflect biological realities. Zayd ibn Haritha stopped going by the name Zayd ibn Muhammad, and Salim, the freed servant of Abu Hudhayfa, stopped referring to himself as Salim ibn Abi Hudhaifa. This showed their full commitment to the revealed law and the truth.

Another verse with an interesting reason for revelation is the verse listing all the qualities of the true believing men and women. Regarding the revelation of this verse, Umm Salama once asked the Prophet why the Qur'an only mentions men when describing the qualities of true believers. Soon thereafter, this verse was revealed.

Muslim men and Muslim women, believing men and believing women, obedient men and obedient women, truthful men and truthful women, patient men and patient women, humble men and humble women, charitable men and charitable women, fasting men and fasting women, men who guard their chastity and women who guard, men who remember Allah frequently and women who remember—Allah has prepared for them a pardon, and an immense reward.[306]

The concept of adopting a child as one's own (tabanni) was abrogated in Surah al-Ahzab and then all such relations were changed to reflect biological realities.

There are many other verses in this *surah* that have clear reasons for revelation. This includes the verses about the Prophet's marriage to Zaynab bint Jahsh, the former wife of Zayd ibn Haritha, the verse on hijab, and the verses addressing the Prophet's wives with rules specific to them. Each of these stories reflect the development of the Shariah in the Medinan era and give us a glimpse of the Prophet's life during that period.

Juz twenty-two

Judgement Day

Surah Fatir is a beautiful reminder about our duties towards our Creator. It includes multiple verses that call on us to remember our Lord, His Favours and our insignificance.

O people! Remember Allah's blessings upon you. Is there a creator other than Allah who provides for you from the heaven and the earth? There is no god but Him. So how are you misled?[307]

O people! The promise of Allah is true; so, let not the lowly life seduce you, and let not the Tempter tempt you away from Allah.[308]

O people! It is you who are the poor, in need of Allah; while Allah is the Independent, the Praiseworthy.[309]

We are reminded that Allah created us from the humblest of origins and that we will return and stand in front of Him on the Last Day. A similar message is repeated in Surah Ya-sin.

Allah created you from dust, then from a small drop; then He made you pairs. No female conceives or delivers except with His knowledge. No living thing advances in years, or its life is shortened, except it be in a Record. That is surely easy for Allah.[310]

It is We who revive the dead; and We write down what they have forwarded, and their traces. We have tallied all things in a Clear Record.[311]

307 Qur'an 35:3.
308 Qur'an 35:5.
309 Qur'an 35:15.
310 Qur'an 35:11.
311 Qur'an 36:12.

The *surah* ends with a reminder that Allah could punish us in this world for our sins and that would be justified. It is part of Allah's mercy that He has delayed our punishment to the Last Day, giving us time and ample opportunities to repent and change our ways.

If Allah were to punish the people for what they have earned, He would not leave a single living creature on its surface. But He defers them until an appointed time. Then, when their time has arrived, Allah is Observant of His creatures.[312]

We are reminded that Allah created us from the humblest of origins and we will return and stand before Him for reckoning on the Last Day.

Surah Ya-sin is one of the most beloved *surahs* in the Qur'an and focuses heavily on the theme of the Last Day. This *surah* reminds us that every nation shall perish and every individual will be raised on the Last Day to account for their beliefs and deeds.

Have they not considered how many generations We destroyed before them; and that unto them they will not return? All of them, every single one of them, will be arranged before Us.[313]

312 Qur'an 35:45.

313 Qur'an 36:31–32.

314 Qur'an 36:48–55.

315 Jami' al-Tirmidhi, no. 2887.

The Day of Judgment is illustrated in detail in Surah Ya-sin, especially in the following passage.

And they say, "When will this promise be, if you are truthful?" All they can expect is a single blast, which will seize them while they argue. They will not be able to make a will, nor will they return to their families.

The Trumpet will be blown, then behold, they will rush from the tombs to their Lord. They will say, "Woe to us! Who resurrected us from our resting-place?" This is what the Most Gracious promised, and the messengers have spoken the truth."

It will be but a single scream; and behold, they will all be brought before Us. On that Day, no soul will be wronged in the least, and you will be recompensed only for what you used to do. The inhabitants of Paradise, on that Day, will be happily busy.[314]

Surah Ya-sin is closely associated with death in many Muslim cultures, as it is a tradition in many cultures to recite it when someone is passing away. Its core message is to recognise the oneness of Allah, obey the Messenger and prepare for the Last Day. Reciting it often serves as a reminder to the believer of these three core tenets of our faith. In this way, it functions as 'the heart of the Qur'an', as stated in a hadith.[315]

Juz twenty-two

Qur'anic worldview

The primary focus in the life of the believer is the pleasure of Allah. Every Muslim must strive to obey the laws of Allah and through doing so, earn the pleasure and blessings of Allah. All the *surahs* in this *juz* focus on the concept of monotheism and our relationship with Allah. The firm focus on a God-centric worldview reminds us to prioritise Allah above everything else.

We grow into the most honourable versions of ourselves by living God-centric lives. An honourable life is its own reward as it protects us from many vices and trials.

Say, "I offer you a single advice: devote yourselves to Allah, in pairs, or individually; and reflect. There is no madness in your friend. He is just a warner to you, before the advent of a severe punishment."[316]

We are reminded in Surah Saba to devote our lives to the worship of Allah. Worship can be done privately or in groups; both types of worship provide their own benefits, and help us fulfil the purpose of life.

O people! Remember Allah's blessings upon you. Is there a creator other than Allah who provides for you from the heaven and the earth? There is no god but He. So how are you misled?[317]

316 Qur'an 34:46.

317 Qur'an 35:3.

318 Qur'an 35:5.

319 Qur'an 35:10.

In Surah Fatir, we are again reminded that all the blessings in our life are from Allah. It is an injustice to praise others for the blessings of Allah. Recognising Allah's blessings in our lives should push us to live God-centric lives.

O people! The promise of Allah is true; so let not the lowly life seduce you, and let not the Tempter tempt you away from Allah.[318]

The biggest distraction from Allah is the allure of this world. As we strive to provide for our families and live good lives, we must be careful that the luxuries and temptations of this world do not distract us from living a God-centric lifestyle.

Whoever desires honour, all honour belongs to Allah. To Him ascends speech that is pure, and He elevates righteous conduct. As for those who plot evil, a terrible punishment awaits them, and the planning of these will fail.[319]

All good is from Allah, including any sense of honour. By living God-centric lives, we grow into the most honourable versions of ourselves. An honourable life is its own reward as it protects us from many vices and trials. This *juz* contains many such reminders to prioritise Allah above all else and the benefits of doing so.

Juz twenty-three

Juz twenty-three

Thematic overview

The twenty-third *juz* of the Qur'an begins at verse twenty-eight of Surah Ya-sin. It contains all of Surah al-Saffat (the Ranged in Rows) and Surah Sad and ends at verse thirty-one of Surah al-Zumar (the Throngs). These are all Meccan *surahs* focused on our primary beliefs. The core themes that flow through this *juz* are faith, repentance, and preparing for the Afterlife.

The theme of the afterlife is strongly emphasised throughout this *juz*. Surah Ya-sin contains several passages about the afterlife. Surah al-Saffat and Surah Sad both describe it in detail. Surah al-Zumar ends with a powerful series of verses describing how people will enter Paradise and Hell. A unique feature found in all four *surahs* are narrations of the conversations of people in Paradise and Hell.

The followers who end up in the fire will curse their leaders and ask Allah to increase their punishment.

In Surah Ya-sin, we learn about the man whose people refused to believe him and killed him instead. Even in Paradise, he thinks about them and wishes they could see his reward so that they would believe. The next *surah* shows us the regret of the disbelievers for following their leaders.

Their excuse will not hold up as each of us have been gifted with free will and a conscience. Choosing to blindly follow leaders down the wrong path is a choice that people will be held responsible for.

They will come to one another, questioning one another. They will say, "You used to come at us from the right." They will say, "You yourselves were not believers. We had no authority over you. You yourselves were rebellious people. The Word of our Lord has been realised against us. We are tasting it. We seduced you. We were seducers." On that Day, they will share in the punishment. Thus, we deal with the sinners.[320]

The same theme continues in Surah Sad. The followers who end up in the fire will curse their leaders and ask Allah to increase their punishment. They will say, "Our Lord, whoever brought this upon us, give him double the torment in the Fire."[321]

In Surah al-Zumar we see the excuses that people will make for not following the truth, excuses that do not hold up in the afterlife.

So that a soul may not say, "How sorry I am, for having neglected my duty to Allah, and for having been of the scoffers." Or say, "Had Allah guided me; I would have been of the pious." Or say, when it sees the penalty, "If only I had another chance, I would be of the virtuous."[322]

320 Qur'an 37:27–34.

321 Qur'an 38:61.

322 Qur'an 39:56–58.

323 Qur'an 39:53.

The regret of the people of the Hellfire is a common theme that flows throughout the *juz*, but Allah does not leave us without hope. In the middle of all of this lies the verse of hope, the most optimistic verse in the Qur'an.

Say, "O My servants who have transgressed against themselves: do not despair of Allah's mercy, for Allah forgives all sins. He is indeed the Forgiver, the Merciful." [323]

In Surah al-Zumar we are reminded that as long as we are alive, we have an opportunity to repent and work towards Paradise.

This verse is a firm reminder that as long as we are alive, we have an opportunity to repent and work towards Paradise. The conversations of the people of Hell should serve as a deterrent against sin and should push us towards repentance and righteousness. For as long as we live, the door of repentance remains open.

These *surahs* discuss Paradise as well. The flow of the Qur'an creates a balance between hope and fear. We require this balance to try and avoid sin, while not losing hope in Allah's mercy. As humans with weaknesses, we cannot function optimally without a balance between hope and fear. To build this balance, these *surahs* contain beautiful descriptions of Paradise and the people of Paradise as well.

This is a reminder. The devout will have a good place of return. The Gardens of Eden, with their doors wide-open for them. Relaxing therein and calling for abundant fruit and beverage. With them will be attendants with modest gaze, of the same age. This is what you are promised for the Day of Account. Such is Our bounty, inexhaustible.[324]

324 Qur'an 38:49–54.

Juz twenty-three

The Seerah

The four *surahs* in this *juz* (Ya-sin, Saffat, Sad and Zumar) are Meccan *surahs* focused on monotheism and other aspects of theology. The one *surah* here that has several interesting reasons for revelation is Surah al-Zumar.

Before the Prophet ﷺ received revelation, there were some men in Mecca who refused to worship idols and were seeking the truth. These men included Waraqa ibn Nawfal and Zayd ibn Amr ibn Nufayl. Waraqa ibn Nawfal accepted a monotheist denomination of Christianity and devoted his life to the scripture. He passed away before the public preaching of the Prophet ﷺ after he had confirmed to the Prophet ﷺ in private that he believed that he was indeed the Messenger of Allah.

Zayd ibn ʻAmr travelled and studied with various Christian and Jewish preachers. However, he felt that they had changed the message of their prophets and did not feel at ease following them. Instead, he devoted his life to the Abrahamic way and tried to revive monotheism in Mecca. He passed away before the Prophet ﷺ received his first revelation.

Two of the earliest converts to Islam were Zayd's son and daughter, Sa'id ibn Zayd ؓ and ʻAtiqa bint Zayd ؓ, the wife of ʻUmar ibn al-Khattab. They were raised as monotheists by their father and he had told them that a prophet was expected in that region soon. Because of this, they embraced Islam very early.

Sa'id ibn Zayd ﷺ and 'Umar ibn al-Khattab ﷺ wondered about the fate of Zayd ibn 'Amr. They knew that he was a righteous man who refused to worship idols, but he did not get a chance to officially embrace Islam. They asked the Prophet ﷺ about the fate of people like Waraqa and Zayd in the afterlife. Regarding the fate of such monotheists, Allah revealed the following verses:

Zayd ibn 'Amr devoted his life to the Abrahamic way and avoided idol worship but he passed away before the first revelation came.

As for those who avoid the worship of idols and devote themselves to Allah—theirs is the good news. So, give good news to My servants.

Those who listen to the Word and follow the best of it. These are they whom Allah has guided. These are the ones who possess great intellect.[325]

These verses give us a glimpse of Allah's mercy. People who did not get to hear the beautiful message of Islam are held responsible to follow the best of what they find. Each person's case is judged on the Last Day based on what they had access to and their sincerity. The message of hope flows throughout this *surah*.

325 Qur'an 39:17–18.

326 Qur'an 39:53.

Another verse in this *surah* is known as the verse of hope. This verse provides hope that sincere repentance will always be accepted, no matter how big our sins are.

Say, "O My servants who have transgressed against themselves: do not despair of Allah's mercy, for Allah forgives all sins. He is indeed the Forgiver, the Merciful."[326]

By Allah's kindness and mercy, people who did not get to hear the beautiful message of Islam are held responsible to follow only the best of what they find.

Some of the companions in Mecca were tortured so much that they were forced to say blasphemous words and pretend to be apostates for years to avoid being killed. When they finally had the opportunity to leave all this behind and embrace Islam openly, they wondered whether they could be forgiven for what they had done. This verse was revealed to provide hope to them and every sinner until the end of time.

Juz twenty-three

Judgement Day

Surah al-Zumar is a powerful and beautiful *surah* full of reminders about the afterlife, and how to attain success on the Last Day. In this *surah*, we learn that the mention of Allah's name has opposite effects on the hearts of believers and hypocrites. The believer's heart is filled with joy while the hypocrite grows resentful and irritated.

When Allah alone is mentioned, the hearts of those who do not believe in the Hereafter shrink with resentment. But when those other than Him are mentioned, they become filled with joy.[327]

We are also reminded that no excuses will be accepted on the Last Day from those who willingly rejected the truth. We cannot blame fate or ask for second chances. This life is our one chance to earn the mercy of Allah.

So that a soul may not say, "How sorry I am, for having neglected my duty to Allah, and for having been of the scoffers." Or say, "Had Allah guided me; I would have been of the pious." Or say, when it sees the penalty, "If only I had another chance, I would be of the virtuous."[328]

The *surah* ends with one of the most powerful descriptions of the main event of the Last Day, entrance into Paradise and Hell. Both are described in extensive detail, giving us a powerful image of how events will play out at the end of the Judgment.

327 Qur'an 39:45.

328 Qur'an 39:56–58.

329 Qur'an 39:71–75.

Those who disbelieved will be driven to Hell in throngs. Until, when they have reached it, and its gates are opened, its keepers will say to them, "Did not messengers from among you come to you, reciting to you the revelations of your Lord, and warning you of the meeting of this Day of yours?" They will say, "Yes, but the verdict of punishment is justified against the disbelievers."

It will be said, "Enter the gates of Hell, to abide therein eternally." How wretched is the destination of the arrogant. And those who feared their Lord will be led to Paradise in throngs. Until, when they have reached it, and its gates are opened, its keepers will say to them, "Peace be upon you, you have been good, so enter it, to abide therein eternally."

And they will say, "Praise be to Allah, who has fulfilled His promise to us, and made us inherit the land, enjoying Paradise as we please." How excellent is the reward of the workers. And you will see the angels hovering around the Throne, glorifying their Lord with praise. And it will be judged between them equitably, and it will be said, "Praise be to Allah, Lord of the Worlds."[329]

Juz twenty-three

Qur'anic worldview

In Surah Ya-sin, the power of Allah is demonstrated many times. We learn from this *surah* that Allah has power over all things. He simply wills it and an entire nation can be erased from existence. Similarly, it takes a single instant for resurrection to begin.

All they can expect is a single blast, which will seize them while they feud. They will not be able to make a will, nor will they return to their families. The Trumpet will be blown, then behold, they will rush from the tombs to their Lord.

They will say, "Woe to us! Who resurrected us from our resting-place? This is what the Most Gracious had promised, and the messengers have spoken the truth."

It will be but a single scream; and behold, they will all be brought before Us.[330]

330 Qur'an 36:48–53.

It is only when we embrace the message of Islam completely that we will get to experience the sweetness of faith, making the paths to Paradise clearer.

[331] Qur'an 36:81–83.

This power is summarised in the word "be" indicating Allah's Perfect Power over all things. This powerful phrase "when He wills a thing, He is to say to it, 'Be,' and it comes to be" has grown into a proverb among Muslims, serving as a reminder that Allah is always in control and nothing happens except by His Will.

Is not He who created the heavens and the earth able to create the like of them? Certainly. He is the Supreme All-Knowing Creator.

His command, when He wills a thing, He says to it, "Be," and it comes to be.

So glory be to Him in whose hand is the dominion of everything, and to Him you will be returned.[331]

This *juz* teaches us to understand the attributes of our Creator and turn to Him in sincere worship. True success in the next life comes from submitting entirely to the Creator and obeying His Law. It is only when we embrace this message completely that we will experience the sweetness of faith and the paths to Paradise will become clearer. At the end of those paths will be doors wide open, with angels waiting to greet us as stated at the end of Surah al-Zumar.

Juz twenty-four

Juz twenty-four

Thematic overview

332 Qur'an 40:55.

This *juz* begins at verse thirty-two of Surah al-Zumar, contains all of Surah Ghafir, and ends at verse forty-six of Surah Fussilat. A common theme that runs throughout these three *surahs* are the conversations of angels with or about the believers. Surah al-Zumar ends with the angels greeting the believers at the gates of Paradise, Surah al-Ghafir mentions the angels under the Throne making *dua* for the believers, and Surah Fussilat shows us the glad tidings of the angels to the righteous at the time of death.

A theme that flows through this *juz* is repentance. Surah al-Zumar contains the verse of hope, and the next *surah* is named Ghafir. Al-Ghafir is one of Allah's Beautiful Names. It means the Most Forgiving. Many of Allah's names and attributes related to punishment and forgiveness are mentioned in this *surah,* creating that balance between hope and fear.

So be patient. The promise of Allah is true. And ask forgiveness for your sins and proclaim the praise of your Lord evening and morning.[332]

At the beginning of this *surah*, we have a powerful passage about the angels around the Throne of Allah and the *dua* they make for the believers.

Those who carry the Throne, and those around it, glorify their Lord with praise, and believe in Him, and ask for forgiveness for those who believe: "Our

Lord, you have encompassed everything in mercy and knowledge; so, forgive those who repent and follow Your path, and protect them from the agony of the Blaze. And admit them, Our Lord, into the Gardens of Eternity, which You have promised them, and the righteous among their parents, and their spouses, and their offspring. You are indeed the Almighty, the Wisest. And shield them from evil deeds. Whomever You shield from the evil deeds, on that Day, You have had mercy on him. That is the supreme achievement."[333]

The angels around the Throne of Allah make dua asking for the believers to be admitted into the Gardens of Eternity which Allah promised them.

Surah Fussilat describes the angels that meet the believer at the time of death and the glad tidings they bring with them.

Surely, those who say: "Our Lord is Allah," and then go straight, the angels will descend upon them: "Do not fear, and do not grieve, but rejoice in the news of the Garden which you were promised. We are your allies in this life and the Hereafter, wherein you will have whatever your souls desire, and you will have therein whatever you call for. As Hospitality from an All-Forgiving, Merciful One."[334]

333 Qur'an 40:7–9.

334 Qur'an 41:30–32.

335 Qur'an 40:28–29.

Themes of redemption, forgiveness, the unseen and punishment all flow together throughout this *juz*. Central to all of this is the story of Musa ﵇ in Surah Ghafir. There is a unique focus in this *surah* on a member of Pharaoh's family who believed in Musa ﵇ and followed him, showing how Allah's guidance and forgiveness reach the hearts of the sincere, no matter what family they come from.

A believing man from Pharaoh's family, who had concealed his faith, said, "Are you going to kill a man for saying, 'My Lord is Allah,' and he has brought you clear proofs from your Lord? If he is a liar, his lying will rebound upon him; but if he is truthful, then some of what he promises you will befall you. Allah does not guide the extravagant imposter. O my people! Yours is the dominion today, supreme in the land; but who will help us against Allah's might, should it fall upon us?" Pharaoh said, "I do not show you except what I see, and I do not guide you except to the path of prudence."[335]

Angels meet the righteous believer at the time of death saying, "Do not fear, and do not grieve, but rejoice in the news of the Garden which you were promised."

Juz twenty-four

The Seerah

The twenty-fourth *juz* and twenty-fifth *juz* consist of the Ha Meem *surahs* which are Meccan *surahs* that share a theme about the message and the qualities of those who embrace it. About these *surahs*, 'Abd Allah ibn Masud ﷺ said, "The Ha Meem *surahs* are the beautiful gardens of the Qur'an."[336]

336 Tafsir al-Qurtubi, 15:253.

337 Qur'an 41:22–23.

Allah warns disbelievers that nothing is hidden from Him. Allah sees all, hears all and knows everything. Nothing could ever escape His Will.

There are various passages in Surah Fussilat that were revealed due to specific incidents in the Meccan era.

You were unable to hide yourselves from your hearing, and your sight, and your skins, to prevent them from testifying against you, and you imagined that Allah was unaware of much of what you do. It is that thought of yours about your Lord that led you to ruin—so you became of the losers.[337]

338 Qur'an 41:30.

These verses were revealed because of the disbelievers who wondered whether Allah could hear them. They would meet in secret and discuss their plots to end the *da'wah* in Mecca. In secret, the Meccan leaders committed great evil and planned greater evils. These verses were revealed to warn them that nothing is hidden from Allah. Our own limbs will testify against us or for us on the Last Day. Allah sees all, hears all and has knowledge of everything, and nothing ever escapes His Will.

Surely, those who say: "Our Lord is Allah," and then remain firm, the angels will descend upon them saying: "Do not fear, and do not grieve, but rejoice in the news of the Garden which you were promised."[338]

This verse was revealed in response to the songs and stories the Quraysh used to interrupt the recitation of the Qur'an. This verse was revealed in praise of Abu Bakr ﷺ who replied to the behaviour of the disbelievers in a dignified manner that brought people to Islam.

The Quraysh did not see the value of Islam, but Abu Bakr did. He knew that the real reward for believing was in the afterlife. This verse also gives us a glimpse of what a good ending looks like. The righteous believer does not face fear or sadness when dying, as the angels will greet him with reassurance and glad tidings.

And who is better in speech than someone who calls to Allah, and acts with integrity, and says, "I am of those who submit"? Good and evil are not equal. Repel evil with good, and the person who was your enemy becomes like an intimate friend.[339]

339 Qur'an 41:33–34.

This verse gives us a glimpse of the *da'wah* methodology of the Prophet ﷺ and the result of his method. The Prophet ﷺ was always kind and polite in his dealings with his enemies. As a result, many of them eventually softened, gave him an honest hearing and finally converted to Islam.

The righteous believer does not face fear or sadness when dying, as the angels will greet him with reassurance and glad tidings.

'Umar ibn al-Khattab, 'Amr ibn Al-'Aas, Khalid ibn al-Walid, Suhayl ibn 'Amr and Abu Sufyan رضي الله عنهم are all examples of people who started as enemies of Islam and later became among its staunchest defenders. This verse also teaches us not to write anyone off. We do not know for whom Allah has written guidance in the future. Our role is to call to Islam with wisdom and always give people hope for redemption through repentance.

Juz twenty-four

Judgement Day

340 Qur'an 40:7–9.

Surah Ghafir focuses primarily on the story of Prophet Musa ﷺ and his *da'wah* to the Pharaoh. This *surah* begins with some scenes from the Last Day. We learn that the angels who carry the Throne of Allah seek forgiveness on behalf of the believers. Their supplication is narrated in full detail in this passage.

Those who carry the Throne, and those around it, glorify their Lord with praise, and believe in Him, and ask for forgiveness for those who believe: "Our Lord, You have encompassed everything in mercy and knowledge; so, forgive those who repent and follow Your path, and protect them from the agony of the Blaze.

"And admit them, Our Lord, into the Gardens of Eternity, which You have promised them, and the righteous among their parents, and their spouses, and their offspring. You are indeed the Almighty, the Most Wise. And shield them from evil deeds. Whomever You shield from evil deeds on that Day, You have had mercy on them. That is the supreme achievement."[340]

This is followed by multiple descriptions of the Day of Judgment. It is described as the Day when all power belongs only to Allah. All Power belongs only to Allah in this world too, but some people are deluded to think they have real power. On that day, nobody will have any doubt that Power and Kingdom belong to Allah alone.

We are also reminded that the Last Day is a day of justice in which every soul will get what it earned and nobody will be treated unjustly. Finally, we are reminded that it is a day in which there will be no friends or alliances that can benefit the disbeliever. Each soul will have to answer for its own deeds.

The Day when they will emerge, nothing about them will be concealed from Allah. "To whom does the sovereignty belong today?" "To Allah, the One, the Irresistible."

On that Day, every soul will be recompensed for what it had earned. There will be no injustice on that Day. Allah is quick to settle accounts.

And warn them of the Day of Imminence, when the hearts are at the throats, choking them. The evildoers will have no intimate friend, and no intercessor to be obeyed.[341]

341 Qur'an 40:16–18.

On the Day of Judgment, there won't be any doubt that Power and Kingdom belong to Allah alone. Each soul will be held accountable for its own deeds.

342 Qur'an 41:19–22.

Surah Fussilat presents a detailed scene from the Last Day. It is the Day when people's own organs and skin will testify against them. This is a reminder that even sins done in private have witnesses, and the very limbs we use to sin can testify against us on that day.

The Day when Allah's enemies are herded into the Fire, forcibly. Until, when they have reached it, their hearing, and their sight, and their skins will testify against them regarding what they used to do.

And they will say to their skins, "Why did you testify against us?" They will say, "Allah, who made all things speak, made us speak. It is He who created you the first time, and to Him you are returned."

You were unable to hide yourselves from your hearing, and your sight, and your skins, to prevent them from testifying against you, and you imagined that Allah was unaware of much of what you do.[342]

Surah Fussilat presents a detailed scene from the Last Day. It is the Day when people's own organs and skin will testify against them.

Juz twenty-four

Qur'anic worldview

Surah Ghafir focuses on the tyranny of Pharaoh, especially to his own relatives who accepted the message of Prophet Musa ﷺ. Throughout history, humanity has been tested with tyrants who oppress the believers and cause mayhem and bloodshed. In our times, there are many examples of such tyrants around the world. The story of Pharaoh in the Qur'an gives us all a glimpse at the wisdom behind the existence of tyrants.

It is common today to question why the punishment of Allah does not descend immediately on tyrants. In our lifetime, we have witnessed terrible acts of genocide and tyranny that shake our faith in humanity. But this should not shake our faith in Allah. It has always been the way of Allah to give tyrants time to repent and change their ways. During this period, the believers are tested, some are returned to their Lord as martyrs, and every act of tyranny is recorded for accounting on the Last Day. Tyrants are a trial for humanity just as Pharaoh was a trial for his people.

Eventually, Allah punished Pharaoh in this world, leaving the greater punishment for the afterlife. This should give the oppressed hope that the same will happen to the tyrants of our time. Eventually, their time will end, and they will have to account to Allah on the Last Day for their crimes. When that day comes, perfect justice will be witnessed.

343 Qur'an 41:49–51.

Surah Fussilat reminds us that life is a series of trials. At times, we are tested with ease and blessings. At other times, we are tested with hardships and calamities. We are reminded that the test of blessings is one that people tend to fail, as they become negligent of Allah and distracted. Others lose hope during times of calamity. Passing the test of life means remaining committed to the obedience of Allah in both good times and bad times and reacting to each trial appropriately.

The human being never tires of praying for good things; but when adversity afflicts him, he despairs and loses hope.

And when We let him taste mercy from Us, after the adversity that had afflicted him, he will say, "This is mine, and I do not think that the Hour is coming; and even if I am returned to my Lord, I will have the very best with Him." We will inform those who disbelieve of what they did, and We will make them taste an awful punishment.

When We provide comfort for the human being, he withdraws and distances himself; but when adversity befalls him, he starts lengthy prayers.[343]

Juz twenty-five

Juz twenty-five

Thematic overview

344 Qur'an 41:3.
345 Qur'an 42:7.
346 Qur'an 43:2–4.

The twenty-fifth *juz* begins at verse forty-seven of Surah Fussilat (the [Verses] Made Distinct). It includes the *surahs* of al-Shura (the Consultation), al-Zukhruf (the Ornament), al-Dukhan (the Smoke) and al-Jathiyah (the Kneeling). A theme that flows throughout this *juz* is the status of the Qur'an and the importance of revelation. All five *surahs* begin with verses about the Qur'an's status.

Caliph 'Umar ibn 'Abd-al-'Aziz, despite being one of the most pious rulers, feared his deeds were not good enough to get him into Paradise. Such is the state of mind of the righteous.

A Scripture whose verses are detailed, a Qur'an in Arabic for people who know.[344]

Thus, we inspired you with an Arabic Qur'an, that you may warn the Central City and whoever is around it and to warn of the Day of Assembly, of which there is no doubt; a group in the Garden, and a group in the Furnace.[345]

By the Book that makes things clear. We made it an Arabic Qur'an, so that you may understand. And it is with Us, in the Source Book, sublime and wise.[346]

We have revealed it on a Blessed Night, we have warned.[347]

The revelation of the Book is from Allah, the Exalted in Might, the Wise.[348]

Verse seven of Surah al-Shura is especially powerful. Fatima bint ʻAbd al-Malik narrates that when her husband ʻUmar ibn Abd al-ʻAziz would recite this verse, he would cry and ask, "Which group am I a part of?" ʻUmar ibn ʻAbd- al-ʻAziz was the eighth Umayyad Caliph and one of the most pious rulers in the history of Islam. Yet he feared his deeds were not good enough to get him into Paradise. This is the heart and mind of the righteous.

Besides verses praising the Qur'an, Surah al-Shura also addresses the criticisms of the Quraysh against the Qur'an. Their arguments about whom the Qur'an was revealed to and why it was revealed to him were directly addressed in the following verses.

It is not for any human that Allah should speak to him, except by inspiration, or from behind a veil, or by sending a messenger to reveal by His permission whatever He wills. He is All-High, All-Wise. We thus inspired you spiritually, by Our command. You did not know what the Scripture is, nor what faith is, but We made it a light, with which We guide whomever We will of Our servants. You surely guide to a straight path.[349]

347 Qur'an 44:3.

348 Qur'an 45:2.

349 Qur'an 42:51–52.

350 Qur'an 43:31–32.

In Surah al-Zukhruf, Allah addresses those who doubted the message, drawing our attention to the real reasons they rejected Islam: tribalism, and arrogance. They were upset that the message was revealed to a man from Banu Hashim and not one of the elite tribes of the cities of Mecca or Taif.

They also said, "If only this Qur'an was sent down to a man of importance from the two cities." Is it they who allocate the mercy of your Lord? It is We who have allocated their livelihood in this life, and We elevated some of them in rank above others, that some of them would take others in service. But your Lord's mercy is better than what they amass.[350]

The theme of the greatness of the Qur'an flows throughout this *juz*. Allah addresses all the arguments raised by the Quraysh against the Qur'an while reminding us of its importance and virtues. In Surah al-Dukhan, Allah reminds us that the Qur'an was revealed on a blessed night, referring to Laylat al-Qadr (The Night of Power) in Ramadan. This is a reminder that the Qur'an is blessed in every way including the date chosen for its initial revelation.

The *juz* ends with Surah al-Jathiyah, a powerful reminder about what happens in the afterlife to those who reject this message. It concludes with a warning that those who reject the book of Allah in this world will face serious consequences on the Last Day. The message is clear: believe in the revelation and follow it, as it is the only path to salvation.

Surah al-Jathiyah concludes with a warning that those who reject the book of Allah in this world will have to face serious consequences on the Last Day.

And it will be said, "Today We forget you, as you forgot the encounter of this Day of yours. Your abode is the Fire, and there are no saviours for you. That is because you took Allah's revelations for a joke, and the worldly life lured you." So today they will not be brought out of it, and they will not be allowed to repent. Praise belongs to Allah, Lord of the heavens, Lord of the earth, Lord of humanity. To Him belongs all supremacy in the heavens and the earth. He is the Majestic, the Wise.[351]

351 Qur'an 45:34–37.

Juz twenty-five

The Seerah

352 Qur'an 44:10–15.

During the Meccan era, a famine hit Mecca that devastated the community. The Quraysh asked the Prophet ﷺ to pray that the famine would end. He did so, and the famine was lifted. Despite this, they remained firm in their disbelief and continued to reject Islam and harm the Muslims. Allah addresses this situation in the opening verses of Surah al-Dukhan.

So, watch out for the Day when the sky produces a visible smoke. Enveloping mankind: this is a painful punishment. "Our Lord, lift the torment from us, we are believers."

But how can they be reminded? An enlightening messenger has already come to them. But they turned away from him, and said, "Educated, but crazy!" We will ease the punishment a little, but you will revert.[352]

Despite witnessing so many clear proofs of prophethood, the Quraysh leaders remained firm in their disbelief. A primary reason for this was arrogance. They could not accept that Allah had chosen an orphan from Banu Hashim as His Messenger over the likes of Waleed ibn Mugheirah. Allah addresses this mindset directly in Surah al-Zukhruf.

But when the truth came to them, they said, "This is sorcery, and we refuse to believe in it." They also said, "If only this Qur'an was sent down to a man of importance from the two cities."[353]

353 Qur'an 43:31.

The leaders of Mecca are warned that wealth is not a sign of Allah's pleasure. It is a trial and a blessing and must be used in ways that are pleasing to Allah. Allah distributes His blessings among His servants based on His divine wisdom. It is this perfect wisdom that we must all trust.

The Quraysh could not accept that Allah chose an orphan from Banu Hashim to become His Messenger over people the likes of Waleed ibn Mugheirah.

Juz twenty-five

Judgement Day

354 Qur'an 42:19–20.

The twenty-fifth *juz* contains multiple descriptions of the Day of Judgment. Each of these *surahs* focuses on various scenes from that day, highlighting different lessons.

Surah al-Shura teaches us that Allah is Kind and Merciful and wants to reward the believers. We are rewarded according to our intentions. Those who intend this world will get their reward here, and those who intend the afterlife will get their reward there. This is a powerful reminder to maintain sincerity in our intentions and work towards the afterlife always.

Allah is kind towards His worshippers. He provides for whomever He wills. He is the Powerful, the Honourable. Whoever desires the harvest of the Hereafter, We increase for him his harvest; and whoever desires the harvest of this world, We give him thereof, and he has no share of the Hereafter.[354]

Surah al-Dukhan reminds us that everything in this world is temporary. Some people may have a lot of wealth in this world, but when they pass away, they leave it all behind and it is deemed worthless. All that matters then are our deeds and beliefs.

How many gardens and fountains did they leave behind? And plantations and splendid buildings. And comforts they used to enjoy. So it was; and We passed it on to another people. Neither heaven nor earth wept over them, nor were they reprieved.[355]

355 Qur'an 44:25–29.

356 Qur'an 44:38–42.

Surah al-Dukhan reminds us that everything in this world is temporary. All that matters ultimately on the Last Day are one's deeds and beliefs.

The world was created as a testing ground for humanity, and on the Last Day we will receive the results of that test. This life is not meant to be all fun and games. This is a core message of this *surah*.

We did not create the heavens and the earth and what is between them to play. We created them only for a specific purpose, but most of them do not know. The Day of Sorting Out is the appointed time for them all. The Day when no friend will avail a friend in any way, and they will not be helped. Except for him upon whom Allah has mercy. He is the Mighty, the Merciful.[356]

357 Qur'an 45:27–32.

Surah al-Jathiyah reminds us that everything belongs to Allah and that all communities will answer to Him on that day.

To Allah belongs the kingship of the heavens and the earth. On the Day when the Hour takes place, on that Day the falsifiers will lose. You will see every community on its knees; every community will be called to its Book: "Today you are being repaid for what you used to do. This Book of Ours speaks about you in truth. We have been transcribing what you have been doing."

As for those who believed and did righteous deeds, their Lord will admit them into His mercy. That is the clear triumph. But as for those who disbelieved: "Were My revelations not recited to you? But you turned arrogant and were guilty people." And when it was said, "The promise of Allah is true, and of the Hour there is no doubt," you said, "We do not know what the Hour is; we think it is only speculation; we are not convinced."[357]

The world was created as a testing ground for humanity, and on the Last Day we will receive the results of that test.

Juz twenty-five

Qur'anic worldview

The luxuries of this world have little value in comparison to the afterlife. This is an important message in Surah al-Zukhruf. In this *surah,* Allah teaches us about the wisdom behind the distribution of wealth in this world. It is the will of Allah that some people will have more than others in this world. This is a test for both the wealthy and the poor.

Is it they who allocate the mercy of your Lord? It is We who have allocated their livelihood in this life, and We elevated some of them in rank above others, that some of them would take others in service. But your Lord's mercy is better than what they amass.[358]

358 Qur'an 43:32.

The believer works hard, yet remains content with whatever Allah provides for him, knowing that this is what is best for him.

Wealth is a trial and those who have wealth will have to account for it all on the Last Day. It is not a reward for righteousness, but a bounty which some people are tested with. Allah then informs us of the wisdom behind not blessing all humans with infinite wealth.

359 Qur'an 43:33–35.

If everyone had access to the luxuries of this world, too many people would fall into disbelief and forget Allah, in the process losing themselves. For many people, a lack of luxuries is a gift that protects their faith and keeps them committed to Allah.

Were it not that humanity would become a single community, We would have provided those who disbelieve in the Most Gracious with roofs of silver to their houses and stairways by which they ascend. And doors to their houses and furnishings on which they recline. And decorations. Yet all that is nothing but the stuff of this life. Yet the Hereafter, with your Lord, is for the righteous.[359]

These verses should not stop us from working hard or pursuing halal sustenance. The believer works hard because a strong work ethic is itself a blessing, but he also knows that sustenance is predetermined. So he works hard, yet remains content with whatever Allah provides for him, knowing that this is what is best for him.

We all must strive to pass the test we are in. Those with wealth should thank Allah for it and use it in a way that is pleasing to Allah. Those who are in difficult financial situations should work hard, be content and be patient with what is not destined for them, trusting Allah's perfect wisdom.

Juz twenty-six

Juz twenty-six

Thematic overview

360 Ismail Kamdar, Themes of the Quran, 77.

361 Qur'an 46:2–3.

The twenty-sixth *juz* contains six *surahs*, all of which represent a variety of themes. These include three Meccan *surahs*; Surah al-Ahqaaf (the Sand Dunes) and the last two *surahs* in the *juz*: Surah Qaf and Surah al-Dhariyat (the Scattering [Winds]). The other three *surahs* in this *juz* are Medinan *surahs*: Surah Muhammad, Surah al-Fath (the Triumph), and Surah al-Hujaraat (the Private Rooms). Each *surah* has its own theme and many powerful lessons.[360]

Surah al-Ahqaf is the final *surah* in a series of *surahs* focused on the importance of the revelation of the Qur'an. It begins with a reminder that Allah did not create the heavens and earth without a purpose; the Qur'an was revealed to show us our purpose.

The sending down of the Scripture is from Allah, the Honourable, the Wise. We did not create the heavens and the earth and what lies between them except with reason, and for a finite period. But the blasphemers continue to ignore the warnings they receive.[361]

The *surah* includes a mention of the people of 'Aad and the consequences of their rejecting the message. This story was relevant to the people of Mecca as they were aware of 'Aad and what had happened to them. The *surah* was a warning that they would face the same consequences if they rejected the truth.

We had empowered them in the same way as We empowered you, and We gave them hearing, sight and minds. But neither their hearing, nor their sight, nor their minds availed them in any way. That is because they disregarded the revelations of Allah; and so, they became surrounded by what they used to ridicule.[362]

362 Qur'an 46:26.

Allah reminds us that He did not create the heavens and the earth without a purpose, and He revealed the Qur'an to show us our purpose.

The next three *surahs* are short Medinan *surahs* focused on a variety of Medinan themes. Surah Muhammad highlights the differences between the believers and hypocrites. Believers are expected to be brave, righteous and steadfast. In return, they are promised Paradise. The hypocrites in contrast pretend to be pious while their hearts are full of cowardice and malice. Their end is disgrace in both worlds. We are supposed to reflect on the two descriptions and ensure we fall on the right side of this description.

363 Qur'an 48:18.

Surah al-Fath was revealed after the treaty of Hudaybiyah (6 AH/630 CE). In this *surah,* Allah declared the treaty a clear victory. This was difficult for the companions to understand at that time, as the treaty seemed unfair against them. Yet it did prove to be the greatest victory as it opened the doors to peace, expansion, mass conversion and eventually the conquest of Mecca.

This *surah* also includes powerful testimony about Allah's acceptance of the deeds of the companions. This verse is considered to be one of the strongest evidence for the high status of the companions in Islam.

Allah was pleased with the believers when they pledged allegiance to you under the tree. He knew what was in their hearts and sent down serenity upon them, and rewarded them with an imminent conquest.[363]

Surah al-Hujarat is also known as the chapter of proper manners. It is an amazing *surah* that summarises the core manners of Islam in eighteen short powerful verses. These verses include the prohibition of gossip, spreading fake news, name-calling, backbiting, spying, unwarranted suspicions and racism. If all Muslims implemented the teachings of this *surah,* it would transform society and rid us of most of our communal problems.

Surah al-Hujarat also includes a warning that the revelation cannot agree with our desires. Had it agreed with our desires, that would defeat the purpose of revelation. The Prophet ﷺ had the mission of conveying the message and implementing it in the land. It was not his job to listen to everyone and treat their opinions as equal to the revelation.

Surah al-Hujarat warns us that the revelation cannot agree with our desires. Had it agreed with our desires, that would defeat the purpose of the revelation.

And know that among you is the Messenger of Allah. Had he obeyed you in many things, you would have suffered hardship. But Allah has given you love of faith, and adorned it in your hearts, and made disbelief, mischief and rebellion hateful to you. These are the rightly guided. Allah knows what is best for us, so we must trust in Allah and obey Him.[364]

364 Qur'an 49:7.

The *juz* ends with a return to the Meccan themes. Surah Qaf begins a new string of *surahs* focused on the afterlife. This remains the core theme for the remaining sections of the Qur'an. Both Surah Qaf and Surah al-Dhariyat contain powerful imagery about the afterlife. The *juz* concludes at verse thirty of Surah al-Dhariyat.

Juz twenty-six

The Seerah

Surah al-Fath was revealed after the Treaty of Hudaybiyah. In Dhul Qa'dah 6 AH/630 CE, the Prophet ﷺ and his companions set off from Medina to Mecca with the intention of performing the minor pilgrimage (*'umrah*). The Prophet had seen a dream in which he entered Mecca in peace and performed *'umrah*. As the dreams of prophets are a form of revelation, he took this as an optimistic sign and travelled to Mecca.

The treaty of Hudaybiyah was a major turning point in the seerah. Thousands flocked to Islam over the following few years as people could experience the beauty of Islam without the tension of war.

The traveling party was stopped outside Mecca in an area called Hudaybiyah, as the Quraysh debated whether to allow them in. On one hand, stopping peaceful pilgrims would be a bad look for the Meccan ruling tribe of Quraysh. On the other, allowing the Prophet ﷺ back in would be a sign of defeat and recognition of the growing power of the Muslims.

After a lot of discussion, the Quraysh's envoy Suhayl ibn 'Amr proposed a peace treaty with the Muslims. The conditions of the treaty were heavily in favour of the Quraysh. The Muslims would have to return home and not perform '*umrah* until a year later. Anyone who left Islam would be allowed to move to Mecca, but nobody from Mecca who accepted Islam would be allowed into Medina, starting with Suhayl's son Abu Jandal who had pleaded with the Muslims to help him escape his father.

The Muslims were shocked when the Prophet ﷺ signed the treaty and returned Abu Jandal to his father. Unable to process what happened, they sat dejected with a sense of defeat. 'Umar ibn al-Khattab رضي الله عنه expressed his concerns verbally, but Abu Bakr رضي الله عنه assured him that anything the Prophet did was always in the best interests of the believers.

On their way back to Medina, the opening verses of Surah al-Fath were revealed, declaring the peace treaty a victory that would lead to even more victories for the believers.

We have granted you a clear victory. That Allah may forgive you your sins, past and to come, and complete His favours upon you, and guide you on a straight path. And help you with unwavering support.

It is He who sent down tranquility into the hearts of the believers, to add faith to their faith. To Allah belong the forces of the heavens and the earth. Allah is Knowing and Wise.[365]

365 Qur'an 48:1–4.

Upon hearing these verses, Umar was so happy and excited that he rode through the ranks of the Muslims repeating them. He knew that if Allah called the treaty a victory, then it must be a victory.

The treaty proved to be a major turning point in the Seerah. With peace finally prevailing between the tribes of Arabia, people could experience the *da'wah* and the beauty of Islam for themselves, without the tension of war. Thousands flocked to Islam over the next few years, as entire tribes accepted Islam.

The next year, the Prophet ﷺ and his companions completed *'umrah* in peace. The dream of the Prophet had come true, and it was just the beginning. Many Meccans converted to Islam. As they were not allowed to migrate to Medina under the terms of the treaty, they formed their own community outside Mecca that proved to be a bigger hindrance for the Meccans. Eventually, the Meccans changed the conditions of the treaty allowing the converts to move to Medina.

After this, Mecca experienced a massive brain drain as many of their leaders, including 'Uthman ibn Talha, Khalid ibn al-Walid, 'Amr ibn al-'Aas and the Prophet's uncle al-'Abbas رضي الله عنهم all eventually migrated to Medina. The ranks of the believers were growing faster than anyone could imagine.

The treaty of Hudaybiyah was one of the greatest victories of the Muslims, proving the power of peaceful da'wah.

Eventually, the Meccans violated the treaty and in return, the Prophet ﷺ marched to Mecca leading an army of ten thousand to a peaceful conquest. The treaty of Hudaybiyah was one of the greatest victories of the Muslims proving the power of peaceful *da'wah*.

Within a short time, all of Arabia was Muslim and the Prophet's mission was complete. The Muslim world continued to grow and continues to grow today over a thousand years later. The victory of Hudaybiyah was the pivotal moment that started this ripple effect across the globe.

Juz twenty-six

Judgement Day

366 Qur'an 46:13–14.

Surah al-Ahqaf teaches us that those who live a righteous life will not experience fear or sadness after death. Part of their reward will be inner peace and glad tidings about the Paradise that awaits them.

Those who say, "Our Lord is Allah," then lead a righteous life, they have nothing to fear, nor shall they grieve. These are the inhabitants of Paradise, where they will dwell forever, a reward for what they used to do.[366]

Surah al-Hujurat teaches us to avoid social sins like spying, backbiting, name-calling and racism. We are also taught to carefully verify facts and not to follow rumours and slander.

Later in this *surah* we are presented with a scene from the Last Day in which the disbelievers will be brought before Hellfire and asked about the bounties they wasted. Allah has given each of us many blessings and opportunities that should be used to please Him. Many of these blessings were wasted by those who did not believe in or prepare for the Last Day.

On the Day when the faithless will be paraded before the Fire: "You have squandered your good in your worldly life, and you took pleasure in them. So today you are being repaid with the torment of shame, because of your unjust arrogance on earth and because you used to sin."[367]

On the Day when those who disbelieved are presented with the Fire: "Is this not real?" They will say, "Yes, indeed, by our Lord." He will say, "Then taste the suffering for having disbelieved."[368]

In the middle of this *juz* is Surah al-Hujurat, an important chapter that summarises the fundamentals of good character. Good character is among the deeds that weigh heaviest on the Last Day. The lessons of this *surah* should be a priority for every believer to learn and apply.

In this *surah*, we learn to avoid disunity, reconcile with our brothers in faith, respect our leaders and elders and to avoid social sins like spying, backbiting, name-calling and racism. We are also reminded to verify facts and not to follow rumours and slander. These are fundamental aspects of Islamic manners that will weigh heavily on the Last Day.

The Prophet ﷺ said, "Nothing is heavier upon the scale of a believer on the Day of Resurrection than his good character. Verily, Allah hates the vulgar and obscene."[369]

367 Qur'an 46:20.

368 Qur'an 46:34.

369 Jami' al-Tirmidhī, no. 2002.

370 Qur'an 51:11–19.

Surah al-Dhariyat directly addresses the disbelievers who questioned the existence of the Last Day. They are presented with a scene from that day to make them reflect on the reality of the afterlife.

This scene is followed by a description of Paradise and the deeds that lead to it: night-prayers, seeking forgiveness in the mornings and generosity.

Those who are dazed in ignorance. They ask, "When is the Day of Judgment?" The Day they are presented to the Fire. "Taste your ordeal. This is what you used to challenge."

But the pious are amidst gardens and springs, receiving what their Lord has given them. They were virtuous before that. They used to sleep little at night. And at dawn, they would pray for pardon. And in their wealth, there was a share for the beggar and the deprived.[370]

Disbelievers who questioned the existence of the Last Day are presented with a scene from that day to make them reflect on the reality of the afterlife.

Juz twenty-six

Qur'anic worldview

The Prophet said, "I was sent to perfect righteous character."[371] The Qur'an and Sunnah focus a lot on the perfection of character and manners. One *surah* that focuses on this topic in detail is Surah al-Hujarat. The teachings of Surah al-Hujarat are crucial for achieving social unity amongst us and for building a strong community.

371 Al-Bukhari, al-Adab al-mufrad, no. 273.

372 Qur'an 49:9–10.

We are told that the believers are brothers, so we must strive to reconcile between our brothers and be conscious of Allah so that we may receive His great mercy.

If two groups of believers fight each other, reconcile between them. But if one group aggresses against the other, fight the aggressing group until it complies with Allah's command. Once it has complied, reconcile between them with justice and be equitable. Allah loves the equitable.

The believers are brothers, so reconcile between your brothers and remain conscious of Allah, so that you may receive mercy.[372]

373 Qur'an 49:11–12.

This *surah* teaches us to respect each other, avoid rumours and fake news, and strive for unity. It also prohibits the primary causes of social problems, including backbiting, slander, name-calling, mockery, unnecessary suspicion, spying and boasting. These prohibitions aim at building a community built on trust, respect, valuing privacy and living together honourably.

O you who believe! No people shall ridicule other people, for they may be better than they. Nor shall any women ridicule other women, for they may be better than they. Nor shall you slander one another, nor shall you insult one another with names. Evil is the return to wickedness after having attained faith. Whoever does not repent—these are the wrongdoers.

O you who believe! Avoid most suspicion—some suspicion is sinful. And do not spy on one another, nor backbite one another. Would any of you like to eat the flesh of his dead brother? You would detest it. So remain mindful of Allah. Allah is Most Relenting, Most Merciful.[373]

These powerful teachings on Islamic manners are an important part of the Islamic worldview and contribute greatly to ummatic unity.

Juz twenty-seven

Juz twenty-seven

Thematic overview

The twenty-seventh *juz* of the Qur'an focuses heavily on the afterlife. This theme is clear in every *surah* in this *juz*, especially in the two famous *surahs*: Surah al-Rahman (the Merciful) and Surah al-Waqi'ah (the Inevitable). The *juz* begins at verse thirty-one of Surah al-Dhariyat (the Scattering [Winds]). It includes *surahs* al-Tur (the Mountain), al-Najm (the Star), al-Qamar (the Moon), al-Rahman, Surah al-Waqi'ah, and ends with al-Hadid (the Iron).

This *juz* marks the beginning of the 'al-Mufassal' (lit. oft-separated) *surahs*, a later part of the Qur'an marked by successive shorter *surahs* separated from one another, according to one opinion. These are the comprehensive *surahs* of the Qur'an mentioned in the famous narration by Aisha ﵂.

The first thing that was revealed thereof was a surah from Al-Mufassal, and in it was mentioned Paradise and the Fire. When the people embraced Islam, the verses regarding legal and illegal things were revealed. If the first thing to be revealed was: "Do not drink alcoholic drinks," people would have said, "We will never leave alcoholic drinks," and if it had been revealed, "Do not commit illegal sexual intercourse," they would have said, "We will never give up illegal sexual intercourse."[374]

374 Sahih al-Bukhari, no. 4993.

The majority of the *surahs* in this *juz* focus on descriptions of Paradise and Hell. Surah Tur describes Paradise in vivid detail.[375] One of the most comforting descriptions mentioned in this *surah* is that we will be with our families and loved ones in Paradise.

Those who believed, and their offspring followed them in faith, We will unite them with their offspring, and We will not deprive them of any of their works. Every person is hostage to what he has earned.[376]

Surah Tur describes Paradise in vivid detail. One of the most comforting descriptions is that we will be with our families and our loved ones in Paradise.

Every *surah* in this *juz* calls on us to urgently embrace the message of truth and follow it completely. Surah Najm reminds us about the moment the Prophet ﷺ saw Jibril. This is followed by a strong warning to embrace the truth revealed in such a powerful rhythmic manner that even the pagans among the Quraysh fell in prostration when they first heard this *surah* recited.

375 Qur'an 52:17–28.

376 Qur'an 52:21.

377 Qur'an 54:17, 22, 32, 40.

378 Qur'an 55:46.

379 Qur'an 55:62.

380 Qur'an 56:10–26.

381 Qur'an 56:27–40.

Surah Qamar reminds us that the Quraysh were shown a clear sign in the splitting of the moon and still rejected the truth. Everyone had been given a clear sign in the Qur'an about which we are repeatedly told throughout this *surah*, "We made the Qur'an easy to learn. Is there anyone who would learn?"[377]

Two different levels of Paradise are described in Surah al-Rahman and Surah al-Waqi'ah. There are various levels of Paradise linked to one's level of piety.

Surah al-Rahman and Surah al-Waqi'ah are unique in their descriptions. These are the only two *surahs* in the Qur'an that describe two different levels of Paradise one after the other. It is from these *surahs* that we learn that there are various levels of Paradise linked to one's level of piety. The righteous will enjoy rewards that the average Muslims will not have access to, but everyone will be content and happy with what they receive.

Surah Rahman first describes the Paradise of those who fear their Lord,[378] then describes a Paradise that is lower than it.[379] Surah al-Waqi'ah likewise first describes the Paradise of the forerunners in piety,[380] then describes the Paradise of the people who receive their books in their right hands.[381] Both *surahs* also contain detailed descriptions of the Hellfire to balance the message of hope with fear of sin.

Juz twenty-seven

The Seerah

The twenty-seventh *juz* contains some of the most powerful imagery in the Qur'an. The *surahs* in this *juz* are generally Meccan *surahs* that provide vivid and detailed descriptions about the afterlife and the world beyond ours. Towards the beginning of this *juz* is the remarkable Surah Najm, a *surah* so powerful that it caused even the pagan Arabs to fall in prostration when they first heard it recited.

Abd Allah ibn 'Abbas* ﷺ *narrates that the Prophet* ﷺ *prostrated while reciting al-Najm and with him prostrated the Muslims, the pagans, the jinn and all human beings.[382]

This incident was so powerful that the news of the pagans prostrating reached the immigrants in Abyssinia who misunderstood that they had all converted to Islam. The immigrants returned to Mecca to find out the rumour was untrue, and many had to migrate to Abyssinia a second time.

When you study the content, rhythm, flow and imagery of Surah al-Najm, its powerful impact becomes very clear. This *surah* was designed to drive home the reality that Muhammad ﷺ is a true messenger, Islam is the true religion and that the afterlife is a reality. It confirms that everything the Prophet said about the religion is based on divine inspiration.

382 Sahih al-Bukhari, no. 1071.

383 Qur'an 53:2–5.
384 Qur'an 53:11–18.

Your friend has not gone astray, nor has he erred. Nor does he speak out of desire. It is but a revelation revealed. Taught to him by the mighty powerful (angel).[383]

This *surah* also describes the Prophet's miraculous interactions with the angel Gabriel whom he saw in his original form twice. This was a special virtue gifted to the final Prophet to confirm his status in the sight of Allah.

The heart did not lie about what it saw. Will you dispute with him concerning what he saw? He saw him on another descent. At the Lotus Tree of the Extremity. Near which is the Garden of Repose. As there covered the Lotus Tree what covered it. The sight did not waver, nor did it exceed. He saw some of the Great Signs of his Lord.[384]

The above verses describe the two occasions on which the Prophet ﷺ saw the angel Gabriel in his true form. The first was on the horizon during the early days of prophethood. The second was during the miraculous journey to Paradise (*mi'raj*), in which he saw things that no other human was gifted with the sight of.

Juz twenty-seven

Judgement Day

The twenty-seventh *juz* is full of *surahs* focused on the Day of Judgment. An entire book would be needed to cover every lesson related to the Last Day in this *juz*. For this chapter, we will focus on a few *surahs* that discuss the Last Day in detail, starting with Surah al-Waqi'ah.

We are given hope that even the weakest believers can still get into Paradise, while also inspiring us to aim to be in the higher ranks with the righteous.

Surah al-Waqi'ah is named after one of the names of the Last Day, *al-Waqi'ah* (The Inevitable Event). This description tells us that the Day of Judgment is inevitable and will be the most important event ever. On that day, the fate of every human will be decided.

When the inevitable occurs. Of its occurrence, there is no denial.[385]

This *surah* divides people on that day into three groups: the righteous who race ahead to do good deeds, the average believer and the disbeliever.

385 Qur'an 56:1–2.

386 Qur'an 56:7–11.
387 Qur'an 56:12–16.
388 Qur'an 56:38–40.
389 Qur'an 56:83–87.

And you become three classes. Those on the right, what of those on the right? And those on the left, what of those on the left? And the forerunners, the forerunners. Those are the nearest.[386]

The division of the people of Paradise into the righteous and the average believer is unique in this *juz*. It gives us hope that even the weakest believers can still get into Paradise, while also inspiring us to aim to be among the righteous.

In Gardens of Bliss. Many of the early generations and a few of the later generations. On luxurious furnishings. Reclining on them, facing one another.[387]

[A reward] For those on the right. Many of the early generations, and many of the later generations.[388]

Surah al-Waqi'ah also gives us a chilling description of death itself that hits the heart and prepares the soul for the reality of the Last Day.

So, when it has reached the throat. As you are looking on, We are nearer to it than you are, but you do not see. If you are not held to account, then bring it back if you are truthful.[389]

The *surah* ends with a description of the state of the soul when it leaves this world in each of the three categories mentioned. Each soul has a different path in the afterlife, based on how it lived.

Surah al-Rahman follows this same pattern and describes two levels of paradise, the paradise of the righteous and the paradise of Muslims of other levels of faith. These two *surahs* flow together like one beautiful message inspiring people to aim for the highest levels of Paradise.

The *juz* ends with Surah al-Hadid, which includes a powerful metaphor about this world and its temporary nature, reminding us that the next world is the real world.

Know that the worldly life is only play, and distraction, and glitter, and boasting among you, and rivalry in wealth and children. It is like a rainfall that produces plants and delights the disbelievers. But then it withers, and you see it yellowing, and then it becomes debris. While in the Hereafter there is severe agony, and forgiveness from Allah, and acceptance. The life of this world is nothing but enjoyment of vanity.[390]

390 Qur'an 57:20.

Surah al-Waqi'ah and Surah al-Rahman flow together like one beautiful message inspiring people to aim for the highest levels of Paradise.

Juz twenty-seven

Qur'anic worldview

The 27th *juz* is full of wondrous descriptions of Paradise, especially in the twin *surahs*, al-Rahman and al-Waqiah. These two *surahs* are the only *surahs* that describe two levels of Paradise for two different types of believers: general paradise for the average Muslim and the higher levels of paradise reserved for the righteous who excelled in worshipping Allah. The *surahs* are placed one after the other in the Qur'an, flowing together with one united theme.

And the people of the Right Hand? What of the people of the Right Hand? (They will be) in lush orchards, with sweet-smelling plants, and extended shade, and outpouring water, and abundant fruit. Neither withheld, nor forbidden.[391]

The verses describing the average believers in Surah al-Waqi'ah bring hope to us all that we too will be among them, because they will be "many of the early generations and many of the latter generations."[392] Yet the description of the Paradise of the righteous should give us a goal to strive for, especially because they are described as "many of the early generation and a few of the latter generations."[393]

A subtle miracle in these verses is that they indicate that the number of believers will increase over time, while the number of righteous will dwindle. This has proven true with each passing generation.

391 Qur'an 56:27–33.
392 Qur'an 56:39–40.
393 Qur'an 56:13–14.

Paradise and Hell are not myths or just beliefs. They are realities that exist in the unseen realm. We must live in such a way that we acknowledge these realities, striving for Paradise and avoiding the paths to Hell. These two *surahs* describe both Paradise and Hell, giving us a balance between hope and fear. That balance is focused more on hope though, as the descriptions of Paradise make up more of this *juz* than the descriptions of the Hellfire.

The descriptions of Paradise in the Qur'an should motivate us to be our best. During difficult times, they remind us that a better life awaits us in the afterlife if we are patient. During good times, they remind us to remain consistent in worshipping Allah and not to prioritise this world over the next. It is extremely beneficial to recite these *surahs* often and reflect on their deep meanings. This will help keep us grounded and motivated to strive for the afterlife, which is the real life.

The descriptions of Paradise in the Qur'an should motivate us to be our best. During our difficult times, they remind us that a better life awaits us in the afterlife if we are patient.

Juz twenty-eight

Juz twenty-eight

Thematic overview

The twenty-eighth *juz* of the Qur'an contains nine *surahs*. Most of these are Meccan *surahs*. As each of these *surahs* are short and revealed at different points in time, their themes are diverse. The *surahs* in this *juz* span everything from family life to warfare and from society to business. The primary focus is on being truthful to our promises and fulfilling the rights of others.

The *juz* begins with Surah al-Mujadalah (the Dispute), the only *surah* in the Qur'an that has the name Allah in every verse. This is followed by Surah al-Hashr (the Gathering [of Forces]).

Surah al-Hashr focuses on the believers who love Allah and assist the immigrants and the prophet, even though they themselves are in need. "And those who, before them, had settled in the homeland, and had accepted faith. They love those who emigrated to them and find no hesitation in their hearts in helping them. They give them priority over themselves, even if they themselves are needy. Whoever is protected from his natural greed, it is they who are the successful."[394]

This verse is about the Medinan Helpers (*ansar*). They went beyond what was expected of them and risked everything to protect the Prophet ﷺ and the Meccan Migrants (*muhajirun*). The *muhajirun* were in a vulnerable state and the kindness of the *ansar* helped and saved them. Contrary to this we see the attitude of the hypocrites who try to violate their promises and harm the Prophet.

394 Qur'an 59:9.

395 Qur'an 61:14.

In Surah al-Saff (Solid Lines), Allah admonishes those who say that which they do not do. When taking a contract with Allah, be sure to honour it. Compare the heroes of the Battle of Uhud (3 AH/ 625 CE) to the hypocrites who abandoned the army at Uhud. The example is given in this *surah* of the disciples of Jesus and their loyalty to him. In this *surah,* Allah praises both the *ansar* of Muhammad and the *ansar* of Jesus.

Surah al-Mujadalah is the only surah in the Qur'an that has the name Allah in every verse. Surah al-Hashr praises the kindness of the Medinan Helpers (ansar) towards the Meccan Migrants (muhajirun).

O you who believe! Be supporters of Allah, like Jesus son of Mary said to the disciples, "Who are my supporters towards Allah?" The disciples said, "We are Allah's supporters." So, a group of the Children of Israel believed, while another group disbelieved. We supported those who believed against their foe, so they became dominant.[395]

Surah al-Munafiqun (the Hypocrites) discusses the hypocrites who broke their promises and undermined the mission of the Prophet. In Surah al-Saff and al-Munafiqun, we see the two opposite types of people, those who obey Allah and those who betray Islam. The focus is on the covenant and fulfilling the rights of Allah and the rights of the believers.

In between these two *surahs* is Surah al-Jum'ah (the Day of Congregation), reminding us to leave our businesses and rush to remember Allah on Fridays (sing. Jum'ah). In these verses, Allah is telling us to remember to focus on our prayer during Jumah, not to drag our feet with our minds still in our businesses. Those who pursue this world will undermine their commitments; those who focus on the afterlife will pursue it with excellence (*ihsan*).

O you who believe! When the call is made for prayer on Congregation Day, hasten to the remembrance of Allah, and drop all business. That is better for you, if you only knew.[396]

Yet whenever they come across some business, or some entertainment, they scramble towards it, and leave you standing. Say, "What is with Allah is better than entertainment and business; and Allah is the Best of providers."[397]

396 Qur'an 62:9.

397 Qur'an 62:11.

The *juz* ends with *Surahs* al-Talaq (Divorce) and al-Tahrim (the Prohibition). Surah al-Talaq teaches us not to mistreat a spouse and to be kind, even when getting divorced. This *juz* teaches us both the right and the wrong ways of dealing with marital problems and ending a marriage.

In Surah al-Jum'ah, Allah reminds us to leave our businesses and rush to remember Allah on Fridays and to prioritise the prayer over the material world at that time.

Surah al-Tahrim teaches us about the kind of people who cling to this world because of those who they associate with, thinking they will protect them. These people are deluded. The example is given of the wives of Prophets Lut and Nuh; their association with their husbands did not protect them in this world or the next, as they were hypocrites.

This is in contrast with Aasiyah and Mary who fulfilled their covenants with Allah. Aasiyah was married to the worst man, the tyrant Pharaoh, but still earned Paradise through her righteousness. She sacrificed everything for Allah. The *juz* begins and ends with a story of a woman making *dua* about her husband mistreating her, and Allah answering her *dua*.

Juz twenty-eight

The Seerah

The twenty-eighth *juz* contains many short Medinan *surahs* that give us a glimpse of the challenges the Muslims faced in Medina. The *surahs* that open and close the *juz* focus on divorce- related topics. The opening *surah* is Surah al-Mujadilah which has a very interesting reason for revelation.

Surah al-Talaq begins with the popular reminder that our sustenance is from Allah and that we should seek it through piety and our trust in Allah.

Khuwlah bint Malik ibn Tha'labah ﷺ narrated, "My husband, Aws ibn al-Samit, pronounced the words, 'You are like my mother.' So, I went to the Messenger of Allah ﷺ, complaining to him about my husband.

The Messenger of Allah ﷺ disputed with me and said, 'Remain dutiful to Allah; he is your cousin.' I continued (complaining) until the Qur'anic verse came down, 'Certainly has Allah heard the speech of the one who argues with you, [O Muhammad], concerning her husband...'[398] till the prescription of expiation.

398 Qur'an 58:1.

399 Sunan Abu Dawud, no. 2214. Authentication grade: fair (hasan).

400 Qur'an 65:2–3.

He ﷺ then said, 'He should set free a slave.'

She said, 'He cannot afford it.'

He said, 'He should fast for two consecutive months.'

She said, 'Messenger of Allah, he is an old man; he cannot keep fasts.'

He said, 'He should feed sixty poor people.'

She said, 'He has nothing which he may give in alms.'

At that moment a date-basket was brought to him. She said, 'I shall help him with another date-basket.'

He said, 'You have done well. Go and feed sixty poor people on his behalf and return to your cousin.' "[399]

This *juz* also includes Surah al-Talaq which begins with the popular reminder that our sustenance is from Allah and that we should seek it through piety and trusting Allah. This reminder is apt as divorce is often a time when people are worried about their future and their financial stability.

And whoever fears Allah, He will make a way out for him. And will provide for him from where he never expected. Whoever relies on Allah, He will suffice him. Allah will accomplish His purpose. Allah has set a measure to all things.[400]

Allah has protected the rights of both men and women, in and out of marriage. Our sustenance is from Allah and nobody can deprive us of that which Allah has written for us.

There are many lessons we can learn from these *surahs*. Allah has protected the rights of both men and women, in and out of marriage. Our sustenance is from Allah and nobody can deprive us of that which Allah has written for us. Allah has revealed a Shariah that protects the rights of both genders and creates an environment of harmony between them. Sometimes marital disputes happen, as this is part of human experience. Even in such cases, Islam has given us a lot of guidance on how to resolve these disputes, while divorce remains permissible for the few cases in which it is impossible to resolve.

Juz twenty-eight

Judgement Day

The twenty-eighth *juz* contains many *surahs* focused on the Day of Judgment. Surah al-Taghabun (Mutual Gain and Loss) gives us one of the names of the Last Day, *Yawm al-Taghabun* (the Day of Mutual Gain and Loss). It is called this because it is the day when there is a huge difference between how much the believer gains and how much the disbeliever loses. There is no bigger division of gain and loss than one group gaining Paradise, while another enters the Hellfire.

The Day when He gathers you for the Day of Gathering, that is the Day of Mutual Gain and Loss. Whoever believes in Allah and acts with integrity, He will remit his misdeeds, and will admit him into gardens beneath which rivers flow, to dwell therein forever. That is the supreme achievement.

But as for those who disbelieve and denounce Our revelations, these are the inmates of the Fire, dwelling therein forever; and what a miserable fate![401]

401 Qur'an 64:9–10.

We are reminded that the trials of this world should not lead us away from the the greater purpose of life.

The path to profiting on that day is clearly mentioned in the next verse: obedience to Allah and His Messenger.

So, obey Allah, and obey the Messenger. But if you turn away, it is only incumbent on Our Messenger to deliver the clear message.[402]

This *surah* also warns us that our own spouses, children, and wealth can be trials in our lives, and sources of misguidance. Some people are tested with difficult spouses or disobedient children, and some are tested with wealth and possessions. We are reminded that these trials should not lead us away from the purpose of life.

O you who believe! Among your spouses and your children are enemies to you, so beware of them. But if you pardon, and overlook, and forgive, Allah is Forgiving and Merciful. Your possessions and your children are a test, but with Allah is a splendid reward.

So be conscious of Allah as much as you can, and listen, and obey, and give for your own good. He who is protected from his stinginess, these are the prosperous.[403]

402 Qur'an 64:12.

403 Qur'an 64:14–16.

404 Qur'an 63:9.

405 Qur'an 66:10–11.

A similar message is repeated in the chapter before it, Surah al-Munafiqun. We are reminded to not let our wealth or children distract us from obeying Allah.

O you who believe! Let neither your possessions nor your children distract you from the remembrance of Allah. Whoever does that, these are the losers.[404]

The topic of spouses as trials continues in the final *surah* of this *juz*. Surah al-Tahrim gives us contrasting examples of this trial. The wife of the Pharaoh was a righteous woman tested with a tyrant husband, while the Prophets Lut and Nuh ﷺ were righteous men tested with rebellious wives. In both cases, the righteous were rewarded for their patience and the disbelievers were punished.

This serves as a reminder that a righteous spouse is not enough to get you into Paradise as we are all responsible for our own deeds and choices.

Allah illustrates an example of those who disbelieve: the wife of Nuh and the wife of Lut. They were under two of Our righteous servants, but they betrayed them. They availed them nothing against Allah, and it was said, "Enter the Fire with those who are entering."

And Allah illustrates an example of those who believe: the wife of Pharaoh, when she said, "My Lord, build for me, with You, a house in Paradise, and save me from Pharaoh and his works, and save me from the wrongdoing people."[405]

Juz twenty-eight
Qur'anic worldview

Taqwa is a concept emphasised throughout the Qur'an, and many times in the 28th *juz*. *Taqwa* is often translated as God-consciousness or fear of Allah. Both translations are acceptable, as it is a comprehensive term that carries a lot of meaning. *Taqwa* is a state of awareness of Allah's Presence and Power, a fear of displeasing Him, and a desire to seek His pleasure. It is often described as a shield that protects a believer from sin and misguidance.

The believers are reassured that if they have taqwa of Allah and trust Him, He will provide for them in truly amazing ways.

Trying to achieve higher levels of *taqwa* is a continuous goal of every Muslim. Along the way, we may slip up and make mistakes, but we keep striving to be better, to be closer to Allah. We do this through our obligatory deeds and build upon that with optional acts of worship. This process and its benefits are outlined in the following powerful Hadith Qudsi, a divine discourse communicated through prophetic wording.

406 Sahih al-Bukhari, no. 6502.

407 Qur'an 65:2–3.

The Messenger of Allah ﷺ said that Allah (mighty and sublime be He) said, "Whosoever shows enmity to someone devoted to Me, I shall be at war with him. My servant draws not near to Me with anything more loved by Me than the religious duties I have enjoined upon him, and My servant continues to draw near to Me with supererogatory works so that I shall love him. When I love him I am his hearing with which he hears, his seeing with which he sees, his hand with which he strikes and his foot with which he walks. Were he to ask [something] of Me, I would surely give it to him, and were he to ask Me for refuge, I would surely grant him it. I do not hesitate about anything as much as I hesitate about [seizing] the soul of My faithful servant: he hates death and I hate hurting him."[406]

The benefits of *taqwa* include having the support of Allah. Allah has promised to aid those who are conscious of Him in ways that they never imagined. Towards the end of the 28th *juz*, in Surah al-Talaq, Allah reassures the believers that if they have *taqwa* of Allah and trust Him, He will provide for them in amazing ways.

And whoever is conscious of Allah, He will make a way out for him. And will provide for him from where he never expected. Whoever relies on Allah, He will suffice him. Allah will accomplish His purpose. Allah has set a measure to all things.[407]

Achieving a high level of *taqwa* is something we must continuously strive for. This will lead to a life that is pleasing to Allah, and a life that is blessed with Allah's Divine Aid.

Juz twenty-nine

Juz twenty-nine

Thematic overview

The twenty-ninth *juz* contains eleven *surahs,* most of which are Meccan *surahs* focused on the afterlife and other aspects of theology. Most of the early revelation is in this *juz* including the *Surahs* al-Qalam (the Pen), al-Muzammil (the Enfolded), and al-Mudathir (The Wrapped in Cloak).

The *juz* begins with Surah al-Mulk (the Dominion) telling us to look at the sky and see how flawless it is, calling on us to ponder over what is beyond that. This is a *juz* that is meant to wake us up to the reality of life. It is recommended to recite Surah Mulk before sleeping to remind us about the reality of life.[408] It reminds us about the greatness of Allah, the beauty of this universe and the difference between those connected to Allah and those who ignore the signs of Allah all around them. The entire *surah* is a reminder of the signs of Allah that we take for granted.

Say, "Have you considered? If your water drains away, who will bring you pure running water?"[409]

The *surah* begins with the bigger signs (the universe) and ends with the daily signs we take for granted (running water). Just as our drinking water is connected to the oceans and the oceans to the rain, the rain comes from Allah. Surah al-Mulk is a reminder of Allah's blessings, our ending and how we will be held accountable for what we did with those blessings.

408 Jami' al-Tirmidhi, no. 2892. Authentication grade: fair (hasan).

409 Qur'an 67:30.

Surah al-Qalam tells us about the insults people made towards the Prophet ﷺ and compares it to how Jonah (Yunus) ﵇ was treated by his people. This was an early *surah*, when the insults were new and the Prophet ﷺ took it hard. He was not accustomed to being treated like this and it was an entirely new situation for him. He is told not to be like Yunus ﵇ who left his people, but to be patient with them and Allah will assist him. An example is given to the Quraysh of the people of the garden who were greedy and refused to help the poor and lost everything.

> *Surah Nuh (Noah) gives us a clear example of people who abandoned their prophet and how Allah destroyed them.*

The people of the garden are given as an example to the tribe of Quraysh, the ruling tribe of Mecca, of their ending if they follow in their footsteps, while Yunus is given as an example to the Prophet as to what not to do, while reminding us that Yunus was elevated and forgiven.

Surah al-Haaqah (the Indisputable) discusses the faith of the perished nations and compares them to the Quraysh. Surah Qalam shows the greed of the Quraysh, while Haaqah focuses on the bigger picture of the destruction of nations. Surah Qalam mentions the insults against the prophets, while Surah al-Haaqah refutes these claims.[410]

410 Qur'an 69:38–50.

Surah Ma'arij (the Ascending Pathways) discusses the qualities of the true believers and how their character sets them apart from their opponents. This is followed by Surah Nuh (Noah) giving a clear example of people who abandoned their prophet and how Allah destroyed them. The next *surah* is Surah Jinn showing that not only humans, but even jinn can replace us as true believers and worshippers of Allah.

Surah al-Mulk reminds us of the greatness of Allah, the beauty of the universe and the difference between those connected to Allah and those who ignore the signs of Allah.

The next two *surahs* are Surah al- Muzammil and Surah al-Mudathir. Surah Muzammil begins by calling to the night vigil worship (*tahajjud*), Surah al-Mudathir begins by calling to *da'wah*, the two sides of the believers: private worship and public calling to the truth. In these two *surahs*, the foundations of the *da'wah* are laid.

The last three *surahs* of this *juz* give us a description of three main parts of the afterlife. Surah al-Qiyamah (the Resurrection) describes the Last Day. Surah al-Insan (Man) describes Paradise in detail. Surah al-Mursalaat (the [Winds] Sent-Forth) describes the Hellfire in detail. The three together give us a strong glimpse of the afterlife.

Juz twenty-nine

The Seerah

The bulk of *surahs* in the twenty-ninth *juz* are early Meccan *surahs* related to the importance of *da'wah*. This *juz* is itself a training manual, teaching us both the practical and spiritual side of *da'wah*. Surah Nuh gives us a blueprint for *da'wah* in the methodology of Prophet Nuh ﷺ. This *surah was* revealed very early in the Meccan era to teach the Prophet Muhammad ﷺ about how the earliest messengers did *da'wah* and how their people reacted.

The Prophet ﷺ was not only sent to humans, but he was also sent to the jinn as well and many of them believed in him and they followed the guidance conveyed to them.

In the story of Nuh ﷺ, we learn about the importance of both public and private *da'wah*, as well as the importance of calling towards Allah's forgiveness and showing the benefits of accepting Islam.

He said, "My Lord, I have called my people night and day. But my call added only to their flight. Whenever I called them to Your forgiveness, they thrust their fingers into their ears, and wrapped themselves in their garments, and insisted, and became more and more arrogant.

411 Qur'an 71:5–12.
412 Qur'an 72:1–2.

"Then I called them openly. Then I appealed to them publicly, and I spoke to them privately. I said, 'Ask your Lord for forgiveness; He is Forgiving. He will let loose the sky upon you in torrents. And provide you with wealth and children, and allot for you gardens, and allot for you rivers.'"[411]

Surah Jinn shows us that this message is truly universal. It is not only for the entire human race but transcends dimensions and reaches the world of the jinn as well. The Prophet ﷺ was not only sent to humans, but he was also sent to the jinn as well and many of them believed in him and followed the guidance.

Say, "It was revealed to me that a band of jinn listened in, and said, 'We have heard a wondrous Qur'an. It guides to rectitude, so we have believed in it, and we will never associate anyone with our Lord.'"[412]

The next two *surahs* are among the earliest revelations, with some scholars stating that they were the second and third *surahs* to be revealed. When the Prophet ﷺ went home after the first revelation, he was shaken and asked his wife to cover him. His blessed wife Khadija ﵂ embraced him, covered him and reassured him. Two *surahs* were revealed back-to-back, addressing him as the covered one, al-Muzammil and al-Mudathir. The first called on him to wake up at night and pray the late-night prayer. The second called on him to stand up and warn the people.

These two *surahs* represent the two sides of *da'wah,* working on our own spirituality while presenting the message of Islam to the world. It is not a matter of choosing one over the other; we need to work on both simultaneously. From day one, the Prophet ﷺ focused on his *salah* and his *da'wah*. This became the golden standard for every flagbearer of Islam, to become a person of regular night-prayer and a caller to Islam.

The *juz* ends with contrasting *surahs* describing the Day of Judgment (Qiyamah), Paradise (al-Dahr) and Hellfire (al-Mursalat). These three *surahs* show us the focus of the early *da'wah* on the afterlife, balancing preparation for the last day with hope in Allah's mercy and fear of disappointing Him.

Surahs al-Muzammil and al-Mudathir call on us to balance our public calling to the religion of Islam with private worship.

Across these *surahs* we learn a variety of lessons about *da'wah*. Surah Nuh shows us a practical role model of calling to Islam in Prophet Nuh ؑ. Surah Jinn reminds us that the message is not for us alone but is for all of humanity and more. *Surahs* al-Muzammil and al-Mudathir call on us to balance our public calling with private worship. Finally, *surahs* al-Qiyamah, al-Dahr, and al-Mursalat remind us to focus on the afterlife as a primary focus of our *da'wah*.

Juz twenty-nine

Judgement Day

413 Qur'an 69:13–22.

As the Qur'an comes closer to its end, the theme of the Last Day weighs heavily as a core theme of the remaining *surahs*. The twenty-ninth *juz* contains multiple *surahs* describing the Last Day in detail.

Surah al-Haaqah contains a powerful description of the Last Day and emphasises the placement of the book of deeds on that day.

Then, when the Trumpet is sounded a single time. And the earth and the mountains are lifted, and crushed, with a single crush. On that Day, the Event will come to pass. And the heaven will crack; so, on that Day it will be frail. And the angels will be ranged around its borders, while eight will be carrying the Throne of your Lord above them that Day. On that Day you will be exposed, and no secret of yours will remain hidden.

As for him who is given his book in his right hand, he will say, "Here, take my book and read it. I knew I would be held accountable." So, he will have a pleasant life. In a lofty Garden.[413]

The end of this *juz* focuses on this theme in a specific order. Surah al-Qiyamah reminds us about the Last Day, and how to prepare for it. Surah al-Dahr describes Paradise in beautiful detail, and Surah al-Mursalat warns us about the Hellfire in terrifying detail. Together, these three *surahs* give us a guided tour of the various phases of the afterlife. Surah al-Qiyamah begins with a warning to those who doubt the resurrection, followed by a detailed description of the Last Day.

Surah al-Dahr provides a beautiful description of Paradise in great detail, while Surah al-Mursalat gives us a warning about Hellfire in terrifying detail.

I swear by the Day of Resurrection. And I swear by the blaming soul. Does man think that We will not reassemble his bones? Yes indeed, We are able to reconstruct his fingertips. But man wants to deny what is ahead of him.

He asks, "When is the Day of Resurrection?" When vision is dazzled. And the moon is eclipsed. And the sun and the moon are joined together. On that Day, man will say, "Where is the escape?" No indeed! There is no refuge. To your Lord on that Day is the settlement. On that Day, man will be informed of everything he put forward, and everything he left behind. And man will be evidence against himself.[414]

414 Qur'an 75:1–14.

Juz twenty-nine

Qur'anic worldview

415 Qur'an 67:1–2.

416 Qur'an 67:9–11.

The 29th *juz*, and especially Surah al-Mulk, reminds us to prioritise the afterlife over worldly desires. This *surah* begins with a reminder that life and death are a test, a test of piety and choices. Every individual will be held accountable for their choices on the Last Day. Notice that in these verses, death is mentioned before life to emphasise its importance.

Blessed is He in whose hand is the sovereignty, and who has power over everything. He who created death and life, to test you as to which of you is better in conduct. He is the Almighty, the Forgiving.[415]

Our attention is then turned to the Last Day. On that day, those who chose to reject the message of Islam will be asked why they rejected the truth. They will admit that they do not have any excuse as they recognised the truth and still rejected it.

They will say, "Yes, a warner did come to us, but we disbelieved, and said, 'Allah did not send down anything; you are very much mistaken.'" And they will say, "Had we listened or reasoned, we would not have been among the inmates of the Blaze." So, they will acknowledge their sins. So away with the inmates of the Blaze.[416]

The bulk of this *surah* focuses on reminders about the power and might of Allah. He controls everything, We all will return to Him and we all will have to account to Him for how we utilised His blessings. The *surah* concludes with a powerful reminder that Allah is both able to punish and Most Merciful. It is our choices that will decide whether we attract His mercy or His justice.

Say, "Have you considered? Should Allah make me perish, and those with me; or else He bestows His mercy on us; who will protect the disbelievers from an agonising torment?"

Say, "He is the Compassionate. We have faith in Him, and in Him we trust. Soon you will know who is in evident error."[417]

417 Qur'an 67:28–29.

This message is repeated through this *juz* in various ways. These *surahs* focus on the Day of Judgment, Paradise and Hell, offering vivid descriptions of all these aspects of the afterlife (*akhirah*). The result of reciting and reflecting on these verses should be the development of an *akhirah*-centric mindset. It is this mindset that will help us make better choices and prepare well for that day.

On the Last Day, those who chose to reject the message of Islam will be asked why they rejected the truth.

Juz thirty

Juz thirty

Thematic overview

The final *juz* of the Qur'an contains thirty-seven *surahs*; most of these are Meccan *Surahs* focused on various aspects of *'aqidah*. The short *surahs* of the Qur'an that are popularly memorised are compiled in this *juz*. Due to the high volume of *surahs* in this *juz*, most of these *surahs*' themes will be summarised in one or two sentences each.

Surah al-Naba (the Announcement) is like a summary of the *juz* covering all the themes found throughout it. Surah al-Naba teaches us that the Last Day is an important event with consequences in both worlds.

Allah tells us that the great news is the Last Day which is the focal point of this *juz*. On that day, everyone will get what they deserve. The righteous will have what they earned, and the disbelievers will have what they earned. Many *surahs* in this *juz* discuss the rewards and punishments of that day.

In Surah al-Naba, Allah refers to the last day as the 'day of sorting' (*yawm al-fasl*) and shows us how everything is perfectly sorted in this world, leading to the conclusion that Allah will sort things perfectly on the Last Day.

The next *surah*, Surah Nazi'at (the Soul-Renders), teaches us how Pharaoh rejected this message and was punished for it. Surah 'Abasa (the Frowned) teaches us not to ignore the weak while focusing on the arrogant oppressors. Our message should reach everyone, especially those whose hearts are opened to hear it.

Surah al-Takwir (the Final Enwrapping) and Surah al-Infitar (the Shattering) discuss details about the Last Day. Surah al-Mutafifin (the Stinters) discusses the importance of ethics in business and not cheating. It also covers the consequences of poor business ethics on the Last Day. Surah al-Inshiqaq (the Splitting Asunder) discusses the tearing up of this world at the end of time.

Surah al-Buruj (the Constellations) reminds us of the story of the oppressed people of the past. Surah al-Tariq (the Nightcomer) reminds us that they plan and Allah plans, but His plan is greatest. Surah al-A'la (the Most High) and Surah al-Ghashiyah (the Whelming Event) remind us that the next life is better than this world.

Surah al-Fajr (the Dawn) reminds us about the Last Day and the good ending of the righteous believer. Surah al-Balad (the City) is a reminder about Allah's favours and how to use them in a way that is pleasing to Allah. Surah al-Shams (the Sun) and Surah al-Layl (the Night) discuss the perfection of day and night, and various contrasts in Allah's creation. Surah al-Duha (the Blazing Morning) and Surah al-Sharh (the Relief) discuss hope and optimism.

Surah al-Tin (the Fig) is a reminder that we are responsible for our deeds on the Last Day. Surah al-'Alaq (the Clinging Form) calls on us to read, reflect and follow the message. Surah al-Qadar highlights the virtues of Laylat al-Qadar (The Night of Power). Surah al-Bayyinah (the Clear Proof) explains the necessity of embracing the true religion. Surah al-Zilzal/al-Zalzala (the Earthquake), Surah al-'Adiyat (the Charging Steeds), and Surah al-Qari'ah (the Hammerer) all describe the Last Day in poetic visuals.

We are told that everyone will get what they deserve in the Afterlife. The righteous will have what they earned and the disbelievers will also get to see what they earned.

Surah al-Takathur (Competing for Worldly Gain) is a reminder against materialism. Surah al-'Asr (the End of the Day) is a reminder that our time on earth is limited. Surah al-Fil (the Elephant) and Surah Quraysh focus on Allah's blessings to the tribe of Quraysh. Surah al-Ma'un (Small Kindness) reminds us that the small deeds also matter. Surah al-Kawthar (the Abundance) reminds us of the high status of the Prophet ﷺ.

The last few *surahs* starting with Kafirun are in a specific order. Surah al-Kafirun (the Unbelievers) confirms the negation part of the Muslim 'Statement of Faith' (*kalima*); i.e., the rejection of polytheism. Surah al-Ikhlas (Sincerity) confirms the core components of monotheism.

Surah al-Nasr (Victorious Help) discusses the improbable victory of the believers, and Surah al-Masad (the Palm Fiber) discusses the humiliation of the one who rejected this message. These two *surahs* are in between the *surahs* of monotheism showing the consequences of belief and disbelief.

The Qur'an begins with a dua for guidance and it also ends with a dua to protect us from misguidance.

The Qur'an ends with the two protectors which we use to ask Allah for protection from the trials of this world and the next. The closing *surahs* are a reminder that we are constantly tested and need to ask Allah for protection daily. The Qur'an begins with a *dua* for guidance (Surah al-Fatiha (the Opening)) and ends with a *dua* for protection from misguidance (Surah al-Nas (the People)). The Qur'an itself is guidance for those who are conscious of Allah and our guidance lies entirely in understanding, reflecting on and living by the teachings of the Qur'an.

May Allah make us from the people of the Qur'an, grant us proper understanding of it, and forgive us our shortcomings.

Juz thirty

The Seerah

The thirtieth *juz* of the Qur'an is one that most readers are familiar with. These *surahs* are among the most memorised and recited in the Qur'an, due to their brevity. The majority of *surahs* in this *juz* were revealed in the early Meccan phase, similar to the twenty-ninth *juz*. Many of these *surahs* have clear reasons for revelation and direct links to the Seerah.

It is unanimously agreed that the first five verses of Surah al-'Alaq were the first revelation given to the Prophet ﷺ in the Cave of Hira.

Surah al-Naba was revealed in response to the Quraysh questioning the concept of the Last Day. Many *surahs* in this *juz* describe the Last Day in vivid detail. The concept of the Last Day and an afterlife was foreign to the pagans of Mecca. Although the Jews and Christians of Arabia believed in this concept, the pagans did not give it much thought. For this reason, early Meccan revelation contained a lot of descriptions and warnings about the end of time. The thirtieth *juz* includes at least ten *surahs* focused on describing the end-times and the resurrection.

418 Muwatta' Malik, 15:480.

Surah ‘Abasa has one of the most famous reasons for revelation. During the early Meccan period, many of the weaker members of society had embraced Islam. To the leaders of Mecca, this was very off-putting, as they had a deep disdain for the poor and weak. Once, the Prophet ﷺ was trying to convince al-Waleed ibn Mughirah, a Meccan chief, to accept Islam when he was approached by a blind companion, Abd Allah ibn Umm Maktum ؓ, for some advice.

Waleed was repulsed by the sight of a blind man, and this incident irritated the Prophet ﷺ who restrained his emotions and limited it to a frown. This was enough for revelation to descend reminding the Prophet ﷺ to prioritise the believers over the disbelievers, even if they seem weaker in the eyes of society.[418] This *surah* can also be considered a proof of prophethood because no false prophet has ever brought revelation correcting himself in such a manner.

Another *surah* with a clear reason for revelation is Surah al-'Alaq. It is unanimously agreed that the first five verses of Surah al-'Alaq were the first revelation. The rest of the *surah* was revealed a few years later after an incident involving Abu Jahl, an archnemesis of the Prophet ﷺ. The first five verses address the importance of knowledge as a foundation of faith; the remainder of the *surah* chastises the stubborn disbeliever. These verses speak directly about Abu Jahl but can apply to anyone who follows in his footsteps until the end of time.

The first revelation occurred in the cave of Hira during the 40th year of the Prophet's ﷺ life. He was reflecting on the purpose of life when the angel Gabriel (Jibril) appeared before him, embraced him, and asked him to recite. Replying that he did not know how to do so, Jibril repeated the question two more times, then recited the first five verses of Surah al-'Alaq to him. These first few verses served as a strong reminder of the rights of the Creator, and the importance of building our faith upon authentic knowledge.

During the early Meccan period, a few months passed during which there was no revelation. This caused the Prophet ﷺ to worry that Allah had abandoned him, and he became very sad. In response to this, Surah al-Duha was revealed, followed quickly by Surah al-Inshirah. These two *surahs* share the theme of optimism about the future. Allah promised the Prophet ﷺ that the future would be better than the past,[419] and that with hardship always comes ease.[420] These *surahs* have over time become proverbs that Muslims remind each other of during difficult times. In recent times, they have also become the foundation of the Islamic approach towards dealing with depression and trauma.[421]

The bulk of the *surahs* in this *juz* show us the Prophet's ﷺ journey in early Meccan Seerah. Surah al-'Alaq reminds us of the first revelation, and his struggles against the likes of Abu Jahl. Surah Abasa shows us the quality of people who embraced Islam, and the arrogance of those who

419 Qur'an 93:5.

420 Qur'an 94:5–6.

421 Najwa Awad and Sarah Sultan, "Your Lord Has Not Forsaken You: Addressing the Impact of Trauma on Faith," Yaqeen, January 10, 2019

rejected Islam. Surah al-Quraysh and al-Feel are reminders that the Quraysh experienced many blessings from Allah, making their disbelief even more severe. Surah al-Masad was a reminder that even in the Prophet's ﷺ own family, there were those who vehemently rejected Islam and caused him grief like his fiery uncle Abu Lahab.

Many surahs are not just reminders, but also powerful duas to recite every day. The message of the Qur'an comes full circle—it begins and ends with a dua.

The *Juz* ends with the two protectors, Surah al-Falaq (the Daybreak) and Surah al-Naas. As it begins with a reminder to seek guidance daily, it ends with a reminder to seek protection from misguidance and the forces of evil daily. These *surahs* are not just important reminders, but also powerful *dua*s that we should recite every day. The message of the Qur'an comes full circle, beginning and ending with *dua*. We ask Allah to keep us firm on the straight path, and to protect us from the whispers of the devils among mankind and jinn. *Ameen.*

Juz thirty

Judgement Day

The final *juz* of the Qur'an focuses heavily on the theme of the Last Day. Various passages in this *juz* describe the events signifying the end of this world and the beginning of the Judgment. These descriptions are vivid and intense. The intention is to drive home the reality and seriousness of these events in the minds of believers.

422 Qur'an 81:1–14.

The Qur'an focuses heavily on the theme of the Last Day. We are given vivid and intense descriptions of the end of this world to drive home its reality.

When the sun is rolled up. When the stars are dimmed. When the mountains are set in motion. When relationships are suspended. When the beasts are gathered. When the oceans are set aflame. When the souls are paired. When the girl, buried alive, is asked: For what crime was she killed? When the records are made public. When the sky is peeled away. When the Fire is set ablaze. When Paradise is brought near. Each soul will know what it has readied.[422]

A core message in each of these passages is that we will be accountable on that day for our deeds and beliefs.

When the sky breaks apart. When the planets are scattered. When the oceans are exploded. When the tombs are strewn around. Each soul will know what it has advanced, and what it has deferred. O man! What deluded you concerning your Lord, the Most Generous? He who created you, and formed you, and proportioned you?[423]

Allah created us, gave us life, and gave us opportunity after opportunity to choose a righteous life. So, what has caused us to neglect our Lord, The Most Generous?

When the sky is ruptured. And hearkens to its Lord, as it must. And when the earth is levelled out. And casts out what is in it and becomes empty. And hearkens to its Lord, as it must. O man! You are laboring towards your Lord, and you will meet Him. As for him who is given his book in his right hand, he will have an easy settlement. And will return to his family delighted.[424]

On that day, everyone will receive their book of deeds. Whoever receives it in their right hand will enter Paradise, and that will be their greatest moment of joy. Our accountability to Allah on that day will be in our favour if we choose to live in a way that is pleasing to Him. On that day of heavy quaking, every little deed will count, both good and bad.

423 Qur'an 82:1–7.
424 Qur'an 84:1–9.

When the earth is shaken with its quake and the earth brings out its loads. And man says, "What is the matter with it?" On that Day, it will tell its tales. For your Lord will have inspired it. On that Day, people will emerge in droves, to be shown their works. Whoever has done an atom's weight of good will see it. And whoever has done an atom's weight of evil will see it. [425]

Our accountability to Allah on the Last Day will be in our favour if we choose to live in a way that is pleasing to Him.

Before our books are presented, our deeds will be weighed on a scale. If the good deeds are heavier, then the outcome will be in our favour.

As for he whose scales are heavy, he will be in a pleasant life. But as for he whose scales are light, his home is the Abyss.[426]

The Qur'an concludes with multiple strong reminders that this world will end. We will face judgment for how we chose to live our lives, and on that day, our beliefs and our deeds will determine our fate.

425 Qur'an 99:1–8.

426 Qur'an 101:6–9.

Juz thirty

Qur'anic worldview

Towards the very end of the last *juz* lies one of the last *surahs* to be revealed, Surah al-Nasr. This *surah* brings the story of the Qur'an full circle. The mission that started with *Iqra* and faced heavy opposition in the beginning, ended with people entering Islam in large numbers.[427] The rapid growth of Islam during this twenty-year mission was miraculous. Even more miraculous is that the growth did not stop with the passing of the Prophet ﷺ. It continued, and continues today over a thousand years later, when a quarter of the earth are Muslim, and more people embrace it every day.

427 Qur'an 110:2.

The impact of the Qur'an's message on the hearts of the believers is the strongest evidence of its divine origins.

There is no other man who claimed prophethood in the past two thousand years who has gained a following the way Prophet Muhammad ﷺ did. The rapid growth of Islam, through both good and bad times, and its continuous growth today when Muslims are in a state of political weakness is yet another proof of the truthfulness of his claim.

The Prophet ﷺ predicted, "This matter will certainly reach every place touched by the night and day. Allah will not leave a house or residence, but that Allah will cause this religion to enter it, by which the honourable will be honoured, and the disgraceful will be disgraced."[428]

He said this at a time when religions were mostly locked to specific regions and no religion had gained a global following yet. Today we see this prediction play out through globalisation, as Islam can be found in almost every country around the world.

As we reach the end of this book, let us reflect on the powerful impact of the Islamic worldview. From this mighty book and message arose a nation that changed the world. Concepts like morality and justice were developed into their best forms through the teachings of Islam. During the best of times, Muslims produced societies that led the world in piety, morality, family values, justice and compassion. In difficult times, Muslims remain models of patience, trust in Allah, acceptance of destiny, resilience, and courage.

The impact of the Qur'an's message on the hearts of the believers is the strongest evidence of its divine origins. The Qur'an remains today the ultimate source of guidance for anyone who seeks the true path to Allah. It is indeed "a guidance for those who are conscious of Allah."[429]

428 Musnad Ahmad, no. 16957.

429 Qur'an 2:2.

Notes

Notes